Series Editors:
Alan Ware (University of Oxford) and
Vincent Hoffmann–Martinot (Sciences Po Bordeaux)

the return of the state of war

a theoretical analysis of operation iraqi freedom

Dario Battistella

Originally published in French under the title *Retour de l'etat de guerre*
© Armand Colin Publisher 2006

First published by the ECPR Press in 2008

The ECPR Press is the publishing imprint of the European Consortium for Political Research (ECPR), an independent, scholarly association, which supports and encourages the training, research and cross–national cooperation of political scientists in institutions throughout Europe and beyond. The ECPR's Central Services are located at the University of Essex, Wivenhoe Park, Colchester, CO4 3SQ, UK

Typeset in Times 10pt by the ECPR Press

British Library Cataloguing in Publication Data
A catalogue record for this book is available from the British Library

ISBN 13: 978-0-9552488-5-6

The ECPR Monographs series is published by the ECPR Press, the publishing imprint of the European Consortium for Political Research (ECPR).

The ECPR is an independent, scholarly association, established in 1970. It supports and encourages the training, research and cross-national co-operation of political scientists throughout Europe and beyond. The ECPR currently has nearly 350 European institutional members and associate members in over 40 countries, from as far afield as New Zealand and Japan. These members together form a network of thousands of individual political scientists, international relations and European studies specialists.

The ECPR Monographs series publishes major new research in all sub-disciplines of political science and includes work from both senior and younger members of the profession and translations of important new research not yet published in English.

contents

| acknowledgements

The original version of this book, *Retour de l'état de guerre*, was first published in France by Editions Armand Colin, on the friendly initiative of Pascal Cauchy from Sciences Po Paris. I owe special thanks to Véronique Sales and Caroline Leclerc, the successive heads of the social science department of Editions Armand Colin, for their unfailing support and patience.

I owe the existence of the English version of this book to Steve Chan and Frank Beer from the University of Colorado at Boulder, who have been prodigal with interest and encouragement. Steve Chan, as well as Pierre Allan from the University of Geneva, evaluated the *Retour de l'état de guerre* for the ECPR Press and recommended its publication. I am also most grateful to Thomas Lindemann and Milos Jovanovic who published two reviews of the French edition in *Défense Nationale and Politique étrangère*. They gave me the impetus to embark on the translation of my book into English.

I am greatly indebted to Jean–François Allafort and Lindsay Holmes, who supervised and substantially improved the present translation with their red pens.

Vincent Hoffmann–Martinot and Alan Ware accepted *The Return of the State of War* for publication in the Monograph Series of the ECPR Press. Special thanks to Rebecca Knappett and Deborah Savage for their generous help in the preparation of this book.

I should like to express very warmly my sense of gratitude to all of them. They cannot be blamed for the many shortcomings which remain: these are all my own.

This book is dedicated to Justine and Simon, citizens of the anarchical society we will pass on to them.

We shall never in any circumstances seek to make an independent people subject to our dominion; because we believe, we passionately believe, in the right of every people to choose their own allegiance and be free of masters altogether.
(Woodrow Wilson[1])

Because things are the way they are, things will not stay the way they are.
(Bertolt Brecht[2])

1 Woodrow Wilson, 4th November, 1915. Quoted in Arnold Wolfers & Lawrence Martin (eds), *The Anglo–American Tradition in Foreign Affairs: Readings from Thomas More to Woodrow Wilson* (New Haven: Yale University Press, 1956), pp. 265–6.
2 Bertolt Brecht, *Leben des Galilei* ('Life of Galileo', 1938), in B. Brecht, *Gesammelte Werke in acht Bänden*, Frankfurt, Suhrkamp, 1967, Band 2, p. 1233.

introduction | operation iraqi freedom and the international order

The past is never dead; it's not even past.
(William Faulkner [1])

On 18 March 2003, the United States attacked Iraq during Operation Iraqi Freedom. Some twelve years before, on 16 January 1991, the US had attacked Iraq during Operation Desert Storm. At first sight, the wars may seem quite comparable. Indeed, they were launched by the same policy makers – or almost the same – Saddam Hussein on the one hand, Bush father and son on the other. They were waged by the same powers – or almost the same – a quasi universally isolated Iraq on the one hand, an overwhelmingly powerful US–led coalition on the other. They ended with the same result – or almost the same – i.e. the total defeat of Iraq, although Saddam Hussein's political fate was very different in 2003.

However, a closer look at both crises immediately reveals a fundamental difference between the two war situations. Contrary to Operation Iraqi Freedom, which was undertaken in the name of 'the sovereign authority ... of the United States of America ... to use force in assuring its own national security'[2], without any formal authorisation from the UN Security Council and against the explicit opposition of some of America's closest Western allies, Operation Desert Storm – decided within the legal framework of a UN Security Council's mandate and with the political support of the Western allies of America – had been launched with the hope that 'out of these troubled times ... a new world order (might) emerge, ... a world where the rule of law supplants the rule of the jungle'.[3]

The purpose of the present theoretical analysis of America's 2003 war against Saddam Hussein is twofold. My objective is first to understand why the optimistic post–cold–war outlook of the early nineties could change into its exact opposite in a short space of a dozen years. In that respect, my aim is to contribute to explaining how the promise of a privileged resort to peaceful inter–state conflict resolution – implied in the US attitude during the first Gulf War – gave way to the explicit triumph of the 'might–is–right' principle during the second Gulf War.[4] I also propose to analyse the potential impact of this return of the state of war on the international order of the twenty–first century. By analysing the possible meanings of

Operation Iraqi Freedom in the light of the past and current evolution of the contemporary international system, the main idea is to address the question whether the shift in America's foreign policy behaviour is but a mere parenthesis in history or potentially the first stage of a long term process.

My argument will be structured in three points – an assumption, a hypothesis, and an analysis – which will be summarised in the introduction before being developed in detail in the subsequent chapters of the book. First, I will set out my theoretical postulate: international politics is characterised by a long–term trend leading to the progressive consolidation of an international society. Then I will present my research hypothesis: Operation Iraqi Freedom upsets this tendency, as it means the return of the state of war, the triumph of Hobbesian values over Lockean values. Lastly, I will look for a causal explanation of America's behaviour during the second Gulf crisis: I will argue that the US has resorted to arms against Iraq, thus breaking with the international norms it contributed to consolidating in the past, because its leaders have perceived a future potential decline of American hegemony.

* * *

As a starting point I postulate that in international politics there exists a long–range tendency towards the expansion and consolidation of an international society. In other words, international politics – which I define as the social realm composed of conflicting interactions between political entities situated in a state of anarchy and bent on advancing their interests and aspirations – is committed to a maturing process characterised by the progressive triumph of peaceful over violent means of conflict resolution.

The idea that international politics takes place in an anarchical setting, typically marked by the absence of any central authority above states, is the bedrock assumption of IR as a discipline. Almost every scholar accepts the postulate of a radical difference between the domestic realm and the international sphere and agrees with Hedley Bull's statement according to which anarchy can be regarded at once 'as the central fact of international life and the starting point of theorizing about it' (Bull, 1995: 75). Whereas domestic politics is characterised by the presence of a central authority claiming – successfully most of the time – the monopoly of legitimate physical violence, 'none is entitled to command; none is required to obey' in international politics (Waltz, 1979: 88).

According to realist thinkers, the state of anarchy is equivalent to a never–ending state of war. Raymond Aron, among many others, asserts that inter–state relations 'take place within the shadow of war' (Aron, 2003: 6). States never exclude the possibility of resorting to arms in order to fulfil their objectives. Consequently 'war is to be found throughout all history and all civilizations' (150). I will, in contrast, postulate a more liberal starting point.[5] Although international politics involves 'in essence, the alternatives of war and peace' (6), it is nevertheless characterised by regulatory efforts undertaken by the states. If indeed 'war occurs because there is nothing to prevent it' (Waltz, 1959: 188), and if it is true that war is 'a mere continuation of policy by other means' (Clausewitz, 1809–1830), states are, all other things being equal, eager to settle their conflicts of interests and aspirations by sending first their diplomats, who 'speak' in their name, before using their soldiers, who 'kill' in their name (Aron, 2003: 5).

In other words, they wage wars only as an *ultima ratio*, after resorting to co–operation and trying 'to adjust their behaviour to the actual or anticipated preferences of others, through a process of policy coordination',[6] and when they have failed to obtain satisfaction by peaceful means of conflict resolution. Obviously, Edward Carr is right in claiming that international politics is, 'in one sense, always power politics'.[7] In their desire to satisfy their own interests and aspirations, political units aim at being in a position to carry out their will despite resistance from other states. But in order to do so and get other states to comply with what they want them to do, more and more states prefer to use 'influence politics' rather than power politics (Wolfers, 1962: 103–15), soft power instead of hard power (Nye, 1990).

To put it briefly, states are far from being 'continuously preparing for, actively involved in, or recovering from organised violence in the form of war' (Morgenthau, 2006: 50). They have successfully transformed the 'immature anarchy' of the past, synonymous with an all–encompassing state of war, into a contemporary 'mature anarchy' (Buzan, 2007: 148). To quote Buzan, the contemporary international system is anarchical not so much because it 'means the absence of government *per se*' but rather because 'government resides in the units of the system' (39) instead of being centralised. States 'have established by dialogue and consent common rules and institutions for the conduct of their relations', thus forming an international society, an anarchical society, recognising 'most of the time their common interest in maintaining these arrangements' (Bull and Watson, 1984: 1).

In the Part I of this book I will defend the idea that the first manifestations of this international society can be traced back to the Westphalian Treaties. While once and for all establishing the sovereign territorial state as the major political unit, in place of the imperial *Respublica Universalis*, the end of the Thirty Years War also inaugurated the conscious practice of the balance of power politics, which was the first expression of states' will to regulate their interactions. The then European powers relied on the defensive doctrine of balance of power politics, or *Realpolitik*, in order to control their destabilising tendency to resort to offensive power politics, or *Machtpolitik*. However, their homage to the Christian community which they claimed they belonged to, as well as their promise to submit their national interests to the rules of international law, did not prevent them from regularly succumbing to the temptation of furthering their own egoistic interests by violent means, calling upon the principle of the balance of power to better hide their expansionist ambitions (Chapter one).

This competitive Westphalian equilibrium, to which the French Revolutionary and Napoleonic Wars put a definitive end, led to the Vienna Congress. In their desire to break with past behaviour patterns, perceived as having provoked more than twenty years of general wars, Napoleon's vanquishers established the

Concert of Europe. This Concert is generally considered to be a kind of institutionalised balance. However, I will show in Chapter two that the stabilisation of the nineteenth–century international system was due less to the presence of a multipolar balance than to the existence of a British primacy. Contrary to appearances, the multipolarity that had prevailed during the seventeenth and eighteenth centuries no longer existed in the nineteenth century, since it was indeed followed by a unipolar power configuration. In accordance with John Ikenberry's theory of the rebuilding of order after major wars (Ikenberry, 2001), I will argue that international society was consolidated thanks to the self–restraint of the preponderant power, the United Kingdom. Thanks to the resources at its disposal, London was both willing to behave moderately and able to organise and manage a stable international system.

The beginning of the twentieth century and the thirty–year period including World War One and World War Two corroborate this analysis. On account of the relative decline of its power, the British hegemon progressively became unable to cope with the German challenge, and the first half of the twentieth century was a transition period from *pax Britannica* to *pax Americana*.

In 1945, the US took over the task of establishing and guaranteeing a peaceful international order. The collective security system of the UN Charter, whose first manifestation – the League of Nations – had totally failed, symbolised this will. However, the USSR refused to accept the new rules of the international game and the US had to wait until the fall of the Berlin Wall and the end of the Cold War to contemplate the prospective success of its project of a universal American order. During the first years following 1989, the American unipolarity, which already existed throughout the Cold War years and which is now obvious to any observer of the international scene, seemed to herald a period of genuine American hegemony, in the sense used by Antonio Gramsci, who defines hegemony as a legitimate domination accepted by those submitted to it[8] (Chapter three).

The central argument of this book is that Operation Iraqi Freedom could well call into question the very idea of the triumph of this American order, explicitly proclaimed by George H. Bush in his 'New World Order' speech in 1990. The first two attempts to establish an American order had failed because of the refusal of the revisionist powers to adjust their behaviour to the institutions imagined by Woodrow Wilson and Franklin D. Roosevelt, even though in 1919 the US Senate itself had impeded US participation in the League of Nations by refusing to ratify the Treaty of Versailles. First the Axis powers, then the USSR, had rejected American post–WWI and post–WWII plans: the Nazis and Japanese by violating the international norms and eventually resorting to arms; the Soviets by accepting the rules without abandoning the promotion of their own counter–project. Things are utterly different nowadays, as is indeed the hegemon itself, which is taking the initiative of calling into question the existing order it has contributed to establishing over the last sixty years. The terrorist attacks of 9/11 clearly prove that some actors, such as the Al'Qaeda terrorist network and its prospective sponsors, do not hesitate to resort to armed force in order to challenge an American order whose legitimacy they are not willing to recognise. It is nonetheless true that the major threat to the survival of contemporary international society originates in the shift in American foreign policy after 9/11.

This is the thesis that I defend in Part II, where I propose an analysis of the three major changes introduced by Operation Iraqi Freedom as regards the long–term tendency towards the consolidation of a mature anarchy. For that purpose, I will complement and enrich the liberal approach used in the Part I with the research tools provided by the modernist constructivist perspective advanced by Alexander Wendt (Wendt, 1992).[9]

The English School, on the one hand, and the American scholar John Ikenberry, on the other, propose different causal mechanisms to explain the emergence of a stable international order. According to Hedley Bull, such an order originates in a common agreement among the major powers of a given period, eager as they are to regulate their interactions, whereas John Ikenberry contends that it is above all the strategic self–restraint of the dominant power emerging from a major war which is conducive to international stability. Despite these differences, Ikenberry and Bull share the same rationalist approach, according to which the will of the great power/s to stabilise the system stems from its/their long–term interest in co–operation rather than confrontation. Wendt does not deny the importance of interests as an explanatory factor of the states' foreign policy behaviour, but he roots states' interests in their identity, shaped by the set of values, beliefs, and ideas they share as regards their respective rank and role on the international scene. These shared beliefs form cultures which, in the absence of any central authority, are fundamentally anarchical cultures – Hobbesian anarchy when political units conceive of themselves as enemies, Lockean anarchy when they see themselves as rivals, or Kantian anarchy when they regard themselves as friends.[10] In the first case, political entities do not recognise each other's right to be a sovereign unit and consequently they will not refrain from violent action against the others. Conversely, in the second case, they conceive of themselves as autonomous entities and may resort to arms for defensive reasons only.

According to Wendt, the Lockean culture has prevailed since the emergence of the Westphalian system. In ancient and medieval times political units used to internalise the resort to armed force as the legitimate norm of their external behaviour but, since 1648, sovereignty has been established as the central institution of the international system, even though there were notable exceptions to this general pattern, such as the bellicose behaviour of Napoleon and Hitler and the systemic consequences, not to mention the Israeli–Palestinian conflict today. Admittedly, in the contemporary Lockean system, there are still outbursts of inter–state violence. It is nonetheless true that Lockean violence is a form of limited violence, constrained by the 'live–and–let–live' principle. States generally accept the status quo. When they resort to violence in order to advance their interests or resolve a conflict in their favour, they do not try to eliminate other states but merely seek to improve their relative position within the existing order.

Now if we compare Operation Iraqi Freedom to this general model, it may be asserted that the war waged by the US and its coalition against Baghdad means the return of Hobbesian values, as it is indeed a triple violation of the norms characterising Lockean anarchy. First, Iraq is perceived by the US as an enemy, and no longer as a rival. Whereas Operation Desert Storm merely sought to roll Iraqi armies back in order to re–establish Kuwait's violated independence, Operation Iraqi Freedom aims to overthrow Saddam Hussein's regime and transform Iraq into a state shaped in accordance with American values and complying with American interests. By acting this way, the US has violated the principle of non–interference – the most visible manifestation of the institution of sovereignty (Chapter four).

The second break is the replacement of the just war doctrine by the preventive war doctrine. Throughout the Cold War, the US consistently led a status quo policy in accordance with the just war tradition, resorting to arms in a defensive perspective and aiming to guarantee its security or consolidate the international order resulting from its victory in World War Two. Washington never tried to impose its order upon the Soviet rival by force, and American politicians were hardly tempted to roll communism back. They mainly wanted to contain Soviet expansionism by adopting a strategy with a view to preserving balances of power between the Western allies and the Soviet block in Europe, the Near and Middle East, and the Far East. In 2002–2003 during the crisis that led to the war opposing the US and Iraq, American policy makers made the opposite choice. They decided to launch a preventive war against an enemy not accused of having arguably upset the existing order, but merely suspected of being anxious to acquire weapons of mass destruction and harbouring aggressive intentions either directly against the US or its allies, or indirectly in co–operating with terrorist networks such as Al'Qaeda (Chapter five).

Third change: American policy during this second Gulf crisis was exclusively and unilaterally decided and coordinated at the White House, regardless of the multilateral procedures of Chapter VII of the UN Charter the US itself promoted in the immediate post–WWII years and abided by during the first Gulf crisis. Furthermore, for the first time since the Western alliance came into existence, the US has not hesitated to act without the consent – and support – of some of its closest allies. It has thus broken with the firmly institutionalized practice of consensual working procedures within the Atlantic Alliance which had prevailed so far, on the occasion of NATO's interventions in Bosnia and Kosovo for instance (Chapter six).

By privileging armed force, Operation Iraqi Freedom is tantamount to a retreat from Lockean values. As such a return of Hobbesian anarchy may mean some form of potential inflection in the long term tendency of maturation of international anarchy, the question raised by America's behaviour during the second Gulf crisis is the following one: is this merely a temporary re–orientation, or may it have a lasting impact on the current pacification process of international politics?

Before trying to answer this question, let me remind the reader that, according to Wendt, an anarchic culture has to be internalised as a legitimate set of beliefs by a significant number of actors before becoming a systemic factor that could shape these actors' international behaviour.[11] In other words, if only one state behaves abnormally in regard to the predominant values, that is not sufficient in itself to lead to the replacement of the existing anarchical culture by the new one adopted by the deviant actor. The other actors also have to adopt the same behaviour, thus contributing to reproducing it at the systemic level.

Contrary to Operation Desert Storm which had almost unanimous support,[12] the attitude adopted by Washington during the crisis preceding Operation Iraqi Freedom was criticised by countries such as Russia and China; but also by France and Germany. The conclusion that can be drawn from this fact is that a non negligible number of contemporary secondary powers are not willing to drop Lockean values and institutions. However, as the return to a Hobbesian behaviour is due to the predominant power, the risk exists that, sooner or later, other states might be tempted to imitate America's example. Indeed, in international politics the predominant power is the core from where, implicitly or explicitly, the standards of legitimate behaviour spread to other parts of the international system.

Anyway, the question of the prospective adoption of Hobbesian logic by other states only comes after. Indeed, this logic must first be internalised by the US itself before having a chance of spreading worldwide. In other words, it is essential to examine the reasons for Washington's decision to go to war against Iraq if we want to apprehend the degree of internationalisation of the Hobbesian logic by the US itself, before trying to infer the potential impact of Operation Iraqi Freedom on the existing international order. Such an impact is likely to depend on whether these reasons are structural or contingent.

According to the Bush administration, the decision to launch an armed attack against Baghdad was motivated by the alleged existence of weapons of mass destruction that Saddam Hussein either already possessed or wanted to acquire. The risk was too high that he might either use these arms or transfer them to terrorist networks hostile to American interests. The underlying logic of this first official reason refers to the doctrine of asymmetric conflict and, more exactly, to the offence–defence balance theory. If Iraq was a threat to America's security, then Operation Iraqi Freedom was a defensive war the US had to wage pre–emptively in order to close the window of vulnerability opened by Iraq's prospective control of destructive weapons. In Chapter seven I will show that this explanation is hardly convincing. Operation Iraqi Freedom is not a form of defensive expansionism but, on the contrary, pertains to an opportunistic expansion due to an offence–dominant balance detrimental to Iraq but favourable to the US, which has taken full advantage of the revolution in conventional military affairs.

I also contend that Washington's decision to resort to such a form of opportunistic expansionism was supported by some specific domestic actors in the US. In other words, Operation Iraqi Freedom is not only an aggressive war but also an imperialist war. It is imperialist in its very nature. This war was launched with a view to exerting political control over the new regime established in the militarily conquered Iraqi territory. It is imperialist in its causes too. The decision to attack Iraq was favoured by some imperialist groups intent on promoting their particular material and ideational interests. Thanks to the presence of some of their representatives in George W. Bush's administration, and on account of the political climate prevailing in the US after 9/11, they successfully managed to persuade public opinion that the strategy adopted was in the national interest of America's security (Chapter eight).

This being said, an analysis of the structural causes of Operation Iraqi Freedom, taking into account the long–term dynamics of the systemic power distribution, shows that there is also a structural factor that may contribute to our understanding of Washington's decision to go to war. This structural factor pertains to the national interest of the US. Indeed, the US is the hegemon of the contemporary system, and the success of its hegemony depends on its capacity to associate the secondary satisfied powers with the benefits of the existing order. Thus the US is bound to control the crucial regions of the world. The Middle East is such a region, both from an economic standpoint – because of the presence of those oil resources that are still vital for a smooth working of the American–led free–market global economy – and also from a strategic standpoint, as it is situated at the periphery of the Asian continent confronted with the rise of America's potential challenger, China. In Chapter nine I will deal with this hidden cause of Operation Iraqi Freedom and argue that it is the major reason for the US political behaviour, all the more so as it has been silenced by America's political authorities.

* * *

If we accept the relevance of the hypothesis that Operation Iraqi Freedom is a proto–systemic war, what then may the impact of this war be on the existing international order? Obviously, any answer to such a question is pure guesswork, as international politics, on account of its very anarchical structure, is undetermined by definition. That is why I will not venture to make any prognosis in my conclusion, but will only content myself with proposing three possible theoretical scenarios – a liberal scenario, a 'declinist' scenario and an imperial scenario.

NOTES

1 William Faulkner, *Requiem for a Nun* (1951), in W. Faulkner, *Novels 1942–1954*, New York, The Library of America, 1994, p. 535.

2 George W. Bush, 17th March, 2003, Address to the Nation. Source: http://www.whitehouse.gov /news/releases/2003/03/20030317–7.html.

3 George H. Bush, 11th September, 1990, Address to a joint session of Congress and the Nation. Source: http://en.wikisource.org/wiki/Toward_a_New_World_Order.

4 Although there was, strictly speaking, a first Gulf War opposing Iraq and Iran in 1980–8, the crisis provoked by Iraq's invasion of Kuwait in 1990 and the ensuing Operation Desert Storm will be called the First Gulf War in this essay, Operation Iraqi Freedom being referred to as the Second Gulf War.

5   For a more comprehensive analysis of liberal international theory, see S. Hoffmann, 'Liberalism and International Affairs', in S. Hoffmann, *Janus & Minerva* (Boulder: Westview, 1987), pp. 394–417; M. Smith, 'Liberalism and International Reform', in T. Nardin & D. Mapel (eds), *Traditions of International Ethics* (Cambridge: Cambridge University Press, 1992), pp. 201–24; M. Zacher & R. Matthews, 'Liberal International Theory: Common Threads, Divergent Trends', in C. Kegley (ed.), *Controversies in International Relations Theory: Realism and the Neo–liberal Challenge* (New York: Saint Martin's, 1995), pp. 107–50.

6   This is the definition of co–operation proposed by Robert Keohane, *After Hegemony: Co–operation and Discord in the World Political Economy* (Princeton: Princeton University Press, 1984), p. 51.

7   Edward Carr, *The Twenty Years' Crisis: 1919–1939* (1946, 2nd edition) (Basingstoke: Palgrave, 2001), p. 97.

8   In ancient Greece, *hegemonia* meant 'direction'. The term was used by Herodotus to designate the direction by, successively, Sparta and Athens of the foreign affairs of the Greek city–states opposed to the Persian Empire. In contemporary social science, this original meaning was rediscovered by the Italian Marxist Antonio Gramsci, *Quaderni del carcere*, Book 3, Notebook 13 (1932–1934) (Turin: Einuadi, 1975), pp. 1636–1638 & 2010–2011, according to whom the presence of a hegemony, defined as the moral and intellectual direction exerted by the bourgeois class over the proletarians, is the key to explaining the stability of the contemporary capitalist societies. In IR, Gramsci's approach has inspired the critical theorist Robert Cox, whose conception of hegemony I share when I use the concept in this essay. See 'Gramsci, Hegemony and International Relations', *Millennium*, 12 (2), Summer 1983, pp. 162–75. The term is often used by realists in the common sense, i.e. as a mere equivalent of material pre–eminence or domination.

9   Alexander Wendt, 'Anarchy Is What States Make of It', *International Organization*, 49, N°2 (Spring 1992), pp. 391–425; *Social Theory of International Politics* (Cambridge: Cambridge University Press), 1999.

10 In this book I will not dwell on Kantian anarchy as the concept is not directly relevant to my analysis. States are friends when they jointly make up a security community and a collective security system. In their own interactions, they exclude the possibility of resorting to arms as a means of conflict resolution. In their relations with third–party states, they spontaneously help each other when one of them is threatened by a third state. According to Wendt, 'the contemporary system is mostly Lockean, with increasing Kantian elements' (Wendt, 1999: 43). The Atlantic Alliance is such a Kantian element as it comprises 'allies who do not use violence to advance their interests to settle their disputes and work as a team against security threats' (258). Since the publication of Wendt's book, his thesis seems to have been corroborated by the European reactions to the terrorist attacks of 9/11. However things have become more complicated since the Iraqi crisis. While the US and the United Kingdom may still be regarded as friends – the 'special relationship' – the refusal of France and Germany to give unconditional support to the American strategy somewhat disproves Wendt's optimism.

11 A. Wendt distinguishes three degrees of internalisation of a norm of conduct. To the first degree, an international norm of behaviour is adopted by a state because it cannot do otherwise, as it is forced to behave according to the existing values by the existing power ratio

and because of the risk of punishment. To the second degree, an actor complies with a norm because it is in his self–interest to do so. And to the third degree, an actor follows a norm of conduct not because of an exogenous cause but because he thinks the norm is legitimate and he therefore wants to respect it, without even wondering whether he might act differently. Logically, in order to be a structural factor shaping the behaviour of agents, an anarchical culture must be internalised to the third degree by a significant number of states.

12 During the first Gulf crisis, no permanent member of the UN Security Council used its veto on resolution 678 (1990) authorising Operation Desert Storm. China abstained from voting, and only two non–permanent members, Cuba and Yemen, used their vetoes.

part one | towards an international society

Politics without history has no roots; history without politics bears no fruits.
(Sir John Robert Seeley[1])

The aim of the present analysis is to evaluate the prospective impact of Operation Iraqi Freedom on the future evolution of the international order. Before any further analysis, it is necessary to recall the past evolution of the international system. In the introduction to this part, I therefore propose to define in detail the epistemological and ontological assumptions implied by such a concept.

The contemporary international political system – which can be referred to as a set of independent political units interacting with each other so as 'to make the behaviour of each a necessary element in the calculations of the other' (Bull, 2002: 10) – finds its origin in the Westphalian Treaties signed in Münster and Osnabrück at the end of the Thirty Years War – a crucial turning point both in terms of changes and historical continuity.

The Westphalian peace in 1648 was indeed a watershed. Not only did it mean the triumph of the territorial sovereign state as the privileged form of political organisation of human societies, in lieu of the imperial form which prevailed during ancient and medieval times, but it also heralded a period of regular interactions between emerging states.

By definition, there can be no international system without nation–states. The diplomatic configurations of the past, such as the Chinese Warring Kingdoms, the Greek city–states, or the Italian pentarchy of the Renaissance, can be regarded as early and 'premature' international systems. But they were at best exceptions to the general pattern that prevailed before 1648, marked by the predominant role of empires as the paramount political systems. If we abide by the strict definition of the empire as a centralised political system acquired through violence by an entity which controls the effective political authority of dominated peripheries conquered by military means, the then prevailing empires typically organised most of their interactions within their borders. The existing interactions were not horizontal interrelations among independent units but vertical relations among integrated entities. Inter–'national' relations, i.e. interactions among imperial units independent of one another, were extremely rare, as empires were self–sufficient. They were generally limited to scattered contacts at the border zones. In other words, from Sumer and Egypt to the Holy Roman Empire, the specific elements defining contemporary international systems were generally missing. These empires were indeed independent political units but, in the absence of any significant interactions, we cannot infer the existence of an inter–'national' system strictly speaking. Any regular interactions that existed mainly concerned hierarchically integrated entities and not sovereign autonomous units.

After 1648, things rapidly changed. The state became the main organiser of the political life of human societies. That is the reason why any analysis of the evolution of the contemporary international political system necessarily implies considering the state as the major actor of international politics and focusing on diplomatic history as an autonomous field of research on its own terms.

Of course, I do not claim that the state is the sole actor on the international political scene; nor do I assert that the state is a rational and unitary actor *per se*. I do take into account the role of transnational actors such as terrorist networks, as well as the role of domestic, sociological and psychological variables that admittedly influence the decision–making process in foreign policy matters. But to the extent that my analysis deals with conflict dynamics and, more precisely, with the impact of the use of armed force on the pacifying process of the contemporary international system, I share Wendt's response to those who criticise his state–centrism. 'It makes no more sense to criticize a theory of international politics as "state–centric" than it does to criticize a theory of forests as "tree–centric", because states are still the primary medium through which the effects of other actors on the regulation of violence are channelled into the world system' (Wendt, 1999: 9).

If we turn to diplomatic history, there is, of course, no doubt that international politics is inextricably interwoven with other elements of collective human activities – economic exchanges, technological discoveries, systemic value shifts and domestic regime changes within the major powers of the international system, etc. Many historians have come to the conclusion that diplomatic history should consequently be dropped, in favour of social or total history. In contrast with this view, I claim that international politics is an autonomous field of research that has to be, and can be, approached from the point of view of its own features, with the help of the tools provided by the discipline of diplomatic history. To quote Paul Schroeder, scholars should first analyse with a critical eye the historical paradigms which are today so much in vogue before accusing specialists in diplomatic history of missing the forest for the trees. 'Marxists usually miss the forests for the roots; *Annalistes* miss the forest for the global landscape; and *Gesellschaftsgeschichtler* miss the forest for the lumber industry' (Schroeder, 1994: VIII).[2]

It remains to be seen that, despite the rise and development of the nation–state and the significant increase in its diplomatic activities, the break with the past does not exclude the existence of hidden historical continuities. Sure enough, from the Westphalian international system onwards, horizontal interactions among independent units have prevailed. Nevertheless the power structure of international politics is still hierarchical. In the pre–Westphalian imperial political systems, the hierarchical power structure, which, by definition, was favourable to the centre of the empire was the means to preserve the long–term stability of the whole system. After 1648, order could no longer be maintained that way. It would indeed be a contradiction in terms if, in an international system composed of equal sovereigns who have horizontal relations with one another, one of these units could explicitly claim to be superior to the other ones. But the absence of a *de jure* hierarchy can hardly conceal the presence of a *de facto* hierarchy.

I will show that in the history of the post–1648 international system there have been two forms of hierarchy. There was first a collective type of hierarchy. Two or more than two 'great powers' consciously sought to establish a balance of power among themselves in order to preserve the stability of the whole system and guarantee the survival of the smaller units of the system. There is a second and more individual type of hierarchy in which one major power implicitly claims the responsibility for managing the long–term stability of the international system. The other powers acknowledge this claim as legitimate, by behaving according to the rules established by the dominant power. I will show in Chapter one how and why the first model – which I call the Westphalian equilibrium – failed, thus paving the way for the one and only efficient means of regulation that has existed in international politics until today, the benevolent hegemony. The United Kingdom in the nineteenth century (Chapter two) and the US since the end of World War Two (Chapter three) have successively exerted such a benign leadership, thus contributing to the definite rise and consolidation of present–day international society.

NOTES

1   John Robert Seeley was a British historian of the nineteenth century (1834–1895). Source: http://www.sowi–online.de/reader/historisch–politisch/lange_politikgeschichte.htm.

2   Schroeder's book *The Transformation of European Politics* 1763–1848 (Cambridge: Cambridge University Press, 1994) is the work of a historian who uses IR concepts and theories in order to successfully combine the tools of both disciplines. Making due allowances, I have adopted a totally reverse approach, using research produced by historians in order to illustrate my theoretical argumentation. For an analysis of the opportunities and limits of combining IR and diplomatic history, see C. Elman & M. F. Elman (eds), *Bridges and Boundaries: Historians, Political Scientists and the Study of International Relations* (Cambridge, MA: MIT Press, 2000), with contributions, among other historians I quote in this research work, from J. Levy, P. Schroeder and J.L. Gaddis.

chapter one | the westphalian equilibrium

A new distemper has spread itself over Europe, infecting our princes, and induc-
ing them to keep up an exorbitant number of troops. ... As soon as one prince aug-
ments his forces, the rest of course do the same; so that nothing is gained thereby
but the public ruin. ... They give the name of peace to this general effort of all
against all.
(Charles de Montesquieu[1])

The origins of the modern international system go back to the Westphalian
Treaties in 1648, which put an end to the Thirty Years War.

The cause of the Thirty Years War was that rival European powers believed that
the Habsburgs aimed to extend their *imperium* over the entire European continent,
at a time when the simultaneously spiritual and political *Respublica Christiana*,
which had ruled Europe throughout the Middle Ages, was progressively being
subverted by the growing importance of the first territorial states and the political
claims of their secular executives. The defeat of Austria established for good the
triumph of the state as the privileged form to which human societies would resort
to organise themselves politically (Gross, 1948).

The rising European states were based on the sovereignty principle with a double dimension. The external dimension of this principle, referred to as *rex est*
imperator in regno suo ('the king is emperor in his own realm'), implied that
states were not subject to any higher political authority. Every state was independent of, and equal to, every other state. The internal dimension – *cujus regio, ejus*
religio ('the ruler determines the religion within his realm') – meant that states
exerted exclusive authority over their territory. Every state determined the legitimate religious beliefs, ideological principles and political regime within its borders and no state had the right to interfere in any other state's domestic affairs.

Once consolidated, first as dynastic states, then as nation–states, European
states progressively became involved in regular diplomatic and military interactions, thus forming the modern international system.

The emergence of this international system, first in Europe, then overseas in
proportion to European expansion (Bull & Watson, 1984), was a turning point in
the norms presiding over the relations among political groupings. Obviously, the

triumph of the sovereignty principle at the unit level implied the triumph of the state of nature – or state of anarchy – at the systemic level, tantamount to the absence of any central authority likely to regulate the international system by punishing a state's deviant behaviour. Political relations were horizontal and decentralised, instead of being vertical and centralised.[2] In such an anarchical arrangement, 'created by states, for states',[3] states had significantly more freedom to act as they were henceforth guided by the principle of raison d'état, and no longer constrained by the religious, moral, or even legal bonds they had been supposed to respect as subordinated members of *Respublica Christiana*. The problem was that increased liberty was potentially synonymous with higher insecurity. If each state felt free to pursue its own egoistic interests without paying attention to common interests, this could jeopardise the security, independence and integrity of the whole community. Thus it is by no means surprising that many contemporary political thinkers, such as Hobbes, Rousseau, or Kant, should have considered that the then prevailing international politics was a state of war.

The European powers were, however, conscious of the potential dangers attached to the sovereignty principle and they strove to regulate the state of anarchy. In the Westphalian Treaties, for instance, they proclaimed their will to respect the 'Christian and universal peace' they wanted to establish among themselves on the basis of their 'sincere, true and perpetual amity'. Even though, of course, such statements may retrospectively appear to have remained a dead letter, there is hardly any doubt that at that time there was a common will among the states to prevent the outbreak of a new systemic war, comparable to the Thirty Years War, which could disrupt the overall stability of the system. The balance of power policy was the means to which they resorted to make sure that no ruler might be tempted to believe that it was profitable for him to attempt to change the system (Gilpin, 1981: 10)[4], as evidenced for instance by the contents of the various treaties signed throughout the whole period, or by the analyses proposed by authors such as Voltaire or de Vattel, who did not agree with Hobbes's description.

I will argue in this chapter that the written references to the principle of the balance of power prove that the European states from that moment on conceived of 'themselves as bound by a common set of rules in their relations with one another' (Bull, 2002: 13). I will also show, however, that this recognition of common interests was insufficient to prevent the states concerned from defending their particular interests and that, despite the internalisation of the shared values they owed to their common Christian legacy, the legitimacy of the system was eventually challenged by the irruption of the French Revolution and the ensuing Revolutionary and Napoleonic wars.

In other words, the Westphalian balance of power may well have been the first rough sketch of a maturing anarchy but it nevertheless could not further the emergence of an international society, defined by Hedley Bull as a group of states 'cooperating in the working of common institutions' (13). The working of the institutions during the 1648–1789 period remained uncertain, for two principal reasons: '*egoismo sacro*' (Schroeder, 1994: 481) still marked the behaviour of the major powers, and the balance of power principle was an intrinsically limited, if not self–contradictory doctrine, as I propose to demonstrate in the following pages.

* * *

Triggered by the Second Defenestration of Prague, the Thirty Years War originated in the will of the Emperor of Vienna to impose the Catholic religion on his Bohemian subjects who, accordingly to the *cujus regio, ejus religio* principle adopted by the Peace of Augsburg signed in 1555, had chosen the Protestant faith. At the outset, the war only affected the various entities which co–existed within the territory of today's Germany, Austria and the Czech Republic. While being nominally united by their common allegiance to the Holy Roman Empire, the rulers concerned were actually divided into Protestant and Catholic camps. Very soon, however, the war was to involve the major powers of continental Europe. Spain supported Austria and the Catholics, whereas Denmark first, then Sweden, and finally France, sided with the Protestants, joined by the recently independent Low Countries, which wanted, once and for all, to put an end to Spain's ambition to re–establish its sovereignty over them.

The Thirty Years War was a total war – a third of the German and Dutch population fell victim to the savagery of mercenary armies, famine and diseases. Within the framework of my analysis of the evolution and pacification of the international system, this war is of utmost importance. Why did major continental powers not directly affected by the initial war issues – the religious dispute and the desire of some German princes to increase their own strength to the detriment of their neighbours or of the Emperor – progressively become involved? Their motivations were clearly of a political nature. The continental powers wanted to seize the opportunity to weaken the Habsburgs, thus forcing them to abandon their claim to dominate continental Europe by controlling the Holy Roman Empire.[5]

This was particularly true for France. In his desire to prevent and oppose Vienna's supremacy,[6] Richelieu, *de facto* maker of French foreign policy, did not shrink from resorting to any means that could help him achieve his aims. Embroiled in its own religious troubles and proud of its reputation as the elder daughter of the Roman Catholic Church, France did not hesitate to support the Bohemian or Swedish Protestants. For that purpose, it formed an alliance with them in order to weaken Catholic Austria. France also helped the Low Countries in their fight against Spain, Austria's main ally, which allegedly wanted to backstab France. In sum, the main signpost guiding France's strategy – and this holds true for any Continental power – was the interest of the state, i.e. the extension of raison d'état in matters of foreign policy,[7] much like the contemporary national interest. Some generations before, Machiavelli had said that 'a prince ... cannot observe all those things for which men are esteemed, being often forced, in order to maintain the state, to act contrary to faith, friendship, humanity, and religion' (Machiavelli, 1513: 18). During the Thirty Years War, the European powers concerned strictly abided by this principle. In interactions with the neighbouring powers, raison d'état meant the primacy of the states' interest over all other considerations, be they ethical values, religious precepts, legal rules, or domestic political interests.[8]

In concrete terms, the promotion of their national interest led European states to adopt offensive as well as defensive power politics. Because of the prevailing international anarchy and the absence of any central authority likely to supervise other states' behaviour, all the states were first and foremost compelled to look for ways to guarantee their physical survival, national security, political independence and territorial integrity.[9] They thus resorted to defensive power politics with a view to defending the existing status quo by preventing any other state from becoming excessively strong and powerful. France, for instance, perceived Austria's prospective supremacy as a threat to its own security. That was why it resorted to armed force against the Habsburgs during the Thirty Years War in order to oppose or contain the growth of a resource gap that would enable Vienna to impose its will. Of course, in the mind of the ruling leaders of the time, it was impossible for a state that merely wanted to survive to 'remain long in the quiet enjoyment of (its) freedom within (its) limited confines; for even if (it) does not molest others, others will molest (it), and from being thus molested will spring the desire and necessity of conquests' (Machiavelli, 1518, Book 2). As a consequence they also tried to accumulate for themselves the greatest possible amount of offensive power compared to their potential adversaries,[10] with a view to altering the status quo when they were in a position to do so. To put it bluntly, France also attacked Austria because the most efficient way to ward off Vienna's power was to preventively force it to accept France's will.

The English philosopher Thomas Hobbes was the first political thinker to observe the autonomy of the political domain from religious and ethical matters, to acknowledge the primacy of the national interest over other interests and to identify the simultaneously defensive and offensive aspects of power politics – *Realpolitik* and *Machtpolitik*. Three years after the Westphalian Peace, in *Leviathan*, he rationalised the political practices at work before his eyes, thus laying down the bedrock assumption of the realist approach in IR – that the state of nature equals a state of war. 'In all times', he wrote,

> kings and persons of sovereign authority, because of their independency, are in continual jealousies, and in the state and posture of gladiators, having their weapons pointing, and their eyes fixed on one another; that is, their forts, garrisons, and guns upon the frontiers of their kingdoms, and continual spies upon their neighbours, which is a posture of war, (Hobbes, 1651: 13)

before adding that

> States and Commonwealths not dependent on one another ... live in the condition of a perpetual war, and upon the confines of battle, with their frontiers armed, and cannons planted against their neighbours round about' (Hobbes, 1651: 21).

Hobbes did not claim that states were permanently involved in effective warfare; he merely asserted that states always kept in mind the possibility of resorting to violence as soon as they believed it was in their interest to do so.

> War consists not in battle only, or the act of fighting, but in a tract of time, wherein the will to contend by battle is sufficiently known. ... War consists not in actual fighting, but in the known disposition thereto during all the time there is no assurance to the contrary' (Hobbes, 1651: 13).

There could be no peace among states. Periods of peace were just truces, during which states recovered from the wars of the past and prepared the wars of the future.

Any observer of the behaviour of the European powers during the 1648–1789 period would spontaneously agree with Hobbes's description of the state of anarchy as a never–ending state of war. There was indeed a succession of major–power wars: the Franco–Spanish War (1635–59); the Franco–Dutch War (1672–8); the War of the League of Augsburg (1688–97); the War of the Spanish Succession (1701–13); the War of the Austrian Succession (1740–8); and the Seven Years War (1756–63), to mention only the most important ones and ignoring the wars which took place at Europe's periphery and mainly involved the Russian and Ottoman empires. The peaceful intervals between these periods of warfare may well seem mere temporary ceasefires during which the 'will to contend by battle' was still strong, because the years that saw no recourse to arms were indeed less numerous than the periods of fighting.

It is thus not really surprising – at least at first sight – that authors as different as Thomas Hobbes, Jean–Jacques Rousseau and Immanuel Kant, should have shared his description of the political situation that prevailed in Europe at that time. According to Rousseau, the state of war,

> the result of a settled intention, manifested on both sides, to destroy the enemy state, or at least to weaken it by all means at their disposal ..., is the natural relation of one power to one another. ... The powers of Europe stand to each other strictly in a state of war and all the separate treaties between them are in the nature rather of a temporary truce than a real peace (Rousseau, 1760, para 62).

Kant, for his part, thought that the 'natural state' of interstate relations 'is one of war', not merely because of 'the rulers of states in particular, who are insatiable of war', but more generally because there existed an 'unceasing threat of war' even if there were no 'open hostilities' (Kant, 1795: §II).[11]

I would contend that Hobbes's paradigm is not totally convincing, however. First of all, his description of international politics cannot be separated from his general political thought, and it is well known that Hobbes mainly sought to justify the existence of a strong political authority within a civil society. Hobbes described the state of nature among states because he wanted to give his readers an idea of what the state of nature was like before men established a sovereign authority by concluding a social contract. He depicted this state of nature as a war of all against all because he wanted to bring home the concept that the only way to guarantee a stable and secure political order was to establish an absolute sovereign representative who would monopolise the legitimate claim to resort to physical violence (Hobbes, 1651: 13). After claiming that, in the state of nature 'every man is enemy to every man', he explicitly admitted that 'it may be thought there was never such a time nor condition of war as this; and I believe it was never generally so, over all the world: but there are many places where they live so now. For the savage people in many places of America, except the government of small families, the concord whereof depends on natural lust, have no government at all, and live at this day in that brutish manner, as I said before. Howsoever, it may be perceived what manner of life there would be, were there no common power to fear, by the manner of life which men that have formerly lived under a peaceful government use to degenerate into a civil war' (Hobbes, 1651: 13). In other words, Hobbes was probably led to paint a rather gloomy picture of international politics for the sake of his domestic political theory.

The most significant feature of this picture is clearly the violent nature of international politics due to its anarchical structure. More than once, Hobbes underlined that states were in a posture of war 'because of their independency' (Hobbes, 1651: 13), because they were 'not dependent on one another' – which is tantamount to inferring that the state of war will probably come to an end once a central authority is established above the political units (Hobbes, 1651: 21). However, in the feudally structured Middle Ages, when such a central authority was perceived as legitimate by the then existing entities, the state of war still prevailed. As a matter of fact, the *Respublica Christiana*, in spite of its hierarchical organisation and communal discourse, was characterised by conflicting practices hardly different from those predominant after the European states' accession to formal sovereignty was legally recognised and their foreign policies justified by the new norms of power politics.

> Believing the world to be a harmonious Christian whole, the people of the feudal age endorsed the legitimacy of universal empire and papal authority while denying legitimacy to separate parts – in contrast to the ideal of sovereignty among modern states. To a small degree, the idea of unity engendered some support for the authority of the church and legitimate kings. On balance, however, political authority fragmented into many separate and autonomous entities under the rule of local strongmen, who strove violently for exclusive control of people and land. ... Thus, while the actors were different, the feudal system was organized by the same fundamental principle as the modern system: the rational propensity to strive for exclusive control over manpower and thus over territory in order to maximize the chances for survival in a condition where central protection is absent. ... The relations among feudal actors were largely governed by the same principle as those of modern states: the pursuit of self–interest by domination and alliance in accordance with the distribution

> of capabilities. ... Conflict resolution was essentially based on the same principle as that among modern states: the arbitrary use and threat of force. ... In sum, feudal politics were not fundamentally different from modern politics, and the communal discourse did not entail corresponding practices (Fischer, 1992: 461–62).

In other words, if the state of war dominated the interstate system of the Westphalian era, this can hardly be ascribed to its anarchical structure. The turning point introduced by the Westphalian system is to be found less in the existence of a ubiquitous state of war than in the explicit recognition of a state of war. Such a state of war of course existed before 1648 but was analytically denied and normatively repressed in the predominant feudal discourse of the time that postulated the existence of a universal community of mankind.

Hobbes finally came to a somewhat self–contradictory conclusion when he admitted that the state of nature among states actually might not be equivalent to a state of war. As a matter of fact, after establishing a parallel between the 'solitary, poor, nasty, brutish, and short' (Hobbes, 1651: 13) life men could expect in the state of nature and the conditions that states had to meet in their interactions – 'as amongst masterless men, there is perpetual war of every man against his neighbour; ... so every Commonwealth has an absolute liberty to do what it shall judge ... most conducing to its benefit', he adopted a more moderate stance and conceded that the state of nature among states was not as miserable as the state of nature among men. But because they ['kings and persons of sovereign authority'] uphold thereby [by the 'posture of war'] the industry of their subjects, there does not follow from it that misery which accompanies the liberty of particular men' (Hobbes, 1651: 21).

To conclude, the description of international politics proposed by Hobbes may aptly reflect political entities' behaviour during the Thirty Years War and before but it is hardly relevant for the understanding of the Westphalian system itself. Furthermore, as Hobbes himself called into question the synonymy between state of nature and state of war, he may have anticipated – against his will to a certain extent – the analyses of the Westphalian system that were to be made some one hundred years later by two observers of the mid–eighteenth century, the French philosopher Voltaire and the Swiss jurist and diplomat de Vattel.

According to Voltaire,

> for some time now it has been possible to consider Christian Europe, give or take Russia, as une espèce de *grande république* ['a sort of great commonwealth'] partitioned into several states, some monarchic, the others mixed, some aristocratic, others popular, but all dealing with one another; all having the same basic religion, though divided into various sects; all having the same principles of public and political law unknown in other parts of the world. Because of these principles the European nations never enslave their prisoners, they respect the ambassadors of their enemies, ... and above all they agree on the wise policy of maintaining an equal balance of power between themselves so far as they can,

> conducting continuous negotiations even in times of war, and exchanging resident ambassadors or less honourable spies, who can warn all the courts of Europe of the designs of any one, give the alarm at the same time and protect the weaker from the invasions which the strongest is always ready to undertake.[12]

De Vattel was of the opinion that

> Europe forms a political system, an integral body, closely connected by the relations and different interests of the nations inhabiting this part of the world. It is not, as formerly, a confused heap of detached pieces, each of which thought itself very little concerned in the fate of the others, and seldom regarded things which did not immediately concern it. The continual attention of sovereigns to every occurrence, the constant residence of ministers, and the perpetual negotiations, make of modern Europe a kind of republic, of which the members – each independent, but all linked together by the ties of common interest – unite for the maintenance of order and liberty. Hence arose that famous scheme of the political balance, or the equilibrium of power; by which is understood such a disposition of things, as that no one potentate be able absolutely to predominate, and prescribe laws to the others. The surest means of preserving that equilibrium would be that no power should be much superior to the others, that all, or at least the greater part, should be nearly equal in force. Such a project has been attributed to Henry the Fourth: but it would have been impossible to carry it into execution without injustice and violence. ... It is a more simple, and easier, and a more equitable plan, to have recourse to the method just mentioned, of forming confederacies in order to oppose the more powerful potentate, and prevent him from giving law to his neighbours. Such is the mode at present pursued by the sovereigns of Europe ...: a system of policy, which is in itself highly just and wise ... as long as ... pursued ... only by means of alliances, confederacies, and other methods equally lawful (de Vattel, 1758: Book III, §§ 47–48).[13]

These descriptions, in which no assimilation is made between periods of peace and periods of truce in a never–ending state of war, offer two advantages over Hobbes's pessimistic outlook. On the one hand, Voltaire and de Vattel took into account the reality of both the power configuration shaping states' behaviour and the regulation efforts the states undertook in order to try to control the negative aspects of this power distribution. On the other hand, they were fully aware of the limits of such efforts. Thus, Voltaire, who asserted that European states considered themselves to form a 'Christian Europe' united by shared values, also emphasised that European states did not go as far as to feel constrained by public law. He recalled that they more modestly looked forward to maintaining a balance of power and to preserving the independence of smaller states 'as far as they can'. De Vattel, too, when he wrote that balance of power politics was 'just and wise' as long as it was practised by 'lawful means', implicitly admitted that the actual behaviour of the European powers did not always correspond to such wisdom and that, actually, the resort to arms was an intrinsical part of this balance of power politics. In other words, Voltaire and de Vattel underscored the intrinsic ambiguity of the stabilisation efforts of the Westphalian powers. There is no doubt that such efforts were really made and that is why, for one and a half centuries, there was no total war on the Continent comparable to the Thirty Years War. But there is also little doubt that these efforts were fragile, and even contradictory: resort to arms was an inherent part of these efforts to maintain stability thus transforming balance of power politics into power politics disguised as balance of power politics.

In the period that followed the Westphalian Treaties, France, ruled by Mazarin and then by Louis XIV, could not help trying to abuse the power at its disposal after its victory in the Thirty Years War against the Habsburgs. The temptation was indeed too great to try to take the place of Austria as Europe's leading power. The first initiatives taken by France and crowned by the – favourable – Treaties of the Pyrenees (1659) with Spain and the Treaties of Nijmwegen (1678) and Rijswijck (1697) with the Low Countries, evidenced France's successful pursuit of its interests. But when Louis XIV seized the opportunity of the death of the last Habsburg king of Spain to build up a Versailles–Madrid axis with the new Spanish king – who happened to be his own grandson – England and the Dutch Republic joined the Holy Roman Empire to form an alliance in order to check what they considered to be French expansionism. Furthermore, they were not satisfied with fighting French ambitions in the name of their refusal of any imperial temptation. Once they had successfully defeated France, they consciously tried to organise the European system on the basis of the balance of power supposed to prevent any destabilising preponderance on the continent. The letter of the Utrecht settlement, signed at the end of the War of the Spanish Succession, was unambiguous. It recalled in its preamble that 'the war ... was at the beginning undertaken, and was carried on for so many years with the utmost force ..., because of the great danger which threatened the liberty and safety of all Europe, from the too close conjunction of the kingdoms of Spain and France' and proclaimed the will of the parties concerned 'to establish the peace and the tranquillity of Christendom by an equal balance of power, which is the best and most solid foundation of a mutual friendship, and of a concord which will be lasting on all sides'.[14]

Where does this confidence in the advantages of the balance of power system come from? At the origin of the supposedly stabilising virtues of the equilibrium – defined by David Hume as a configuration of powers within which no state benefits from such a force 'as to incapacitate the neighbouring states from defending their rights against it' (Hume, 1752) – lies what Henry Kissinger has called 'the classic expression of the lesson of history that no order is safe without physical safeguards against aggression' (Kissinger, 1957: 318). States are convinced that

a superior power cannot remain within the bounds of true moderation inasmuch as the natural ambition of sovereigns, the flatteries of their councillors and the prejudice of all nations make it impossible to believe that a nation that can conquer the others will abstain from doing so for whole centuries[15] and so they alternately build up their military capacities and try to maintain an equilibrium of forces among themselves, calculating that if no state knows that it is stronger than others, either individually or in a coalition, all will be deterred from launching a war that would be very hard to win.[16]

The doctrine of the balance of power is consistent with the deterrence doctrine, based on the principle *si vis pacem, para bellum* ['if you wish for peace, prepare for war'], conceived by the Roman general Vegetius, which suggests the only way to deter a potential adversary from attacking is to match his military capacities. 'The political objective of military preparations of any kind is to deter other nations from using military force by making it too risky for them to do so. The political aim of military preparations is, in other words, to make the actual application of military force unnecessary by inducing the prospective enemy to desist from the use of military force' (Morgenthau, 2005: 34). There is an inherent problem in this strategy, however. As a matter of fact, a state confronted with an adversary having at its disposal almost the same military capacities knows it is unlikely to win a war. But it also knows that it has equally little chance of losing the war. By definition, such a state is not weaker than the other one and may consequently bet on a victory rather than on a defeat in case of armed confrontation. It is all the more tempted to abide by this doctrine as, according to the basic postulate underlying the balance of power doctrine, states have a general inclination to behave offensively. There would otherwise be no need for mutual balancing. Given this supposed initial war–proneness, it is not clear why a state, looking for supremacy, should perceive an equality of resources as an obstacle instead of an asset. In other words, the balance of power is far from guaranteeing diplomatic prudence. It may encourage risky behaviour, a conclusion already drawn by Rousseau. 'A prince who stakes his cause on the hazards of war knows well enough that he is running risks. But he is less struck with the risks than with the gains on which he reckons, because he is much less afraid of fortune than he is confident in his own wisdom. If he is strong, he counts upon his armies; if weak, upon his allies' (Rousseau, 1760).[17]

Moreover, in Hobbes's analysis, the state of war is the immediate result of the equality of power capacities between men. It is the 'equality of ability', due to the fact that 'nature has made men so equal in the faculties of body and mind', which originates 'equality of hope in the attaining of our ends' and makes men invade their fellow–men 'for gain, for safety, and for reputation' or 'endeavour to destroy or subdue one another' (Hobbes, 1651: 13). Even if the analogy of the state of nature among men cannot be directly transposed to the state of anarchy among states, the observers of the Westphalian equilibrium themselves deduced the stability of nineteenth–century Europe from the inequality among powers, in contrast with the equality prevailing during the seventeenth and eighteenth centuries: 'Had the surface of the globe been divided into equal parts, no such union would ever have taken place; and an eternal war of each against the whole is probably the only event we should have heard of'.[18] In the Westphalian system, states perceived themselves to be roughly equal in military force and, far from being incited to act prudently, they constantly sought to improve their relative positions by resorting to violence.

Let us now consider the concrete strategies adopted by the major European powers to maintain a general balance, a strategy that de Vattel summed up as follows: 'Forming confederacies in order to oppose the more powerful potentate, and prevent him from giving law to his neighbours' is a better means of preserving the equilibrium than trying to maintain a system in which all are 'nearly equal in force'. Instead of practising internal balancing, i.e. increasing their own capacities, European rulers preferred to resort to external balancing, i.e. joining in alliances in order to deal with the stronger among them (de Vattel, 1758: Book III, § 48).[19] Does this choice not mean that general equality is not tantamount to stability?

In any case, external balancing is hardly more favourable to stability. Indeed, states join alliances in order to further their own national interests,[20] which are likely to clash not only with the interests of their adversaries but also with those of their own allies. According to the upholders of the balance of power doctrine, fluidity and flexibility are necessary requirements for successful alliances. In more concrete terms, any state belonging to a coalition will leave its partner(s) and join its former adversary/ies in case of a shift in the balance. To quote Morgenthau, 'any nation will shun alliances if it believes that it is strong enough to hold its own unaided or that the burden of the commitments resulting from the alliance is likely to outweigh the advantages to be expected' (Morgenthau, 2005: 193). A state, even while being an ally, will not exclude the possibility of preferring its own egoistic national interest to the common interest of the alliance. Its commitment to an alliance is, by definition, 'conditional in its foundations and putative in its results' (Haine, 2004: 111). On the one hand, an ally will hardly hesitate to adopt a 'buck–passing' strategy by trying to get another member of the coalition to bear the burden of deterring or even fighting a potential aggressor.[21] On the other hand, this allied state is likely to be tempted to choose a 'bandwagon' policy, i.e. joining forces with a former adversary, if such a strategy might give it a share in this power's anticipated victory.[22] An offensive power has thus another obvious reason to hope that a possible equality of forces with its adversary/ies will not last very long once it has launched its attack, and it is far from evident that it will adopt self–restraint in its relations with its present or prospective adversaries.

To sum up, if from a logical standpoint a balanced distribution of military resources is likely to incite a state to aggressive behaviour as much as to prudent action, depending on the risk–tolerance or risk–aversion of its rulers, then a balanced distribution of capabilities will engender stability on the only condition that the major powers adopt a status quo policy because they are satisfied with the existing system. But in that case, the main cause for stability is less the balanced configuration of power than the internalised legitimacy of the existing order.

According to Adam Watson, the eighteenth century, an 'age of reason and of balance' tantamount to 'order and progress', was precisely characterised by such a balanced distribution of power internalised as legitimate. The hegemonic ambitions of Louis XIV were checked by a coalition including no predominant power, and the initially bipolar order hinging on the Habsburgs and the Bourbons was progressively transformed into a multipolar system including, in addition to France and Austria, three other great powers, Great Britain, Prussia and Russia (which had taken the place of Spain and Sweden), plus a number of medium and smaller powers – the Low Countries, Bavaria, Saxony, Denmark, Poland (Watson, 1992: 198).

If Watson is right, why then did the Seven Years War take place, pitting a Franco–Austrian coalition against an English–Prussian alliance from 1756 to 1763? Either this war was a mere war of adjustment, through which England, according to the balance of power doctrine, checked France's expansionist policy: in which case France could not be considered to be a satisfied power accepting the legitimacy of the status quo established by the Utrecht and Rastatt Treaties. Or France, indeed, was a satisfied power and it was England which regarded France's satisfaction as an opportunity to try to change the status quo in favour of its own interests. Whatever the answer to this enigma may be – and let me remind the reader that the war was initiated by the British – there is hardly any doubt that 'the idea of a viable and commonly accepted status quo [was] decisively rejected by all the major powers throughout [this] century' (Sofka, 2001: 151).

The same strategies prevailed after 1768 as, indeed, 'the struggle for mastery between Britain and France' continued to be 'the dominant idea running right through the century' (153). Given the exhaustion of the protagonists and the distribution of power resources, a period of peace following the Treaty of Paris would have seemed a plausible prediction. After its victory in North America, Great Britain was invulnerable; defeated France was weakened; Russia was safe and could exert its domination in Northern and Eastern Europe; Austria and Prussia, caught between France and Russia, were paralysed by their rivalry in the German territory. And yet, there was an escalation of violence. Considered to be a zero–sum game,[23] the balance of power game turned out to be 'one of pure balance of conquests' favouring 'the *beati possidentes* ['blessed are those who have power'] and the big battalions' (Schroeder, 1994: 33, 537). The various European leaders internalised Russian Tsarina Catherine's aphorism 'Who gains nothing, loses',[24] and the strategy of balancing was tantamount to offensive *Machtpolitik* and not to defensive *Realpolitik*. It consisted in taking the leadership of an offensive coalition favouring conquest instead of a defensive alliance fostering stability, asking for compensation and indemnification at the least sustained loss and resorting to preventive strikes at the least anticipated imbalance.[25]

The result was the exact opposite of the proclaimed aims.[26] Far from being stable, the Westphalian equilibrium was marked by a succession of violent conflicts involving all the major powers in opposition to each other, but nevertheless agreeing on the fate of the smaller powers whose independence was supposed to be guaranteed by the balance of power principle. Three times was Poland divided among its Russian, Prussian and Austrian neighbours;[27] Bavaria and other German entities were regularly acquired by the selfsame powers through exchange or donation, regardless of the local populations' aspirations, and the territory of the

Ottoman Empire was progressively curtailed.

To conclude, the history of European international politics from the end of the Thirty Years War to the outbreak of the French Revolution proves that the Westphalian equilibrium was less constitutive of an international society than of an international system, i.e., to quote Raymond Aron, a set of 'political units that maintain regular relations with each other and that are all capable of being implicated in a generalized war' (Aron, 2003: 94). Paul Schroeder sees the Westphalian system as 'a balance of competition' instead of 'satisfaction', provoking 'innumerable and fruitless wars'[28] which 'refutes the notion that balancing practices and techniques promote equilibrium, limited conflict, and preserve the independence of essential actors, or can do so. Instead, they naturally tend to produce imbalance, hegemony, and systemic conflict' (Schroeder, 1994: 48).[29]

*   *   *

The French Revolution triggered the last of the systemic conflicts of this period – the cycle of the French Revolutionary and Napoleonic Wars from 1792 to 1815.[30] During these years, the amoral foreign policy behaviour of the seventeenth and eighteenth centuries progressively evolved, first into a pseudo–moral crusade of the popularly legitimised national sovereignty principle,[31] and then into the essentially imperial–colonialist expansionism of Napoleon, who feared neither God nor man.

The first wars of this cycle largely fall into traditional categories though, after their victory at Valmy, the French dropped their defensive posture in favour of a more messianic offensive. Beyond the diversionary motivations which may have guided the Girondins at the very outset of their resort to arms,[32] French expansionism, at least until the Directoire, was due to the country's will to spread the new national sovereignty principle instead of the dynastically legitimated principle of monarchical sovereignty; as well as to its long–time anti–Habsburg feelings, to its assertive military ambitions and to more traditional security aims – the consolidation of the so–called natural borders and the establishment of satellite regimes in the neighbouring states. During this first phase, the various protagonists' behaviour was perfectly in tune with previous patterns. The prevailing rhetoric appealed to the necessity of preserving the balance of power. For example, according to the First Coalition's manifesto, 'no power interested in the maintenance of the balance of power in Europe could see with indifference the Kingdom of France, which at one time formed so important a weight in this great balance, delivered any longer to domestic agitations and to the horrors of disorder and anarchy[33] which, so to speak, have destroyed her political existence'.[34] But the policy followed was more akin to a balance of competition. France's convincing victory in 1795 led to no stable diplomatic success. Every power talked peace and balance but meant victory and domination. The discourse–practice gap had nothing to do with cynicism or hypocrisy. Quite simply, nobody wanted peace or, to be more precise, nobody had internalised the idea of stable peace, as the only conceivable plan of peace was an armed truce.

The Napoleonic episode both confirmed and changed these practices. After

Napoleon's successive triumphs, the Treaty of Amiens signed with the United Kingdom in 1802, as well as the Treaties of Tilsit concluded with Russia in 1807, might have been conducive to an at least temporarily stabilised international system, comparable to the periods of limited peace characteristic of the Westphalian equilibrium. These accords were indeed based on an implicit recognition of the coexistence of three great powers – France, Great Britain, Russia – each one separated from the others by geographic boundaries (the Channel) or buffer–zones (Austria and Prussia), and founded on the spoliation of Poland, Venice, the Piedmont and various German ecclesiastical entities.

However Napoleon was not satisfied with mere co–preponderance. He wanted to get rid of any British presence through the implementation of the Continental Embargo,[35] and sought to create an empire overseas in order to exert effective control over the external and internal sovereignty of the conquered entities. Napoleon's ambition knew no limits.[36] His aggressive behaviour was constitutive of an imperialist policy in the strict sense of the word, i.e. in the sense of military conquests with a view to exerting political sway over the conquered territories.[37] He was looking for something else than traditional domination and supremacy and wanted to transform Europe, organised on the basis of independent states since 1648, into a set of colonies, which was incompatible with the existence of a system founded on the mutual recognition of sovereign entities.

To put it bluntly, during the Napoleonic era, the European system was no longer homogeneous but heterogeneous. According to Aron, a homogeneous system is a system in which 'the states belong to the same type, obey the same conception of policy', whereas in a heterogeneous system 'the states are organized according to different principles and appeal to contradictory values' (Aron, 2003: 100). Seen from this perspective, the Westphalian equilibrium was homogeneous, as indeed the various powers perceived international politics from the same perspective, i.e. as a competitive equilibrium. Conversely the Napoleonic episode was a heterogeneous moment, as Napoleonic France appealed to 'contradictory values' in its will to subordinate the sovereignty principle to the imperial principle.

It was precisely the awareness of this heterogeneity, the consciousness of the immense cost of the spell of violence unchained by Napoleonic France, which led European powers to establish a new regulation method of international politics after Napoleon's defeat. The Concert of Europe was proposed at the Vienna Congress by the United Kingdom, the country which had brought about Napoleon's downfall.

NOTES

1   Charles de Montesquieu, *The Spirit of Laws, Book 13* (1748). Source: http://www.constitution.org /cm/sol.txt.

2   The awareness of, and the legitimacy of the difference between, the hierarchical imperial structure and the anarchical international structure date back to the time of the Westphalian

Treaties. That is the reason why I have chosen to start my analysis in 1648, and not in 1495, i.e. at the outset of the Italian wars opposing France and the two branches of the Habsburgs. These wars are sometimes considered to be the first manifestation of the contemporary inter-state system: see, for instance, Jack Levy, *War in the Modern Great Power System 1495–1975* (Lexington: Kentucky University Press, 1983). However, a quick look at Machiavelli's and Bodin's writings proves that during this transition period, the then major actors still did not make any clear distinction between the centralised domestic order and the decentralised international milieu.

3   Kalevi J. Holsti, *Peace and War: Armed Conflicts and International Order 1648–1989* (Cambridge: Cambridge University Press, 1991), p. 25.

4   According to Robert Gilpin, *War and Change in War Politics* (Princeton: Princeton University Press, 1981), p. 10, 'an international system is stable (i.e., in a state of equilibrium) if no state believes it profitable to attempt to change the system'.

5   This ambitious plan, which dated back to 1519, was successively endorsed by Charles V and Philip II of Spain during the sixteenth century, and their respective successors, Ferdinand II and Philip IV during the first half of the seventeenth century. It was once and for all abandoned in 1659, when Spain, which was not concerned by the Treaties of 1648, acknowledged its defeat towards France and accepted the Treaty of the Pyrenees.

6   Most contemporary scholars agree with the idea that the Habsburg ambitions were a real threat to the other European powers. See, for instance, Bull, 1977: 31 or K. Holsti, *Peace and War*, *op. cit.*, p. 26. Conversely, Andreas Osiander, 'Sovereignty, International Relations and the Westphalian Myth', *International Organization*, 55, N°2 (Spring 2001), pp. 251–287, thinks that the Austrian supremacy was actually exaggerated by the Swedish and French propaganda in order to justify their intervention in the war which, at the outset, did not directly affect them.

7   To my knowledge, the Italian Giovanni Botero was the first author to use the concept of 'reason of state' in his essay called *Della ragione di stato*, published in 1589. The idea however was already implicitly present in Machiavelli's *The Prince*, written in 1513 and published in 1532. The best presentation of the reason of state doctrine remains Friedrich Meinecke, *Machiavellism: The Doctrine of Raison d'Etat and its Place in Modern History* (1924) (London: Transaction Publishers, 1997). See also Etienne Thuau, *Raison d'Etat et pensée politique à l'époque de Richelieu* (1966) (Paris: Albin Michel, 2000), as well as N. Keohane, *Philosophy and State in France: The Renaissance to the Enlightenment* (Princeton: Princeton University Press, 1980).

8   The essay 'Of the Interest of the Princes and States of Christianity', which was published in 1639 by one of the main leaders of the French Protestants, the Viscount Henry de Rohan, perfectly illustrates the primacy of foreign policy interests over domestic considerations, and the ensuing differentiation between the so-called high politics and low politics. Despite being a fierce domestic opponent to Richelieu, de Rohan accepted to become Richelieu's right hand man during the Thirty Years War, an attitude he justified by invoking the superior interests of France's national security. See the French edition of his essay: Duc Henri de Rohan, *De l'intérêt des Princes et Etats de la Chrétienté* (Paris: PUF, 1995).

9   See Waltz, (1979), according to whom states are security-seekers.

10   See Mearsheimer 2001, according to whom states are power-maximisers.

11 Immanuel Kant, *Perpetual Peace: A Philosophical Sketch* (1795, Section II). In spite of his description of the existing European political landscape of the eighteenth century as a state of war, Kant was convinced that a perpetual peace could be established. He did not share the tradition of despair characterising Hobbes and believed, quite on the contrary, that wars were a vehicle through which a cosmopolitan peace would finally arise. See also his *Idea of a Universal History* (1784).

12 Voltaire, *Siècle de Louis XIV* (1751–1756), quoted in Watson, 1992: 206–7.

13 Jack Levy, 'What Do Great Powers Balance Against?', in Paul, Wirtz & Fortmann, 2004: 29–51, recalls that the balance of power principle goes back to the Greek historian Polybius: 'We should never contribute to the attainment by one state of a power so preponderant, that none dare dispute with it even for their acknowledged rights'.

14 Quoted in Watson, 1992: 199.

15 *Fénélon, Supplément à L'Examen de conscience sur les devoirs de la royauté* (1734), quoted in French in Bull, 2001: 106.

16 For a defence of the supposed advantages of the balance of power, see Ludwig Dehio, *The Precarious Balance. The Politics of Power in Europe 1494–1945* (1948) (London: Chatto and Windus, 1963), as well as Edward Gulick, *Europe's Classical Balance of Power* (New York: Norton, 1967).

17 Rousseau took his inspiration from Abbé de Saint–Pierre, *Projet pour rendre la paix perpétuelle en Europe* (1713).

18 F. Gentz, *Fragments upon the Balance of Power in Europe*, quoted by H. Bull, 'Society and Anarchy in International Relations', in James Der Derian, 1995: 88.

19 On internal and external balancing, see Waltz, 1979: 168.

20 On alliances, see Walt, 1987 and Glenn Snyder, *Alliance Politics* (Ithaca: Cornell University Press, 1997).

21 On the notion of buck–passing, see Christensen & Snyder, 1990 and Mearsheimer 2001: 157–63 and 267–333.

22 The key works on bandwagon strategy include Eric Labs, 'Do Weak States Bandwagon?', *Security Studies*, 1, N°3 (Spring 1992), pp. 383–416; Randall Schweller, 'Bandwagoning For Profit: Bringing the Revisionist State Back In', *International Security*, 19, N°1 (Summer 1994), pp. 72–107; and S. Walt, *The Origins of Alliances, op. cit.*

23 The mercantilist ethos underpinning the trade policies of the contemporary main powers sharpened their international rivalries. International trade was perceived to be a zero–sum game, and economic policy and power politics were interchangeable terms, 'no man (profiting) but by the loss of others' according to the French author Montaigne.

24 Quoted in Sofka, 2001: 160.

25 In the *Preliminary Articles* of his *Perpetual Peace*, Kant denounced the various practices implied by the balance of power doctrine as so many obstacles to a perpetual peace, be they the 'secret reservations' included in many peace treaties, the acquisitions of territories by other states 'through inheritance, exchange, purchase or donation', the 'debts contracted in connection with the external affairs', or the interferences in another state's domestic affairs. More broadly speaking, he held the balance of power principle in contempt because of its inability to guarantee stability. In an essay called *The Principle of Progress Considered in Connection with the Relation of Theory to Practice of International Law*, he went as far as

to assert that 'a lasting universal peace on the basis of the so–called balance of power in Europe is a mere chimera. It is like the house described by Swift, which was built by an architect so perfectly in accordance with all the laws of equilibrium, that when a sparrow lighted upon it, it immediately fell'.

26 On the – ideological – ambiguities of the balance of power doctrine, see Ernst Haas, 'The Balance of Power. Prescription, Concept or Propaganda?', *World Politics* 5, N°3 (April 1953), pp. 442–477. These ambiguities are of course still valid concerning today's invocations of the balance of power principle. For instance, the National Security Strategy of the USA adopted in September 2002 claims on the one hand that 'the great struggles of the twentieth century between liberty and totalitarianism ended with a decisive victory of the forces of freedom', that 'the US enjoys a position of unparalleled military strength and great economic and political influence', and on the other asserts that the US seeks 'to create a balance of power that favours human freedom'. Obviously, if the forces of freedom are prevailing and if the US enjoys unparalleled influence, then there is no need to re–establish a balance of power favouring freedom.

27 In fact, Poland was partitioned only one time before the French Revolutionary Wars, in 1772, by Austria, Prussia and Russia. The other two partitions took place in 1793 and 1795. Furthermore, the partition of Poland between Hitler's Germany and Stalin's Soviet Union, planned in the Molotov–von Ribbentrop Pact signed in 1939, eventually occurred after Poland's invasion by the Nazis in September 1939, with the USSR controlling a third of its Eastern territory.

28 Statement made by E. Burke, quoted by Herbert Butterfield, 'The Balance of Power', in H. Butterfield and M. Wight (eds), *Diplomatic Investigations*, London: Allen and Unwin, 1966, pp. 132–48.

29 Schroeder uses the term 'hegemony' in the traditionally realist, non–Gramscian, sense of material pre–eminence, preponderance, supremacy and illegitimate domination.

30 The wars that took place before the Treaty of Amiens signed in 1802 are called the Revolutionary Wars; the post–1802 wars are referred to as the Napoleonic Wars.

31 See Mlada Bukovansky, *Legitimacy and Power Politics: The American and French Revolution in International Relations* (Princeton: Princeton University Press, 2002).

32 On the diversionary theory of war, see Jack Levy, 'The Diversionary Theory of War: A Critique', in Magnus Midlarsky (Ed.), *Handbook of War Studies* (London: Unwin Hyman, 1989), 1st edition, pp. 259–88.

33 Needless to say that in this quote 'anarchy' is used in the common sense, equivalent to trouble and disorder.

34 Quoted in Morgenthau, 2006: 200.

35 The *Grand Empire* reached its apex in 1810. On the Continent, Sweden and Portugal were the only territories that were not under Napoleon's control, and Great Britain and Russia were the only powers which could resist his ambitions. It was precisely his planned invasion of Russia which brought about his defeat, together with the United Kingdom's insular security.

36 Napoleon himself acknowledged that 'my power depends on my glory and my glories on the victories I have won. My power will fail if I do not feed it on new glories and new victories. Conquest has made me what I am and only conquest can enable me to hold my position.' Quoted in Kennedy, 1989:170.

37 The notion of imperialism was invented by Napoleon's political supporters in France. 'Imperialists' was the name given to the members of the political faction favourable to Napoleon's empire. Some three generations later, the British supporters of Disraeli's foreign policy were also called 'imperialists'.

chapter two | the 'british concert'

England appeared in Vienna with all the glamour which she owed to her immense successes, to the eminent part she had played in the Coalition, to her limitless influence, to a solid basis of prosperity and power such as no other country has acquired in our days – in fact to the respect and fear which she inspired and which affected her relations with all the other governments. Profiting by this, England could have imposed her will on Europe.
(Friedrich von Gentz[1])

The 'long nineteenth century' (Meadwell, 2001) which started with Napoleon's final defeat, was the most stable international order since the contemporary international system came into existence. Indeed for a period of ninety–nine years there was no war simultaneously opposing all the major powers and the comparatively few armed conflicts in which a couple of major powers were involved were short, caused relatively few victims and limited material damage.[2] Furthermore, the impact of the major powers' armed interventions in the domestic affairs of small and middle powers was somewhat constrained by their will to preserve the overall status quo.

Various explanations of this overall stability can be proposed. A first explanation relates to Lewis Richardson's well known war–weariness hypothesis.[3] The disaster caused by the French Revolutionary and Napoleonic Wars conferred some form of immunity on most European peoples and elites and induced them to drop, at least for a certain lapse of time, war as a rational means for conflict resolution.[4] A second explanation refers to the peace–through–economic–interdependence thesis. The nineteenth century was the century of industrial revolution and of capitalist expansion, and the free–trade doctrine which replaced mercantilism contributed to the pacification of international politics, as war was henceforth perceived to be irrational and counterproductive.[5] Lastly, a third explanation, mainly advanced by Marxist authors, emphasises the importance of the colonial wars fought by the major European powers. Acting as a kind of safety valve, they indirectly stabilised the European system by diverting European states from resorting to armed force in their mutual interactions.[6]

In this chapter I will argue that, notwithstanding the importance of these factors, the most crucial cause of the peaceful nineteenth century is the fundamental change that took place in the field of diplomatic ideas and collective mentalities. European states progressively became conscious that the competitive and conflicting balance of power politics, which had led to a twenty–three–year cycle of wars from 1792 to 1815, could no longer be pursued. They thus established a set of specific devices with a view to regulating their interactions through a concert of quasi–institutionalised co–operation procedures. Certainly, the balance of power principle was not abandoned; but it was embedded in a legal–institutional framework whose objective was to prevent the militarisation of great–power conflicts through the adoption of consensual norms of appropriate behaviour, while simultaneously guaranteeing the independence and integrity of the smaller entities, in total contrast to the frequent partition schemes of the past.

At the time of the Vienna Congress, this new mode of regulation was essentially favoured by the United Kingdom and Tsarist Russia, the two lateral powers which had been the main players in Napoleon's defeat. Considering the fact that their leadership was accepted by the other victorious powers, Austria and Prussia, and ratified by post–Napoleonic France, it is generally admitted that the stability of the nineteenth century was due to the multipolar structure of the then international system (Watson, 1992: 238 *sqq*),[7] whether or not it is considered to have been homogeneous (Aron, 1962: 99 *sqq*) or legitimate (Kissinger, 1957). However, even when the Crimean War tolled the knell of the Concert of Europe,[8] the international anarchy continued to be regulated, as proved by the successful integration of the new Italian, and above all German, unified states within the status quo.

The continuity of the process of maturing from international anarchy to international society was not at all due to multipolarity. The most important factor, I argue, was British supremacy. The United Kingdom had benefited from a resource superiority from the very first days of its involvement in the Napoleonic wars and, during the first half of the nineteenth century, London could exert a self–interested but nevertheless benign leadership in Europe, thus paving the way for the stabilisation and consolidation of international society. After a while however, Britain went back in its European policy to the more traditional *Realpolitikal* practices it had followed overseas. From that moment onwards, the ongoing European stability was less due to Britain's benign leadership than to the deterrent effect of its supremacy on the states tempted to challenge by force the existing status quo.

At the end of the nineteenth century, Great Britain's resource advantage progressively vanished, because of the growing prosperity of the United States and the rise of a dissatisfied power, Germany. The period of parity between the rising revisionist contender and the declining hegemonic power led to London's growing inability to deter Germany's expansive ambitions, which explains the increasing instability of the international system. More exactly, the double challenge to British hegemony by both Imperial Germany in 1914 and Nazi Germany in 1939 marked the end of *pax Britannica*, as the United Kingdom could no longer profit from the same overwhelming resource advantage that, one century before, had allowed the country to successfully foil Napoleon's plans.

* * *

'In the beginning was Napoleon', Paul Schroeder writes, thus stressing the decisive impact of the French Revolutionary and Napoleonic Wars on the evolution of the European political system.

> Napoleon … finally convinced the statesmen of Europe, hard persons to teach, that what was at risk was not merely certain goods in international politics (peace, security, territorial integrity) but the very life of principles of European politics which made these goods and others possible, the independence of European states, the existence of a European states system. He made them see that the kind of politics they had hitherto practised themselves had made his rise to power and his colonial rule possible; that to preserve the international system … they would have not only to defeat or curb him but also to abandon their own old politics, and discover or invent something else (Schroeder, 1994: 371, 395).[9]

The Vienna Congress held in 1815 symbolised this learning process. It was a deliberate effort to reconcile 'great–power demands for influence and control with small–power requirements for independence', balance 'the needs of the international community against the needs and the claims of the individual states', secure and legitimise 'international rights while also allowing room for international change' (577). Whereas during the Westphalian equilibrium the European powers had exclusively relied upon balance of power techniques to regulate their mutual interactions, they would from now on call upon common institutions.

Two main institutional devices were set up in order to guarantee long–term stability. The first one was the establishment of a number of associations composed of various states committed to coordinating their behaviour instead of acting egoistically as before. The German Confederation, for instance, aimed both at creating a defensive union against the risk of French retaliation, and reconciling the rival ambitions of Prussia and Austria which, in the past, had torn apart Germany's territory. The Holy Alliance was a paternalist union of the Russian, Prussian and Austrian monarchs over their respective populations, purporting to preserve the survival of the absolute regimes in Europe. Its role in maintaining international stability cannot be neglected (Kissinger, 1957) as it was favourably viewed by the British. Indeed, and despite his suspicions about Tsar Alexander I of Russia – he did not hesitate to call the Holy Alliance a 'sublime mysticism and nonsense' (quoted in Ikenberry, 2001: 101), Castlereagh was conscious that there had been a link between the outbreak of the French Revolution and the ensuing wars of 1792–1815. But the most important international association was, of course, the Quadruple Alliance.

The Quadruple Alliance was created in 1814 by the Treaty of Chaumont. Great Britain, Russia, Austria and Prussia renounced furthering their national interests at the price of sacrificing common objectives and united

> not on the goal of military victory or an abstract vision of peace, but on a practical concept of peace: a Europe of independent sovereign states, equal in

rights, status, and security, if vastly unequal in power, responsibility and influence, protected by a balance of power on the one hand and rights, law, morality, and consensus on the other (504).[10]

They bound themselves to remain united for twenty years within a defensive alliance and guarantee mutual protection against any new threat from France caused by a potential revival of French expansionism or the possible accession to power of a member of the Bonaparte family. It is true that, at the time of the conclusion of the Treaty of Chaumont, Napoleon had not been completely defeated and the four allied powers were mainly guided by their common will to continue the struggle until Napoleon's downfall. They were indeed motivated by *Realpolitikal* considerations, in their wish to prevent any power from succumbing to the temptation of getting on the bandwagon with Napoleon, or signing a separate peace treaty with France. To quote Andreas Osiander, 'they had to co–operate precisely because they could not trust one another'.[11] Nevertheless there were provisions for a lasting European settlement in the Treaty of Chaumont.

In the past, the European powers had looked forward to limiting and constraining their respective power by balancing efforts and territorial partitions. Henceforth, they would try to bind themselves in permanent unions with a view to controlling one another, which was indeed a revolutionary change. Friedrich Gentz, Metternich's counsellor, gave a very precise description of this point. 'The principle of equilibrium or, rather, counterweights formed by particular alliances – the principle which has governed, and too often troubled and engulfed, Europe for three centuries – has been succeeded by a principle of general union, uniting all the states by a federal bond under the direction of the five principal powers' (quoted in Ikenberry, 2001: 105–6).[12]

The 'federal bond' Gentz alluded to was the second institutional device of the Vienna agreement. It mainly consisted in the regular organisation of diplomatic summits and conferences aiming at a collective management of conflicting interests and territorial disputes. The idea arose during the iterated encounters of the various representatives of the allies in the last two years of the Napoleonic Wars. Castlereagh and Metternich became aware that the most appropriate means of maintaining constructive links was to meet regularly and have personal contacts, instead of waiting for the outbreak of a crisis before calling for the organisation of a diplomatic summit. They acknowledged that such encounters offered the opportunity for every participant to express their views and agreed that such meetings increased transparency while reducing the risks of unilateral temptations. In accordance with Article V of the Treaty of Chaumont, which stipulated that the allies promised to 'concert together … as the means best adapted to guaranteeing to Europe, and to themselves reciprocally, the continuance of the Peace' (quoted in Ikenberry: 104), Article VI of the Treaty of the Quadruple Alliance signed in Paris in 1815 enshrined the practice of great power meetings.

The High Contracting Parties (agree) to renew their meetings at fixed periods ..., for the purpose of consulting upon their common interests, and for the considerations of the measures which at each of these periods shall be considered the most salutary for the repose and prosperity of Nations, and for the maintenance of the Peace of Europe. (104)

This conference diplomacy paved the way for a continuous management of the international order by the European great powers. Instead of relying upon force, the Concert resorted to moral persuasion to prevent aggressive actions, limit revisionist demands on territorial redrawing, define appropriate behaviour with regard to small powers, and privilege peaceful means of conflict resolution. By combining 'elements of the old European logic of balance with new legal–institutional arrangements meant to manage and restrain power' (Ikenberry, 2001: 114), the Concert was the expression of the new collective awareness of the great powers in their desire to be responsible and guided by their duties as well as by their rights, by their obligations as well as by their interests.

During the three decades following Waterloo, European international politics was in all logic marked

> by an unusually high and self–conscious level of co–operation among the major European powers. The states did not play the game as hard as they could; they did not take advantage of others' short–run vulnerabilities. ... Each state co–operated in the expectation that the others would do the same. Multilateral and self–restraint methods of handling their problems were preferred to the more common unilateral and less restrained methods (Jervis, 1985: 59).

France was the first great power to benefit from the new regime once the country was no longer perceived as a potential threat after the Bourbon Restoration. As early as 1816, it obtained a reduction of the war indemnities which it was in a position to pay thanks to a loan granted by British bankers. At the Conference of Aix–la–Chapelle in 1818 it was decided to anticipate the withdrawal of the army of occupation from the French territory and, more significantly, to accept France's integration into the Concert. This led to the creation of the Quintuple Alliance, though the Quadruple Alliance was maintained as a precaution against any threat from France.

The middle powers, such as the Low Countries and Spain, as well as the peripheral Ottoman Empire, also benefited from such prevailing moderation. Contrary to what had been the case throughout the eighteenth century, they were no longer the classic victims of the great powers' rivalries. Although 'military actions were initiated to defend the existing socio–political order from revolutionary threat' (Kennedy, 1989: 205), there was a significant difference from eighteenth–century practices. In 1823, for instance, France, with the tacit agreement of the Holy Alliance and the benign neglect of the United Kingdom, intervened in

Spain in order to restore King Ferdinand to the throne. Once it had re–established order, its armies left Spanish territory, without trying to profit from this military intervention at the expense of the other Great Powers, contrary to what had happened in the reign of Louis XIV.[13]

If we turn to the territorial modifications which took place on the Continent when Greece and Belgium attained independence, the very existence of the European Concert prevented any excessive weakening of the Ottoman Empire or the Low Countries. In that respect, French self–restraint during Belgian independence was quite revealing of the smooth working of the Vienna regulation. France played the role of an honest broker in its own sphere of influence as acknowledged by the Concert, thus showing that it had accepted its integration in the existing order, and internalised the idea that its prestige and grandeur no longer resided in its capacity of overthrowing the status quo but in its willingness to co–operate with the other powers.

Considering its capacity to preserve the independence, vital interests and status of the major actors, reconcile their rights and claims with their obligations, and allow them to pursue their individual aims without threatening the existing European order in its totality, there is no doubt that the European Concert was the first successful manifestation of an international society, thanks to the goodwill of the states concerned to adopt strategic self–restraint, accept mutual constraints, respect established norms of appropriate behaviour and even give proof of loyalty.

The Concert came to a close in 1848 at the outbreak of the Spring of Nations,[14] a result of the countries' incapacity to satisfy the material needs of their people and embody a legitimate political authority for their subjects. From the perspective of the present book, it matters little whether the revolutions of 1848 originated in Marx and Engels's *Manifesto of the Communist Party* or in the principle of national sovereignty diffused by Napoleon during his bloody conquest of Europe. Indeed, the disappearance of the Concert had no impact whatsoever on the long–term stability of the international system established in 1815. Quite on the contrary, neither the Crimean War nor the Wars of Italian and German unifications threatened to upset the international status quo, despite the successive implications of the major powers – France, Great Britain and Russia, France and Austria, Austria and Prussia, Prussia and France.

The main question is therefore to determine and define the missing link that could help us explain the stability of the international system concomitant to the existence of the European Concert before 1848 and the persistence of the same stable environment after 1848 and the end of the European Concert. I uphold the idea that the common feature was British supremacy, the unipolar structure which marked the apparently multipolar international system of the nineteenth century. In the first half of the nineteenth century, the prevailing role of the United Kingdom had prompted London to lay the foundations of an international society. After 1848, the evolution of British supremacy led Britain's rulers to resort to a more classical form of *Realpolitik*.

At the end of the Napoleonic Wars in 1815, two countries, Great Britain and

Russia, clearly seemed to exert supremacy in the organisation of the post–war order. The United Kingdom emerged as the leading global power, thanks to its industrial development, its financial networks, its navy and its colonial empire. Russia was the predominant Continental power, because of its huge territory, its vast population, and its large standing army. There is hardly any doubt that such a general feeling made it impossible for the re–emergence of the competitive multi-polar equilibrium that had marked the eighteenth century, especially as the other three powers, including victorious Prussia and Austria, were comparatively weak in comparison with Russia and Great Britain. But can we really speak of an Anglo–Russian leadership?

Admittedly, London and Saint–Petersburg shared the main responsibility for Napoleon's final defeat, and during the years 1813–15, both Alexander I and Castlereagh successfully led the fight against *La Grande Armée* and saw to the organisation of the Vienna settlement. For instance, Russia agreed with Great Britain to grant France the right to recover its 1789 frontiers and both favoured the emergence of a joint Austrian–Prussian leadership in the German Confederation. Russia also successfully negotiated with London the recognition of its sphere of influence in Eastern Europe by imposing its territorial and constitutional claims upon Poland, in exchange of its own recognition of Prussia's domination over Saxony. All these elements support the idea of a kind of Anglo–Russian co–lead-ership in the early stage of the long nineteenth century. However, they cannot hide the fact that the United Kingdom was undoubtedly 'the deciding voice' (Schroeder, 1984: 553) in Vienna.

As a matter of fact, the Vienna agreement was proposed and imposed by Great Britain, as exemplified by its sustained efforts to finance the costs of the wars fought by the coalesced forces against Napoleon – Sweden, Portugal, Sicily, but also Austria, Prussia, and Russia. On the one hand, it was Pitt's gold, managed by Castlereagh from 1813 onwards, which prevented any member of the coalition from leaving the alliance and adopting either a bandwagon or a buck–passing strategy. Metternich, for instance, who left Napoleon's Continental system in 1814, had been tempted to sign a separate peace with France after Napoleon's transitory victories in spring 1814. Without Great Britain's 'sterling diplomacy', he would not have hesitated very long, as he was a convinced supporter of the tra-ditional balance of power practices. On the other hand, London granted its finan-cial aid on the very condition that the allies should accept the post–war settlement Castlereagh's Foreign Office administration was preparing. In other words, while the United Kingdom could not win the war alone without the help of Russia – or, more precisely, the Russian winter – Russia on its part could not afford to dispense with Britain's subsidies. London's role during the French Revolutionary and Napoleonic Wars cannot be under–estimated. Indeed, though the total amount of the financial aid provided by London to its allies was higher than the contributions paid during all the previous wars taken together, it remained lower than England's own war effort.[15] In other words, Great Britain was more than a mere ally, which is tantamount to saying that the post–Napoleonic Wars international system was characterized neither by a bipolar structure opposing London and Saint–Petersburg, nor by a multipolar configuration including the four Continental powers and the United Kingdom, but rather by a unipolar hierarchy in favour of Great Britain.

In order to explain such a situation which, according to the balance of power principle, should never have happened, we have to go back to the definition of the balance of power and to the actual balance of power policies adopted by the European powers during the eighteenth century.

During the Westphalian equilibrium, the various European states, in accordance with the balance of power doctrine, aimed at preventing any other state "from accumulating forces superior to those of its allied rivals" (Aron, 2003: 128). In order to do so, they both increased their own military capacities, thus resorting to an internal balancing strategy, and formed alliances against the state they perceived as potentially predominant or threatening, thus adopting an external balancing strategy. Given that the "usual suspect", i.e. the state suspected of behaving aggressively, was always the same, namely France, it was in all logic against this country that the other European powers formed alliances. By way of consequence, the state which, within the anti–French alliances, best succeeded in its own internal balancing strategy, progressively improved its power position, all the more so as those alliances focussed all their efforts to check France's rise, even though the result may have been at odds with the objectives respectively pursued by each member of the anti–French coalition. Obviously, the state better apt to increase its own capacities was the United Kingdom. London increased its power in proportion to the allies' victories against France in the War of the Spanish Succession, the Seven Years War and, of course, the French Revolutionary and Napoleonic Wars.[16]

To a certain extent, the general configuration which emerged after the Vienna Congress was still a balanced one, if we abide by de Vattel's definition of the concept of balance, i.e. "a disposition of things as that no one potentate be able absolutely to predominate and prescribe laws to the others" (de Vattel, 1758: Book III, § 47), which is tantamount to saying that the equilibrium will still prevail even if one predominant power is as powerful as all the other existing powers taken together, because, in such a configuration, it does not control more resources than the others and cannot thus "prescribe laws" to them. However, if we consider the reality of the situation of Europe from the middle of the eighteenth century onwards, it clearly appears that there was a single preponderant power during that period, namely Great Britain. As British supremacy was not checked by any alliance between the four Continental powers, it can hardly be denied that London profited from such disequilibrium to the detriment of the other states.

In the years that immediately followed the Vienna Congress, this imbalance did not rule out British moderation, quite on the contrary. Under the impulse of Castlereagh and Wellington, the United Kingdom stopped short of using Europe as a means of global domination. British leaders had drawn the lesson from Napoleon's Continental Empire in its attempts to keep Great Britain off the Continent. They were fully aware that England's global supremacy depended on its capacity to appear to the satisfied European states as a power which could guarantee their independence. British self–restraint was the logical result of this awareness. In strategic matters, London avoided reducing the Low Countries to the status of a satellite state, thus proving its willingness to use its supremacy to reconstruct Europe on the basis of the sovereignty principle. In the economic domain, the United Kingdom exerted a benign leadership, by assuming the costs of maintaining free trade, protecting the freedom of the seas, and associating the other European societies with the benefits of these global public goods.

> Most of the time most European states considered Britain's use of its naval power tolerable, even beneficial. It kept the sea lanes open, encouraged and protected commerce, which was not used to monopolize overseas expansion for Britain. There were problems over the slave trade and colonies, ... but the way the British after 1815 ran their formal land and informal overseas empire clearly contributed to stability, at least in Europe (Schroeder, 1984: 575. See also, Kindleberger, 1973).

The scope of this benign hegemony however, remained limited. The British Parliament stuck to its isolationist policy for fear of being entangled on the Continent. Above all, as implied by Schroeder's nuance, the Vienna settlement exclusively concerned European affairs and did not apply to Britain's overseas expansionism, notably in Asia, with the so–called Great Game opposing London and Saint–Petersburg from the Bosporus to India and Central Asia. Moreover, and independently of British intentions, various structural factors combined to subvert the consensus on the necessity of a collective regime organizing the post–Napoleonic order. The Concert had stemmed from the collective awareness that the old balance of power politics had contributed to facilitating the cycle of the French Revolutionary and Napoleonic Wars, but after a time, the memory of the past disaster progressively faded away. The former enemy was no longer perceived as a threat, and the various powers wondered whether it was still in their interest to maintain the post–war alliance. Finally, the leading power was tempted to abandon its self–restraint or, at least, ask its allies to share the burden of maintaining the existing order, and the resulting troubled partnership in its turn encouraged everybody to return to unilateralism. Thus, progressively, the United Kingdom tended to resort once again to its traditional *Realpolitik*.[17]

In 1848, Lord Palmerston clearly summed up the situation. Britain, he said, had 'no eternal friends and no perpetual enemies', but only 'eternal and perpetual interests' it was its 'duty to follow'.[18] In other words, British foreign policy essentially consisted in keeping the balance. However the distribution of power in the mid nineteenth century was hardly comparable to the one prevailing before the end of the eighteenth century, because of Britain's acknowledged primacy. The meaning of the balance of power concept and of the balance of power practice significantly differed from what they had meant during the period of the Westphalian equilibrium.

There were two types of equilibria in the contemporary balance of power.

There was first, if we abide by the definition proposed by de Vattel, a kind of global balance of power between Great Britain and the other – Continental – states, as indeed Great Britain was not more powerful than Russia, France, Austria and Prussia taken together. There was secondly a regional balance of power between the four Continental powers, as their respective resources were roughly equal after France's defeat in 1815. However, since the four Continental powers did not form an alliance to counterbalance Britain's capacities but engaged in a succession of small wars against each other throughout the second half of the nineteenth century, the global balance was actually an imbalance – synonymous with British supremacy and a unipolar structure.

The balancing policy was also twofold. On the one hand, Britain sought to maintain the regional balance on the Continent, with a view to preventing any one of the four Continental powers from becoming preponderant in Europe. 'Of Europe, not in Europe', to quote Carl Schmitt (Schmitt, 2001: 173)[19], Britain adopted the role of the offshore–balancer, also called holder of the balance[20], for that purpose. Obviously, the global imbalance depended on the Continental balance, and London's desire to preserve the Continental balance was thus due to its will to preserve its global financial, commercial, and colonial supremacy. 'The principle of equilibrium which Pitt and Castlereagh held so high was one which applied to European territorial arrangements, not to the colonial and commercial spheres' (Kennedy, 1989: 180).

According to Paul Kennedy, throughout the first two–thirds of the nineteenth century, London succeeded in expanding its global advantage, notably at the expense of Russia. When the Crimean War broke out, the British navy needed only three weeks to reach Sebastopol, 'whereas Russian troops from Moscow sometimes took three months to reach the front' (Kennedy, 1989: 224). Thanks to the industrial revolution, Britain's share of the World Gross Product rose from 1.9 per cent in 1760 to 19.6 per cent one century later, transforming the United Kingdom into a preponderant power fully aware that it was 'a different sort of power' (187). As British economist William Jevons said:

> The plains of North America and Russia are our corn fields; Chicago and Odessa our granaries; Canada and the Baltic are our timber forests; Australasia contains our sheep farms, and in Argentina and on the western prairies of North America are our herds of oxen; Peru sends her silver, and the gold of South Africa and Australia flows to London; the Hindus and the Chinese grow tea for us, and our coffee, sugar and spice plantations are in all the Indies. Spain and France are our vineyards and the Mediterranean our fruit garden; and our cotton grounds, which for long have occupied the Southern United States, are now being extended everywhere in the warm regions of the earth (quoted in Kennedy, 1989: 194).[21]

It was this advantage in resources which allowed Great Britain to maintain the stability of the international order during this period, despite the disappearance of the Concert. In theoretical terms, a balanced configuration is tantamount to stability on the explicit condition that the powers concerned accept the status quo as legitimate and adopt a moderate strategy (see Chapter one), whereas a unipolar structure is peace–prone[22] whatever the attitude of the states, be they security seekers or power–maximisers.[23] First, satisfied powers, which consider the possibility of going to war exclusively for security reasons, are not incited to resort to arms. They are right to believe that the predominant power, which by definition benefits from the existing status quo, has neither interest nor need to resort to arms. It has no need to resort to arms because it can impose its will by the mere demonstration of its excess of power, and it has no interest in resorting to arms because such a strategy would be counterproductive, undermining the existing order by encouraging the secondary status quo powers to form an alliance against it. There are thus two reasons for status quo powers to feel safe in a unipolar structure. Secondly, if we turn to potentially revisionist or aggressive states, in an imbalanced distribution of power the resource gap which separates them from the predominant power logically deters them from resorting to armed force in order to change the status quo, as such a move is likely to have a negative expected utility.[24]

This being said, once a preponderant power resorts to a *Realpolitik* based on the *divide et impera* principle, rather than to an institutionalised concert, the stability of the system depends on its material capacities, i.e. the dynamics of the demographical, economic and technological resources on which its military power is based. In other words, after the end of the Concert system, the continuity of *pax Britannica* was dependent on favourable changes in the overall distribution of material resources among the powers concerned, as there were no more institutional devices collectively managing international affairs. Unfortunately for Britain, at the end of the nineteenth century, changes in this distribution did not favour the existing order. Following America's and Germany's rise, Great Britain had to face up to a relative decline; this was at the origin of the new hegemonic war cycle from 1914 to 1945.[25]

Admittedly, Britain's achievements were still impressive at the beginning of the twentieth century. The British Empire included a quarter of the world's population; the Royal Navy was by far the largest and most powerful navy in the world; and the most dynamic investors, the most important raw material negotiators as well as the world's richest traders, bankers and insurers were to be met in the City of London. But in 1900, the German share of the World Manufacturing Output reached 13.2 per cent, and America's share 23.6 per cent, compared to Britain's 18.5 per cent, and the eve of the First World War saw Great Britain's share fall to a mere 13.6 per cent, overtaken by both America (32 per cent) and Germany (14.8 per cent) (Ikenberry, 2001: 120).

America's overwhelming power capacities had no immediate impact on Britain's predominance, as the US, in spite of its resources, did not yet take part in the international power system. Notwithstanding MacKinley's and Theodore Roosevelt's 'big stick' policy towards Spain in Cuba and the Philippines, the US was a satisfied power, accepting the current status quo. The rise of Germany was a more direct threat to British supremacy, as German unification changed the power distribution among the Continental powers. Contrary to France weakened by the loss of Alsace–Lorraine after its defeat in the Franco–Prussian War of 1870, contrary to Austria–Hungary thrown out from the German territory after the Prussian victory in the Austrian–Prussian War of 1866 and entangled in the Balkans, contrary to Russia severely affected by underdevelopment and caught in revolutionary troubles after its humiliating defeat during the Russian–Japanese War of 1905, the rapidly industrialising Germany increasingly emerged as the one and only great power on the Continent, favoured by its location at the heart of Europe. Germany's rapid development modified the relative positions of all the other Continental powers, thus affecting Britain's supremacy, because global unipolarity depended on the persistence of the regional balance on the Continent. Bismarck may have moderated Germany's expansionism once Germany had become unified, but Kaiser Wilhelm II, in the mid 1890s – from 1895 onwards – declared that Germany had 'great tasks to accomplish outside the narrow boundaries of old Europe', and strove to exert some sort of peaceful 'Napoleonic supremacy over the continent' (Kennedy, 1989: 272). Such a revisionist *Weltpolitik* was not radically different from the expansionist drives characterising the US – though temporarily – or Japan, or even Italy at that time. But dissatisfied Germany was the only great power to possess 'the instruments of power to alter the status quo', and combine 'the modern, industrialized strength of the Western democracies with the autocratic decision–making features of the Eastern monarchies'.[26] It was the only rising power whose continuous growth and potential expansionism to the East or to the West by necessity undermined 'directly, rather than indirectly, the European balance' (Kennedy: 276). The colonial cake was shared between France and the United Kingdom in Africa, the Near and Middle East, and South and South–East Asia; the Western Hemisphere was America's backyard, as stated by Roosevelt's corollary to the Monroe Doctrine; Japan had clearly demonstrated during its war with Russia its ambition and capacities to control the Far East. Germany's potential expansion could therefore only take place on the Continent, to the detriment of its neighbouring powers.

To sum up, the European system, after a period of British primacy, entered a new phase, marked by power parity between a declining status quo hegemon – the UK – and a rising challenger – revisionist Germany. According to the power transition and the hegemonic war theories, such a phase of parity is significantly war–prone. First, a war can break out as a direct consequence of the evolution of the power ratio between the still pre–eminent but already declining hegemon and the rapidly rising dissatisfied challenger. Perceiving the relative rise of the ascending power as a threat either to its own security or to the existing world order, the still–dominant power can be tempted to launch a preventive war against the rising challenger in order to impede an undertaking tantamount to putting an end to its hegemony. Secondly, the expansionist policy of the rising challenger, striving to topple the still predominant hegemon, compels the hegemonic power to intervene and to wage war in order to try to preserve the existing order and its own supremacy, correlated with this order, thus transforming an initially limited local conflict into an escalating major war.

The Peloponnesian War is a good illustration of the first hypothesis: 'As Thucydides explains, the Spartans initiated the Peloponnesian War in an attempt to crush the rising Athenian challenger while Sparta still had the power to do so' (Gilpin, 1981: 191).[27] An illustration of the second hypothesis is the cycle comprising both World Wars. Twice did the United Kingdom declare war on an expansionist Germany: in 1914 because Imperial Germany joined Austria–Hungary's war against Serbia; and in 1939 because Nazi Germany attacked Poland after having invaded Austria and Czechoslovakia.

* * *

World War One tolled the knell of *pax Britannica*. It was indeed the American President Woodrow Wilson, the head of what was, potentially, the greatest power because of its superiority in material resources, and not the British Prime Minister, as had been the case in 1815, who took the initiative of assuming the responsibility for outlining a project for the organisation of the post–war world, founded on a collective security system.

Wilson was inspired by a liberal vision of international politics. In his desire to make the world 'safe for democracy',[28] he believed that war was not a form of human instinct but a specific way of conducting foreign policy, i.e. an inherent part of a political programme, which could thus be replaced by alternative means of conflict resolution. These convictions, empirically corroborated by German U–Boote attacks against the Lusitania and American commercial vessels, was at the origin of his decision to join the Triple Entente powers in their fight against Germany, despite his pledge to remain neutral during the electoral campaign.[29] As there was a genuine risk of seeing autocracies defeat democracies, the US was compelled to get involved in the war and commit itself in favour of the creation of a 'community of democratic countries' (Haine, 2004: 167) which could both win the war and organise a new peaceful order.[30]

In his Fourteen Points Speech, Wilson purported to replace the European Concert of powers grounded on the balance of power by 'a general association of nations' based on the respect of international law. The objective was to put an end to the arms races implied by the equilibrium principle through a generalised disarmament process; to prefer 'open covenants of peace, openly arrived at', to the secret arrangements characteristic of the old diplomacy; to promote free trade and freedom of navigation of the seas in order to prevent any worsening of political rivalries by economic conflicts; and, finally, to abandon the common practice of the great powers – the creation and control of colonial–imperialistic spheres of interest – in favour of the collective right of nations to self–determination.

Wilson's very ambitious proposal was put into practice, at least partially and temporarily, with the notable exception of public diplomacy. The self–determination principle led to the independence of the peoples of the Russian, Austrian and

Ottoman empires. Free trade triumphed over protectionism. The dollar superseded the pound sterling as the international currency. And last, but not least, a League of Nations was established.

Striving 'to promote international co–operation and to achieve international peace and security by the acceptance of obligations not to resort to war' and willing 'to respect and preserve as against external aggression the territorial integrity and existing political independence' of all its members, the League of Nations was the first attempt to institutionalise a collective security system. It was based on the belief that it was possible to limit the use of armed force through 'arbitration or judicial settlement', although aggressive states were most unlikely to be punished because such sanctions had to be decided unanimously by all the members of an international organisation with no international military force at its disposal.

The League of Nations was unfortunately a failure, for a variety of reasons, including the economic depression of 1929 and the expansion and increased heterogeneity of the international system beyond Europe and including democratic powers such as the US, Great Britain and France, right–wing totalitarian or at least authoritarian powers such as Nazi Germany, Fascist Italy and Imperial Japan, and one left–wing totalitarian state, the USSR. I uphold the hypothesis that, from the perspective of the process by which international anarchy matures into international society, the most important cause of this setback was the American decision not to join the League of Nations, despite its American origin. Following the US Senate's refusal to ratify the Treaty of Versailles, the United States withdrew into the Western Hemisphere. Britain, and France to a lesser extent, could still believe that they were sitting on the top of the world.

Things were to change after World War Two, whose outbreak was facilitated by Britain's appeasement policy[31] and by the buck–passing strategies adopted in turn by the three Continental powers opposed to Hitler.[32] American policy–makers who were aware, after Pearl Harbour, that the security of their country could no longer be guaranteed without committing themselves on the international scene, would from then on assume their responsibility for constructing a new world order.

NOTES

1   F. Gentz, quoted in Ikenberry, 2001: 85.

2   See, among numerous empirical and statistical inquiries on the evolution of war in the contemporary international system, K. Holsti, *Peace and War: Armed Conflicts and International Order 1648–1989* (Cambridge: Cambridge University Press, 1991); Jack Levy, *War in the Modern Great Power System*, (Lexington: Kentucky University Press, 1983); Evan Luard, *War in International Society* (London: Tauris, 1986).

3   See Lewis Richardson, *Arms and Insecurity* (Chicago: Quadrangle, 1960).

4   For an empirical refutation of the war–weariness hypothesis, see Jack Levy & Clifton Morgan, 'The War–Weariness Hypothesis: An Empirical Test', *American Journal of Political Science*, 30, N°1 (February 1986), pp. 26–49.

5   The 'peace–through–free trade' hypothesis is generally associated with the *doux commerce* thesis of C. de Montesquieu, *The Spirit of the Laws*. Contemporary upholders of this theory include Richard Rosecrance, *The Rise of the Trading State* (New York: Basic Books, 1986), and *The Rise of the Virtual State* (New York: Basic Books, 1999), as well as Solomon Polachek, 'Conflict and Trade', *Journal of Conflict Resolution*, 24, N°1 (March 1980), pp. 55–78. Contemporary critics include Katherine Barbieri, *The Liberal Illusion: Does Trade Promote Peace?* (Ann Arbor: University of Michigan Press, 2002). See also Edward Mansfield & Brian Pollins (eds), *Economic Interdependence and International Conflict: New Perspectives on an Enduring Debate* (Ann Arbor: University of Michigan Press, 2003), and G. Schneider, K. Barbieri & N.P. Gleditsch (eds), *Globalization and Armed Conflict* (Lanham: Rowman & Littlefield, 2003).

6   On the absolute and relative importance of colonial, or extra–systemic, wars, see David Singer & Melvin Small, *The Wages of War: 1816–1965* (New York: Wiley, 1972); Melvin Small & David Singer, *Resort to Arms: International and Civil Wars: 1816–1980* (London: Sage, 1982); Daniel Geller & David Singer, *Nations at War* (Cambridge: Cambridge University Press, 1998).

7   See A. Watson, *The Evolution of International Society, op. cit.*, pp. 238 *sqq.*

8   According to some scholars, the multipolar balance still prevailed until the eve of World War One. See, for instance, Kalevi Holsti, 'Governance without Government: Polyarchy in Nineteenth–Century European International Politics', in James Rosenau & Ernst–Otto Czempiel (eds), *Governance without Government: Order and Change in World Politics* (Cambridge: Cambridge University Press, 1992), pp. 30–57.

9   The expression 'In the beginning was Napoleon' was first used by the German historian Thomas Nipperdey, *Deutsche Geschichte 1800–1866: Bürgerwelt und starker Staat* (Munich: Beck, 1994), in his analysis of Napoleon's impact on the domestic evolution of nineteenth century Germany.

10 While arguing that the British Foreign Secretary Viscount Castlereagh played a leading part in negotiating the Treaty of Chaumont, the first manifestation of the European powers' will to moderate their diplomatic behaviour, I do not underestimate the role of Prince Metternich in the emergence of a new statecraft. In 1813 indeed, the Treaty of Ried signed with Bavaria when it left the *Grand Empire*, redefined the patterns of security policy between a great power and a small one, by promising a peace without annexations or compensations, and founded on mutual interests, consensus and legal norms. We should not forget that, according to John Ikenberry, (2001: 104) the ideas applied in the Treaty of Chaumont in order to rebuild Europe after the Napoleonic Wars had already been expressed by William Pitt as early as 1805.

11 Andreas Osiander, *The States System of Europe 1440–1990: Peacemaking and the Conditions of International Stability* (Oxford: Clarendon, 1994), p. 234.

12 Gentz mentions five powers instead of four, because he refers to the Quintuple Alliance including France from 1818 onwards.

13 Needless to say, the most numerous interventions were made by the armies of the Holy Alliance in order to preserve the survival of the political regimes in Central Europe, such as the Austrian repression of the Polish upheaval of 1846 in Galicia, or the intervention of the Russian troops to crush the Hungarian revolt in 1848.

14 Inis Claude, *Swords into Ploughshares* (New York: Random House, 1956), asserts that the Vienna Concert stopped functioning as early as 1823.

15 Paul Schroeder (1994: 485) notes that 'the Napoleonic Wars put a proportionately greater burden on Britain in terms of lives and resources than the First World War'. Without anticipating the arguments advanced in Chapter three, it can be argued that, in its war effort, Britain's role during the Napoleonic Wars is quite comparable to the role played by the US during World War Two.

16 Britain's behaviour at the very beginning of the French Revolutionary Wars (1792–5) corroborates the idea that London's supremacy already existed at the end of the eighteenth century. When the war broke out, England did not feel involved either by the change of the French political regime or by the stake of the battles opposing France and the First Coalition. Things began to change after France's invasion of Belgium. Not because England feared the potential contagion of French revolutionary ideas, but because of British security interests. France's search for natural frontiers and its desire to establish satellite regimes from the Low Countries to Italy and from the Rhineland to Switzerland was perceived by British authorities as evidence of a French expansionist ambition likely to disrupt the Continental balance. Such a risk could not be accepted, as it was a direct threat to overall British supremacy.

17 Obviously, Great Britain was not the only state to return to unilateralism. In its relations with the Ottoman Empire for instance, Russia had never abandoned its *Machtpolitik*.

18 Quoted in Evan Luard (ed.), *Basic Texts in International Relations* (London: MacMillan, 1992), p. 166.

19 I use the French translation of Carl Schmitt's book *Der Nomos der Erde im Völkerrecht des Jus Publicum Europaneum*. As early as 1758, Emer de Vattel had written that 'England, whose opulence and formidable fleets have a powerful influence, without alarming any state on the score of its liberty, because that nation seems cured of the rage for conquest, ... has the glory of holding the political balance' (de Vattel, 1758: Book III, § 48).

20 For an analysis of the role and strategy of an 'offshore balancer', see Mearsheimer, 2001: 234–266. Hans Morgenthau uses the expression 'holder of the balance' (Morgenthau, 2005: 204). Paul Schroeder implicitly admits the 'balancer'–hypothesis, as he writes that 'only actual or aspiring hegemonic powers can consistently practice balance of power techniques' (Schroeder, 1994: 48).

21 Far from being partial, Jevons' statement was shared by all the contemporary observers of the world economy. For instance, in his essay called *The National System of Political Economy*, the German economist Friedrich List claimed in 1841 the right for the German Confederation to resort to protectionism: according to him, 'under the existing conditions of the world, the result of general free trade would be ... a universal subjection of the less advanced nations to the predominant manufacturing, commercial, and naval power', i.e. Great Britain.

22 See the various versions of the power cycle theory, particularly the hegemonic war theory proposed by R. Gilpin, *op. cit.*, as well as 'The Theory of Hegemonic War', in Robert Rotberg & Theodore Rabb (eds), *The Origin and Prevention of Major Wars* (Cambridge: Cambridge University Press, 1989), pp. 15–37, and the power transition theory due to A. F. Kenneth Organski, *World Politics* (New York: Knopf, 1958), A.F.K. Organski & Jacek Kugler, *The War Ledger* (Chicago: The University of Chicago Press, 1980), J. Kugler &

Douglas Lemke (eds), *Parity and War: Evaluations and Extensions of The War Ledger* (Ann Arbor: University of Michigan Press), 1996, Ronald Tammen *et al., Power Transitions: Strategies for the 21st Century* (New York: Chatham House Publishers, 2000).

23 Beyond Waltz's *Theory of International Politics* and Mearsheimer's *Tragedy of Great Power Politics*, the main references on defensive vs. offensive realism are Eric Labs, 'Beyond Victory: Offensive Realism and the Expansion of War Aims', *Security Studies*, 6, N°4 (Summer 1997), pp. 1–49; Andrew Kydd, 'Sheep in Sheep's Clothing: Why Security Seekers Do Not Fight Each Other', *Security Studies*, 7, N°1 (Fall 1997), pp. 114–155; Stephen Brooks, 'Duelling Realisms', *International Organization*, 51, N°3 (Summer 1997), pp. 445–77.

24 On the positive expected utility of going to war, see Bruce Bueno de Mesquita, *The War Trap* (New Haven: Yale University Press, 1981), as well as B. Bueno de Mesquita & David Lalman, *War and Reason* (New Haven: Yale University Press, 1992).

25 Recent research has shown that the relative decline of Great Britain was due to the sole law of uneven economic growth, and not to imperial overstretch, as stated by Paul Kennedy. According to John Hobson, 'Two Hegemonies or One? A Historical Sociological Critique of Hegemonic Stability Theory', in Patrick O'Brien & Armand Clesse (eds), *Two Hegemonies: Britain 1846–1914 and the United States 1941–2001* (Aldershot: Ashgate, 2002), pp. 305–325, military expenditure amounted to 3.2 per cent of the British Gross National Product between 1870 and 1913, that is, a ratio three times less than the American one during the high tension periods of the Cold War.

26 Needless to say, the autocratic nature of Imperial Germany's regime regarded its foreign policy decision–making process. In matters of social policy for instance, Germany was probably the most progressive state of that time, because of the importance of the social–democratic movement pushing for social reforms.

27 Gilpin grounds his analysis on the famous statement made by Thucydides, *The Peloponnesian Wars:* 'The growth of the power of the Athenians, and the alarm which this inspired in the Lacedaemonians, made war inevitable' (Thucydides 411 BC). Gilpin's interpretation of Thucydides's essay is not shared by the majority of realist scholars, who rather adhere to David Hume's interpretation. According to Hume, *Of the Balance of Power*, the rise of Athens did not represent a threat to Sparta's hegemony but to the existing bipolar balance between the two city–states: 'In all the politics of Greece, the anxiety, with regard to the balance of power, is apparent, and is expressly pointed out to us, even by the ancient historians. Thucydides presents the league, which was formed against Athens, and which produced the Peloponnesian War, as entirely owing to this principle' (Hume, 1752).

28 Woodrow Wilson, 2nd April, 1917, speech before a joint session of the US Congress, quoted in A. Wolfers & L. Martin (eds), *The Anglo–American Tradition in Foreign Affairs* (New Haven, Connecticut: Yale University Press, 1956) p. 279.

29 Robert Jervis, 'Understanding the Bush Doctrine', *Political Science Quarterly*, 118, N°3 (Fall 2003), pp. 365–388, quotes Wilson's claim according to which America's goal should be 'the destruction of every arbitrary power anywhere in the world that can ... disturb the peace in the world'. Given this Wilsonian statement, it is hardly surprising that Wilson should have been referred to by George W. Bush when he declared that he had to wage a war against Iraq because Saddam Hussein's regime was a threat to global peace. Without

anticipating the arguments advanced in the next chapters, there is a fundamental difference between Bush and Wilson. Wilson fought against a country guilty of having attacked US vessels, whereas Iraq had not attacked the US nor its allies in the Near and Middle East. Furthermore, Wilson acted in concert with Germany's adversaries, whereas Bush scorned those among his allies who did not agree with him. To sum up, Wilson and Bush may have pursued the same aim – the defence and promotion of American values – but Wilson acted multilaterally and behaved defensively, whereas Bush has acted unilaterally and behaved offensively.

30　On Wilson and its influence, see Frank Ninkovich, *The Wilsonian Century: US Foreign Policy since 1900* (Chicago: University of Chicago Press, 1999).

31　While being based on an inadequate perception of Hitler's expansionist ambitions, the British appeasement policy was also the continuation of the traditional British off–shore balancing policy aiming at preserving a rough balance between France, Germany, and Russia. In the eyes of London, the three Continental powers were potential adversaries of Britain, and there was no reason to focus on and privilege opposition against Germany, be it Nazi Germany. In 1936, Winston Churchill, despite his opposition to Chamberlain's policy, evoked the permanent objectives of British foreign policy: 'For four hundred years the foreign policy of England has been to oppose the strongest, most aggressive, most dominating power on the Continent …. Observe that the policy of England takes no account of which nation it is that seeks the overlordship of Europe. The question is not whether it is Spain, or the French Monarchy, or the French Empire, or the German Empire, or the Hitler regime; it is concerned solely with whoever is the strongest or the potentially dominating tyrant' (quoted in Morgenthau, 2005, 207–8).

32　See Chapter six for a detailed analysis of this point.

chapter | the american order
three |

America as the dynamic center of ever widening spheres of enterprise, America as the training center of skillful servants of mankind, America as the Good Samaritan, ... and America as the powerhouse of the ideals of Freedom and Justice ... It is in this spirit that all of us are called ... to create the first great American Century.
(Henry Luce[1])

The year 1945 marked the end of the transition phase between two stable international orders, *pax Britannica* and *pax Americana*. From the perspective of the maturing process of international anarchy towards the consolidation of international society, the two World Wars were the repetition of one and the same hegemonic war, not so much as regards their immediate causes or explicit purposes, as in the extent and stakes of these wars. Indeed a new international order emerged after 1945, structured by a new power hierarchy and regulated by new rules and norms proposed by a new dominating power[2] – the United States of America.

At the turn of the twentieth century, US economic production had overtaken that of Great Britain. Nevertheless this new situation had not led the US to challenge British supremacy because the US was a satisfied power and American civil society was not really interested in bringing American diplomacy into line with the potential of its massive material resources.[3] However, US involvement in both World Wars had been essential for Britain's victories against the Germans in 1914–18 and, to an even greater extent, in 1939–45. This clearly evidenced British decline, thus offering the US a new opportunity to rebuild a post–war order – an opportunity it had passed up in the aftermath of World War One.

The Atlantic Charter, the first draft of the American project, epitomised Wilson's idea and ideal of a liberal–democratic post–war order. It was based on the principles of political liberty and right to self–determination, 'freedom from want and fear' in domestic affairs, free trade and 'abandonment of the use of force' in international affairs. Considering the power relations of 1945, and the dictatorial nature of the Soviet regime, Franklin Roosevelt was led to give up his predecessor's hope of converting the whole world to democracy but he held fast to the Wilsonian project of a multilateral management of the post–war order in economic and security matters. The phrase 'One world, four policemen' is, in that respect, an excellent illustration of his vision of the new order in which America, Britain, Soviet Russia and China would guarantee and enforce peace around the world.

The Soviet refusal stymied the American plan but only partially and temporarily. In fact, two American orders were to coexist during the period from 1946–7 to 1989–91. First there was a *de jure* agreement among Western states, perceived as an adequate response to the troubled period of the thirties, which was held to be one of the major causes of the disaster of 1939–45. This agreement was based on economic openness, political reciprocity and multilateral regulation of a liberal–democratic order under American pre–eminence. As for the *de facto* settlement with the USSR, which governed day–to–day reactions to the progressive deterioration of relations with the former war ally during the first years of the Cold War, it was buttressed by ideological rivalry but tamed by a defensive *Realpolitik* grounded on both a containment and deterrence policy and the recognition of the adversary's right to exert control over a security zone.

The causes of the forty–year long Cold War were numerous – reciprocal misperceptions, irreconcilable forms of messianism, and power rivalries. It is generally admitted that the Cold War was a state of war in the Hobbesian sense of the concept, as the Soviet–American confrontation took place 'within the shadow of war', to quote Raymond Aron (Aron, 2003: 6). However, the Cold War has also been analysed as a 'long peace' (Gaddis, 1987), and even a 'bipolar society' (Watson, 1992: 290) made up of two great powers, each well aware of their common interests, despite their desire to promote their national interests, and agreeing to be bound by rules in their interactions and to co–operate in the working of common institutions. I argue in this chapter that, much like the international society of the nineteenth century, the stability of the bipolar society was due to the overwhelming power asymmetry, favourable for the US and the Western camp to the detriment of the USSR and the Soviet bloc. While such asymmetry progressively decreased as regards their respective military capacities, the gap widened in the economic and technological domains. The US thus had the necessary means to propose security regimes to the Soviets, with a view to temporarily perpetuating the status quo, along the lines of Kennan's containment strategy adopted in 1947, until the USSR finally disappeared, buried under its own contradictions.

The collapse finally occurred in 1989–91. The Soviet leader, Mikhail Gorbachev, was convinced that the USSR would never be a serious 'contender'[4] (Organski and Kugler, 1980) as a convincing alternative to the American order. He thus decided to put an end to the Cold War. The fall of the Berlin Wall and the breakdown of the Soviet Union two years later did not mean 'the end of history'[5], though. It was rather, to quote Charles Krauthammer, a 'unipolar moment' (Krauthammer, 1990–1),[6] a potential stepping stone to the worldwide *pax Americana* that would emerge in the next century.[7] When George H. Bush made his 'New World Order' Speech in 1990, America's 'third try at world order' (Ruggie, 1994), after Wilson's and Roosevelt's attempts, seemed to be the good one.

* * *

In 1945, the strategic dimension of the new international configuration was marked by a huge disparity of power resources between the three major victorious countries of World War Two. The US alone accounted for almost half of the world's economic production and accounted for some 75 per cent of the great powers' total military expenditure. Its navy and its air force were by far the most powerful. It controlled a global network of military bases and was the only power to have a nuclear arsenal. Comparatively, Great Britain and the USSR were dwarfs on the international scene. Indeed the USSR represented roughly one–fifth of America's economy and one–tenth of its military budget, and the United Kingdom just about 20 per cent of America's economy and military budget. In other words, the US benefited from 'a sort of windfall of power assets' (Ikenberry, 2001: 4), and could afford to choose among three strategic options: it could either make use of its abundant resources to further its advantage at the price of an endless series of conflicts, following the example of France after its victory in the Thirty Years War; it could try to use these assets in order to shape a new and durable world order with a view to promoting its own long–term interest while associating as many states as possible with the benefits of this order, the strategic choice made by Britain after its victory in the Napoleonic Wars; or it could shirk any responsibility and return to isolation, just as it had done after the US Senate's refusal to ratify the Treaty of Versailles in 1919.

Roosevelt's position was actually much closer to the stance adopted by Castlereagh in 1815 than to Wilson's position in 1918. In the immediate post–WWI period, the US was already the pre–eminent power and its President had proposed to establish 'not a balance of power, but a community of power; not an organized rivalry, but an organized, common peace'.[8] But American war sacrifices had been more symbolic than effective. The 'peace without victory' that Wilson had striven after had not actually bound the US. America had entered the war fairly late and was not yet a major player in the international system. It believed quite innocently that it could transform European politics without getting involved in Europe. Conversely, during the Second World War, the US played a most prominent role in the fight against Nazi Germany and Imperial Japan. Thanks to the economic and military resources of the country, American policy–makers were in a position to shape the coalition's strategic initiatives, set the agenda of warfare, and ask the allied nations to accept the post–war order they were planning, on the model of what the British had done in the closing years of the Napoleonic Wars.

At first sight, the position of the Soviet Union was also quite comparable with Russia's situation in 1815. Just as the great Tsarist army 'had been the gendarme of East–Central Europe' after Napoleon's downfall (Kennedy, 1989: 464), the Red Army had liberated the Eastern half of Europe from Nazi occupation. But there was one major difference. Stalin was not Alexander I. Convinced as he was that 'this war is not as in the past; whoever occupies a territory also imposes on it his own social system. Everyone imposes his own system as far as his army can reach. It cannot be otherwise',[9] Stalin opposed Roosevelt's post–war plans and the USSR, though it was 'economically poor, deprived, and unbalanced' (467), used all possible means to advance its interests. In 1950, its military expenditure exceeded that of America, which heralded an endless arms race between the two powers.

While, in the course of World War Two, 'the US did not at all think to divide the world according to ideological criteria, but quite on the contrary planned to include the USSR in the set of international organizations it planned to establish in order to preserve future peace' (Soutou, 2001: 24), it was in all logic that the "layer–cake" of regional and global, multilateral and bilateral institutions' (Ikenberry, 2001: 164) imagined by the Americans in economic, commercial, financial, and strategic matters, only took shape among Western powers.

In the economic domain, the Bretton Woods and GATT regimes perfectly corresponded to America's enlightened national interests, in so far as an open world economy, with the US dollar as the international currency, was the best means to preserve and expand America's huge production capacities developed during the wartime economy. It was, of course, quite normal for a pre–eminent power, intent on establishing a durable post–war order, to diffuse its model to the societies accepting the new order. However, it should also be stressed that the multilateral order set up by the US in the domain of international economic relations also proved America's self–restraint. 'Embedded liberalism', which marked the international economic relations between capitalist states throughout the thirty years following the end of World War Two, was a compromise between the advocates of a purely liberal free–market economy and the upholders of a more social market economy. It was in fact the projection on an international scale of the partially regulated economic system of Roosevelt's New Deal. Furthermore, it was inspired by the 'welfare–internationalism' (Zacher & Matthews, 1995: 116) proposed during the interwar period by British liberal internationalists. Far from calling for the advent of some form of nineteenth century laissez–faire liberalism, authors such as John Hobson and John M. Keynes rather favoured the establishment of an international government that would manage international economic relations rather than be the mere guarantor for free trade. The advantages of free trade were to accrue to everyone on the condition that there should be international institutions in charge of maintaining and monitoring 'states' adherence to certain rules of free trade, particularly the open door to trade and investment' and delivering 'the economic goods', i.e. controlling 'the development of world–resources in the interests of humanity'.[10]

In other words, the Western post–war economic order was indeed hegemonic insofar as it hinged on the US and reflected American political mechanisms and ideological values. But it was a form of 'consensual hegemony',[11] both penetrating and benevolent. Penetrating because the US offered its allies an opportunity to vote within the established organisations; benevolent because the US agreed to pay the costs of ensuring the smooth working of an international economy beneficial to its allies, while showing self–restraint, as indeed it accepted beforehand the idea of having to support the negative consequences even if they chose to exit the system.

A similar form of self–restraint – as opposed to the alternative choice of a ruthless domination – was adopted by the US in political and military matters. In this domain, too, the US domination was a hegemony 'wanted by Europeans, exerted through consent, and ratified by consensus' (Haine, 2004: 103). Georges–Henri Soutou is right when he recalls that, 'contrary to a commonplace idea, it was not the Americans who imposed a military alliance on the Europeans. The Europeans implored the fairly reluctant Americans to complement their almost exclusively economic actions in Europe by a formal political and military commitment' (Soutou, 2001: 197).

For mainstream realists, the attitude adopted by the Western European states was a surprise. According to the balance of power theory, the emergence of a predominant power necessarily gives rise to a counterbalancing strategy on behalf of the secondary powers, they should have done anything but ally with the US. Waltz, for instance, asserts that the anarchical structure of international politics 'stimulates states to behave in ways that tend toward the creation of balances of power' (Waltz, 1979: 118). Actually, the Western European countries, or at least the policy–makers deciding in their name, were much less afraid of being dominated by America than of being abandoned by Washington, as they bore in mind the precedent the Americans had set in 1919. In their efforts to balance the threat from the USSR and the international communist movement,[12] they adopted a bandwagon strategy in favour of the US, perceived as the sole power both able to help them recover their economic well–being and protect them from any potential expansionist temptation on the part of the Soviet Union.

The US, however, needed persuading to accept the idea of becoming an 'empire by invitation' or 'by integration' (Lundestad, 1986, 1998). Military regionalism was adopted quite late, two years after the Marshall Plan in fact, which had meant the acceptance of Atlanticism in place of globalism in economic matters. The Vandenberg Resolution, which was at the origin of the NATO Treaty, consistently referred to the UN Charter and its explicit recognition of regional security pacts – the potentially isolationist US Senate would not have accepted a peacetime binding alliance without any reference to the collective security system of the United Nations. Moreover, by stipulating that in the case of 'an armed attack against one or more of them in Europe or North America … each of them, in exercise of the right of individual or collective self–defence recognised by Article 51 of the Charter of the United Nations, will assist the Party or Parties so attacked by taking forthwith, individually and in concert with the other Parties, such action *as it deems necessary*, including the use of armed force, to restore and maintain the security of the North Atlantic area' (emphasis added). Article 5 of the Treaty explicitly held that the US refused any automatic commitment on its behalf and did not consider its participation in the Atlantic Alliance as a permanent security guarantee in favour of its European allies.

America admittedly delayed its commitment in Europe because its policy–makers only reluctantly agreed to abandon their global post–war order plans, after being compelled to tone down their ambitions because of Moscow's refusal to accept the rules of the game dictated by Washington. I contend that it was nevertheless America's self–restraint in its post–war behaviour that explains why the Cold War was actually a long peace or, better still, a bipolar society, instead of a state of war, as claimed by the realist analysts of contemporary international politics.[13]

There have been endless debates on the origins of the Cold War. Did it originate in the creation of the Kominform by Stalin and the communist coup in Prague or in the American containment doctrine enshrined in the Marshall Plan? Does it date back to the Iron Curtain Speech delivered by Winston Churchill in Fulton, Missouri, on 5th March, 1946, or to Stalin's declaration on 16th February, 1946, that there could be no stable peace between socialists and imperialists? Was the outbreak of the Cold War due to Britain's initiative when British policy–makers invited the Americans to help their allies in the Greek civil war, as they were fully aware that they would not be in a position to go on practising their traditional off–shore balancing strategy on the Continent? Was it caused by Stalin's paranoia or Truman's basic anti–communism? Did the Cold War start in Europe, because of the German question? In the Far East, because of the American nuclear bomb on Hiroshima? Or in the Middle East, because of the Soviets' designs to exert control over the straits between the Black Sea and the Mediterranean Sea, and over the oil fields of Northern Iran with the help of Azeri communists?

There have been as many contending approaches to the fundamental causes of the outbreak and persistence of the Cold War, depending on the level of analysis adopted – individual actor, collective actor or systemic level.[14]

At the individual actor level of analysis – relative to the personality, psychology, beliefs and convictions of the decision makers – the inadequate perceptions, called 'misperceptions' by Robert Jervis,[15] held by American and Soviet leaders, played a most significant part. For instance, the Soviet leadership, whose economy had been ruined by the war operations on Russian territory, was obsessed by the idea of reconstruction. In that respect, it considered the dismantling of German and Central European industrial plants and their rebuilding in the USSR to be legitimate. Conversely, American leaders, whose economy had prospered during the war, and who were preparing to propose the Marshall Plan to the devastated European economies, perceived Moscow's attitude as evidence of its will to exert control over its satellite states. Interested in the quick economic recovery of the European societies, perceived to be as many prospective markets for their products, they viewed the Marshall Plan as the best means of avoiding the errors committed in the thirties. For Moscow, the Marshall Plan embodied America's thirst for power and imperialism, all the more so as it was also proposed to the countries liberated by the Red Army. In a way, both the American and Soviet policy–makers were tempted to take a black–and–white, Manichaean view of each other's actions. They credited themselves with being motivated by the best intentions and they attributed the worst imaginable motivations to their adversary, thus finally transforming their misperceptions into self–fulfilling prophecies. For instance, when the Western allies formed the Atlantic Alliance in 1949, they perceived this alliance to be a defensive organisation functioning as a deterrence device against potential Soviet expansion, and when in 1950, North Korea attacked South Korea with the approval of Stalin, the creation of NATO retrospectively seemed justified by Moscow's expansionism. Conversely, the creation of NATO, seen by the USSR as a hostile and offensive decision, subsequently justified Moscow's decision to exert political authority over its satellites' sovereignty. If they had not established control over their Central European neighbours, the Soviets argued, NATO would have integrated them, thus extending its reach up to Russia's national borders.

Such biased perceptions obviously referred to the negative image that Washington had of Moscow, and vice versa. This image was relative to the domestic regimes of both protagonists. At the collective actor level of analysis – i.e. the political regime of a state, its ideological values, the principles of its economic organisation, its origin and history – the Cold War can be explained by the confrontation of two messianic projects. According to Aron, the national interests a state seeks to satisfy on the international scene cannot be 'defined apart from the internal regime, the aspirations characteristic of the different classes, the political ideal of the state' (Aron, 2003: 92). If we abide by this hypothesis, the socialist Soviet Union and the liberal–democratic US were then bound to be adversaries. The mission of the Soviet Union was to spread the Communist revolution in order to put an end to capitalist exploitation, whereas the aim of the US was to promote freedom in order to preserve the world from totalitarianism. Seen from Washington, a communist regime could not but expand its social model through violent means, and inherently peaceful democracies thus had to adopt a containment strategy with a view to diminishing the ensuing risks of armed confrontations. Seen from Moscow, capitalism systematically resorted to arms in order to prevent the final triumph of socialism – as indeed the end of history meant the rise of a communist, classless society – and socialist states thus had to use any available means to fight the anti–communist crusade. To sum up, the Cold War was a heterogeneous system, opposing two powers and their respective allies who adhered to contradictory values and principles.

Of course, the heterogeneous nature of the post–World–War–Two system cannot be separated from the structure of the power distribution which, at the systemic level of analysis, was at the origin of another set of factors that may contribute to explaining the Cold War. In the years following 1945, there emerged a new, unprecedented power configuration. The traditional European powers were no longer relevant and the situation seemed to prove true the famous prediction made in the 1830s by Alexis de Tocqueville in his conclusion to the first volume of *Democracy in America*:

There are, at the present time, two great nations in the world which seem to tend towards the same end, although they started from different points: I allude to the Russians and the Americans. ... The American struggles against the natural obstacles which oppose him; the adversaries of the Russian are men; the former combats the wilderness and wild life; the latter, civilization with all its weapons and its arts: the conquests of the one are therefore gained by the ploughshare; those of the other by the sword. The Anglo–American relies upon

> personal interest to accomplish his ends, and gives free scope to the unguided exertions and common–sense of the citizens; the Russian centres all the authority of society in a single arm; the principal instrument of the former is freedom; of the latter servitude. Their starting–point is different, and their courses are not the same; yet each of them seems to be marked out by the will of Heaven to sway the destinies of half the globe.[16]

The US and the USSR were, indeed, the only powers which could be called superpowers.[17] According to the vast majority of realists, such as Morgenthau, Aron, Kissinger, or Waltz, the Soviet–American relationship was a bipolar system opposing two powers controlling a roughly equal amount of power. The Cold War was thus the logical result of two interacting sets of policies whose respective aim was to maintain the existing balance and prevent the other power from acquiring a pre–eminent amount of military capacities. On the contrary, according to a minority of realist scholars, such as Organski or Gilpin, who emphasise the resource asymmetry favourable to the US, the post–WWII system was in fact a unipolar system, in spite of appearances, and the Cold War was caused by the interaction of an American policy aiming at preserving the existing hierarchy with a Soviet strategy seeking to make up its resource gap.

Whatever interpretations realists may propose of the fundamental causes of the Cold War, they agree in considering it to be the perfect empirical illustration of Hobbes's state of war concept. According to them, the Cold War[18] was a cold, instead of a hot, war, precisely because the US and the USSR lived 'in continual jealousies, and in the state and posture of gladiators, having their weapons pointing, and their eyes fixed on one another, … in the condition of a perpetual war, and upon the confines of battle, with their frontiers armed, and cannons planted against their neighbours round about'. The White House and the Kremlin indeed adopted the same behaviour as the kings and princes of the middle of the seventeenth century, 'having forts, garrisons, and guns upon the frontiers of their kingdoms, and continual spies upon their neighbours' (Hobbes, 1651: 13).

Admittedly, the two superpowers avoided any direct armed confrontation, preferring to rely on the proxy wars fought by their allies in the Third World. However, throughout the second half of the 'short' twentieth century, they still had 'the will to contend by battle', 'the disposition to actual fighting', and thus the Cold War can be perfectly defined in Aron's short but accurate phrase: 'Peace impossible, War improbable'.[19] A major war was indeed improbable, because it would have meant the suicide of humanity; but peace was not possible either because of the security dilemma in which both the US and the USSR were caught.

Realists uphold the idea that no state can ever be sure of the behaviour of any other state – as there is no central supra–national authority above them – and that all the states are permanently afraid of 'being attacked, subjected, dominated, or annihilated' by other states (Herz, 1950: 157). As a logical consequence each state has to guarantee its own security. 'In anarchy security is the highest end. Only if survival is assured can states safely seek other goals such as tranquillity, profit, and power. ... The goal the system encourages them to seek is security' (Waltz, 1979: 126). In concrete terms, each state tries to increase its military resources in order to protect itself from 'the impact of power' of the other states. Unfortunately, this leads to increased insecurity for the other states, because they cannot be absolutely sure of the purely defensive – or potentially offensive – nature of such military preparations. They are thus compelled to prepare for the worst, what Herbert Butterfield calls the 'Hobbesian fear',[20] and John Herz the 'security dilemma'.

> Wherever (an) anarchic society has existed, ... there has arisen what may be called the "security dilemma" of men, groups, or their leaders. Groups or individuals living in such a constellation must be, and usually are, concerned about their security from being attacked, subjected, dominated, or annihilated by other groups and individuals. Striving to attain security from such attack, they are driven to acquire more and more power in order to escape the impact of the power of others. This, in turn, renders the others more insecure and compels them to prepare for the worst. Since none can feel entirely secure in such a world of competing units, power competition ensues, and the vicious circle of security and power accumulation is on (Herz, 1950: 157).[21]

To a certain extent, a state will always feel insecure whatever it may do when confronted with another state's growing power. If it does not respond accordingly, it will necessarily have less power than its adversary, and of course insecurity will increase. But even if it decides to strengthen its own military capacities, the result in terms of insecurity will be the same, as there is a definite risk of provoking an escalation in the power race. According to realists, states tend to always imagine the second, worst–case scenario, because any error about an adversary's relative power may have dramatic consequences for their own survival. A military build–up in one state will eventually lead to a similar military build–up in the other state. 'In an anarchic domain, the source of one's comfort is the source of another's worry. Hence a state that is amassing instruments of war, even for its own defence, is cast by others as a threat requiring response. The response itself then serves to confirm the first state's belief that it had reason to worry' (Waltz, 1989: 43). International politics is of necessity a tragedy. The rational unilateral actions each state performs individually, because of its subjective uncertainty about the intentions of other states, end up in producing and reproducing an irrational state of collective objective insecurity.

The security dilemma model seems to correspond exactly to the development of the US–USSR relationship from 1946–7 onwards. The USSR did not withdraw from the countries liberated by the Red Army: Moscow asserted that it aimed at establishing a defensive perimeter on its Western frontiers, as the Russian territory had already been invaded from this border twice in less than thirty years. Western leaders, however, did not accept such an interpretation of Moscow's decision, suspicious as they were that Moscow's deployment might not obey purely defensive goals. As a precaution, they decided to form an alliance and re-arm in order to be able to preserve their security in case of a new military threat from Moscow. Obviously, Western rearmament, the creation of NATO, and the integration of Germany in the Atlantic Alliance, were perceived by Soviet leaders as so many offensive gestures. They consequently decided to launch their own military pact, build their own atomic weapons, and improve their arsenal. The ensuing arms race, marked by the acquisition of thousands of nuclear warheads in both camps, was the necessary outcome of the Soviet–American security dilemma.

In the past, arms races which involved 'simultaneous abnormal rates of growth in the military outlays of two or more than two rival states resulting from the competitive pressure of the military rivalry itself' (Wallace, 1979: 5),[22] had regularly led to the outbreak of violent conflicts. Far from corroborating the deterrence model according to which a state has to match its adversary's amount of military preparedness in order to deter it from resorting to arms, arms races had furthered escalation processes, as in the two World Wars, for instance. That was not the case during the Cold War. The state of war, tantamount to a latent war according to realist scholars, did not turn into an effective war. This apparent miracle – actually it was not a miracle as indeed periods of high tension were not more frequent than periods of détente[23] – was due to the American will and capacity to change the Cold War into a bipolar society.

When elaborating his post–war plans, Roosevelt was convinced that the US and USSR would be the main peace enforcers of the coming order, flanked by the United Kingdom and China. Roosevelt was far from being fooled by the Soviet Union's designs on Eastern and Central Europe, whatever these designs may have been – the establishment of a buffer zone to protect Soviet Russia or the creation of a zone in order to spread the socialist model, still confined to one country. But contrary to Winston Churchill, who was still desperately looking for spheres of influence in accordance with Britain's past off–shore balance policy from Palmerston to Chamberlain,[24] the American President hoped to 'limit Soviet expansionism by committing Stalin to a global co–operation within the framework of the United Nations' (Soutou, 2001: 32). In actual fact, the American leadership endeavoured to influence the Soviets' security policy,[25] but it nevertheless agreed to make concessions. For instance, the initial version of the 'One world; four policemen' plan stipulated that if one of the four policemen was involved in a conflict, he could not take part in the vote relative to the actions to be undertaken in order to find a solution to this conflict. Obviously, this meant that the US accepted the hypothesis of being forced to submit to a multilateral decision. Moreover, when the Soviets refused this point, in the name of the sovereignty principle, the US agreed to withdraw it, in order to prove its goodwill and find a viable compromise with the USSR. At last, when the Greek and Turkish crises broke out – a serious strain in relations between the former war allies – Truman referred the matters to the Security Council, thus showing his desire to hold fast to Roosevelt's attitude towards the Soviets.

Admittedly, the power ratio within the UN was favourable to the US which could count on a quasi–automatic majority. But the fact that the US should have striven to defend its national interest was less crucial than the way it behaved in doing so. America's goals were, of course, the same as any other power's objectives, but its strategy was different from the strategy adopted by any great power in the past, if we except Castlereagh's Britain in 1815.[26] With their immense material resources, American policy–makers looked forward to organising a durable post–war settlement by establishing multilateral institutions for conflict resolution – such as the United Nations, constitutive of a genuine *pacto de contrahendo*. Only the repeated vetoes of the Soviets, which paralysed Chapter VII of the UN Charter, persuaded Truman to abandon Cordell Hull's internationalist vision in favour of a 'more strictly Atlantic vision' (Soutou, 2001: 10).

Moreover, though the US resorted to an off–shore balancing strategy towards the USSR, much like Britain's behaviour towards the Continental powers after the end of the European Concert,[27] this defensive *Realpolitik* never led to abandoning the idea of seeing the USSR re–integrated into the American order sooner or later. In accordance with George Kennan's containment doctrine,[28] America's policy towards the USSR over forty years consisted in proposing negotiations to the Soviets while at the same time maintaining the US resource advantage, in order to reveal the Soviet Union's inner contradictions and favour a long–term deterioration of the rival regime.

At the outset, the 'containment by exclusion' that succeeded the 'containment by cooptation' only took a military turn after its first economic stage. The multiplication of regional alliances – NATO, CENTO, SEATO, and ANZUS – and of bilateral security treaties – with Japan and South Korea – remained essentially defensive. Likewise, throughout the crises occurring during the first fifteen years of the Cold War, such as the Berlin blockade in 1949 or the Cuban missile crisis in 1962, the US successfully managed to hold the Soviet Union responsible for a possible escalation, which the Soviets consciously avoided. Afterwards, 'the explicit refusal of the preventive war option' (Soutou, 2001: 231) as well as the implicit rejection of the roll–back strategy, gave way to univocal offers of negotiations in order to stabilise the US–Soviet nuclear relationship. From Eisenhower's proposal to start negotiations on a nuclear test ban to the Non–Proliferation Treaty and the ABM, SALT and START agreements, the successive American administrations were guided by their desire to further the arms–control process, whatever clash might occur, as for instance during the Vietnam War, the invasion of Afghanistan, or the Euro–missile crisis.

The American–Soviet nuclear learning process (Nye, 1987) was one of the most striking manifestations of the bipolar society. Among other illustrations, we may also quote the survival of the Potsdam agreements, relative to the German question, which led to peaceful German unification in 1990 through the '2 + 4'–Treaty, or the reciprocal respect of the non–interference principle. This was what the Budapest insurgents in 1956, the trade unionists of Gdansk in 1981, and Che Guevara and Salvadore Allende in the sixties and seventies[29] learnt at their own expense. The whole process climaxed in the Final Helsinki Act in 1975 whose 'Declaration on Principles Guiding Relations between Participating States' listed the following ten points: sovereign equality, respect for the rights inherent in sovereignty, refraining from the threat or use of force, inviolability of frontiers, territorial integrity of states, peaceful settlement of disputes, non–intervention in domestic affairs, respect for human rights and fundamental freedoms, including the freedom of thought, conscience, religion or belief, equal rights and self–determination of peoples, co–operation among states and fulfilment in good faith of obligations under international law.

Through this decalogue we may indirectly determine the fundamental reason for the transformation of the Cold War into a bipolar society. The values enshrined in the Act mirrored the American vision expressed in 1919 and in 1945 through the Yalta Freed Europe Declaration, the Declaration of Potsdam and the treaties signed with Nazi Germany's former allies in 1945. In other words, the bipolar society was concomitant with America's preponderance,[30] and not with an intrinsically stable bipolar system as claimed by Waltz (Waltz, 1979: 161 *sqq*).[31] It is, more specifically, the analysis of the nuclear question which gives us supportive evidence of this hypothesis, thanks to the concept of relative gains developed by Joseph Grieco.

According to Grieco, anarchy means the absence of an 'overarching authority to prevent others from using violence, or the threat of violence, to destroy or enslave' other states (Grieco, 1988: 126). Logically, the security of a state depends on its relative position within the international distribution of power. Any state is a 'defensive positionalist'. Before engaging in a co–operation process with another state, it must first consider the relative gains of the potential partner state, as they will necessarily have an impact on its own current and, above all, future position. In concrete terms, 'states fear that their partners will achieve relatively greater gains; that, as a result, the partners will surge ahead of them in relative capabilities; and finally, that their increasingly powerful partners in the present could become all the more formidable foes at some point in the future' (128). Consequently, states agree to co–operate only if they are convinced that such co–operation will allow them to obtain positive – or nil – relative gains, as in both cases their relative position after co–operation will be, at least, as good as before co–operation. In other words, a state accepts to co–operate if co–operation reproduces, or improves, the existing status quo.

In the specific case of the Cold War, one great power was interested in reproducing the status quo tantamount to American supremacy, namely the United States. It was thus quite rational for American leaders to take the initiative in the arms control process.[32] Through this initiative, they aimed at 'rationalizing the strategic East–West relationship to avoid a nuclear war at the same time as maintaining the deterrence', as they knew that this process would never 'call into question America's strategic primacy' (Soutou, 2001: 397, 545). For instance, when Robert McNamara invited the Soviets to armour their nuclear silos and take a large percentage of their long–range missiles aboard their submarines, in order to make them invulnerable – which meant mutual destruction in the case of a first strike – he knew perfectly well that the US retained the possibility of a second strike, unlike the Soviets.[33]

* * *

It is true that American pre–eminence was exclusively material in its relation with the USSR. The absence of any symbolic recognition by the USSR of the United States' supremacy explains why the Cold War was a bipolar, rather than an international, society. International society consolidated among Western liberal–democratic states, whereas the society concerned by East–West relations remained divided into two camps, instead of progressively uniting. However things were to change rapidly from 1985, when Gorbachev came to power at the Kremlin.[34]

The Communist Party's new First Secretary was well aware of the Soviet Union's numerous handicaps, which led him to start an ambitious reform programme of the Soviet economy, society, and even polity – at least partially – hoping that his *glasnost* and *perestroika* policy could give a boost to the USSR, rather as Lenin had done with his New Political Economy in the early twenties. In spite of the failure of his political reforms and the eventual implosion of the Soviet Union in 1991, his 'new approach' put a definitive end to the Cold War. By proposing a general disarmament process to Ronald Reagan instead of a mere arms–control process; by withdrawing the Red Army from Afghanistan; by replacing Brezhnev's limited–sovereignty doctrine by the so–called 'Sinatra doctrine', which granted more autonomy to the East European popular democracies; he signalled his willingness to abandon the traditional Soviet dream of trying to spread the communist model beyond the limits of the territories liberated by the Red Army during the Second World War. In other words, he acknowledged the legitimacy of the American order.[35]

Gorbachev's acknowledgement of the American order was facilitated by the US's consistent self–restraint,[36] and by the existence of the international institutions established by the US in the aftermath of World War Two. He could thus take the risk of liberating the Soviet Union's satellites for several reasons: first because 'the American promise(d) not to profit from the situation by aggravating the instability in the Eastern camp' (Soutou, 2001: 714); secondly, because 'the Western victory (took) place within the framework of a global set of legal norms' (730) integrating Yalta, Potsdam, Helsinki and the arms–control regimes; and finally, because the existing institutions such as the Atlantic Alliance and the European Community absorbed Germany's unification, which made it acceptable to Moscow.[37]

The peaceful end of the Cold War – which nobody had foreseen – retrospectively proved that the Cold War had been a mere parenthesis within the process of an emerging American order dating back to Wilson and Roosevelt. The American order was part of the process by which international anarchy was maturing and of the consolidation process of the international society whose foundations were laid in 1815, if not in 1648.[38] In 1990, the US was indeed the first great power with such material and ideological resource pre–eminence that it could become a hegemonic power in the Gramscian sense of the concept, legitimate enough 'to found and protect a world order which (is) universal in conception, ... an order which most other states (can) find compatible with their interests' (Cox, 1983: 36).

In the immediate post–Cold–War years, the first Gulf War and Clinton's two consecutive presidential mandates corroborated this general feeling. American behaviour during the first Gulf crisis and the Yugoslavian Wars showed that the US had internalised the classic lesson of history, according to which 'so long as a hegemonic power (keeps) its exercise of hegemony within reasonable bounds, no one (is) willing to challenge it' (Schroeder, 1994: 635). However, the second Iraqi crisis saw America reintroducing Hobbesian values into its international behaviour: this called into question the continuation of the process by which international anarchy matures into international society that I have hypothesised. This reintroduction is the subject of the analysis in Part II.

NOTES

1   Henry Luce, 'The American Century', *Time Magazine*, 17th February, 1941.

2   The concept of 'hegemonic war' was used by R. Gilpin, *War and Change in World Politics*, *op. cit.*, pp. 197–198, inspired by an essay called *War and Industrial Society*, published by Raymond Aron in 1959.

3   On the domestic causes of America's confinement within the Western hemisphere until World War Two, see Fareed Zakaria, *From Wealth to Power: The Unusual Origins of America's World Role* (Princeton: Princeton University Press, 1998).

4   According to A. F. K. Organski, a contender is a dissatisfied or revisionist power whose power resources amount to at least 80 per cent of the power capacities of the hegemonic power. At the systemic level, the emergence of a contender provokes the passage of a hierarchical and stable unipolar system to a parity phase tantamount to an unstable transition period characterised by higher war risks.

5   See Francis Fukuyama, 'The End of History?', *The National Interest*, N°16 (Summer 1989), pp. 3–18; *The End of History and the Last Man* (New York: The Free Press, 1992).

6   I use Krauthammer's expression in an exclusively descriptive sense, as a mere statement of the power hierarchy after the end of the Cold War. I do not share the normative prescriptions Krauthammer deduces from his statement – which he updated after 9/11, on the eve of Operation Iraqi Freedom, in his article 'The Unipolar Moment Revisited', *The National Interest*, N°70 (Winter 2002–2003), pp. 5–17.

7   See Alfredo G. Valladao, *The Twenty–First Century Will Be American* (London: Verso, 1996).

8   Woodrow Wilson, 22nd January, 1917, address to the Senate, quoted in A. Wolfers & L. Martin (eds), *The Anglo–American Tradition in Foreign Affairs* (New Haven, Connecticut: Yale University Press, 1956), p. 272.

9   Stalin's statement, expressed in 1945, is reported by Milovan Djilas, in his *Conversations with Stalin*. Source: http://en.wikiquote.org/wiki/Joseph_Stalin.

10   John Hobson, quoted in David Long, 'John Hobson and Economic Internationalism', in Peter Wilson & David Long (eds), *Thinkers of the Twenty Years' Crisis: Inter-war Idealism Reassessed* (Oxford: Clarendon, 1995), pp. 161–188. See also Jaap de Wilde, *Saved from Oblivion: Interdependence Theory in the First Half of the Twentieth Century* (Aldershot: Dartmouth, 1991).

11   Charles Maier, *In Search of Stability: Explorations in Historical Political Economy*

(Cambridge: Cambridge University Press, 1987), p. 148.

12 Logically, while Kenneth Waltz's balance of power theory is refuted by the Western European states in the aftermath of World War Two, Stephen Walt's balance of threat theory is corroborated. See *The Origins of Alliances*.

13 In fact, the American commitment became irreversible after the Korean War and the failure of the project of a European Defence Community. The US needed to integrate Western Germany into its defence plans against Soviet Russia, and the only way to make German rearmament acceptable for the French and the British was to set up American bases and deploy troops in Western Europe.

14 See Kenneth Waltz, *Man, the State and War* (New York: Columbia University Press, 1959), pp. 1–15; David Singer, 'The Level–of–Analysis Problem in International Relations', in K. Knorr & S. Verba (eds), *The International System: Theoretical Essays* (Princeton: Princeton University Press, 1961), pp. 77–92; Barry Buzan, 'The Level–of–Analysis Problem in International Relations Reconsidered', in K. Booth and S. Smith (eds), *International Relations Theory Today* (Cambridge: Polity Press, 1995), pp. 198–216.

15 See Robert Jervis, 'Hypotheses on Misperception', *World Politics*, 20, N°3 (April 1968), pp. 454–479, and *Perception and Misperception in International Relations* (Princeton: Princeton University Press, 1976). Misperceptions are defined as subjective perceptions which do not correspond to the objective reality of the perceived situation. They are provoked by processes of cognitive consonance and dissonance.

16 Alexis de Tocqueville, *Democracy in America,* Volume 1, 'Conclusion'. Source: http://xroads. virginia.edu/~HYPER/ DETOC/home.html

17 The expression was first used by William Fox, *The Superpowers: The United States, Britain, and the Soviet Union* (New York: Harcourt Brace, 1944). It is interesting to notice that the subtitle of this book published in 1944 includes Great Britain as a superpower. Obviously, after 1945 the United Kingdom was no longer a member of this very select superpower club.

18 The expression 'Cold War' was coined by Roosevelt's adviser, Bernard Baruch, and by the American journalist Bob Swope, before being popularised by Walter Lippmann. Interestingly, the Spanish equivalent *'guerra fria'* was used during the *Reconquista* of the Iberian Peninsula against the Arabs, the Moors and the Jews under the reign of King Ferdinand II of Aragon and Queen Isabella I of Castile.

19 R. Aron, *Le grand schisme* (Paris: Gallimard, 1948), p. 13.

20 See Herbert Butterfield, *History and Human Relations* (London: Collins, 1951).

21 150 years before Butterfield and Herz, Jeremy Bentham had anticipated the idea of the security dilemma. 'Measures of mere self–defence are naturally taken for projects of aggression', with the result that 'each makes haste to begin for fear of being forestalled' (quoted in Arnold Wolfers, 'National Security as an Ambiguous Symbol', in Wolfers, 1962: 159).

22 Wallace's major findings are the following ones: during the period spanning from 1815 to 1965, 23 out of 28 interstate disputes accompanied by arms races led to war, whereas only 3 out of 71 conflicts which were not accompanied by arms races still resulted in war. Wallace's research has been criticised by Paul Diehl, 'Arms Races and Escalation: A Closer Look', *Journal of Peace Research*, 20, N°3 (September 1983), pp. 205–212.

23 It is generally admitted that there were three periods of high tension during the Cold War: from the Communist coup in Prague to the death of Stalin and the end of the Korean War;

from the second Berlin crisis beginning in 1958 to the Cuban Missile Crisis in 1962; from the Soviet invasion of Afghanistan in 1979 to the end of the Euro–missile crisis in 1983. The periods of *détente* were just as numerous: from Stalin's death to the double crisis of Budapest and Suez in 1956; from the peaceful end of the Cuban missile crisis to the Helsinki Conference on Security and Co–operation in Europe in 1975; from 1985 when Gorbachev came to power until the fall of the Berlin Wall which heralded the end of the Cold War. All in all, the periods that may be compared to a state of war, in the sense of Hobbes, totalled up a maximum of fifteen years, i.e. roughly a third of the whole Cold War.

24 In October 1944, Churchill and Stalin sealed by handshake the so–called secret 'percentages–agreement' dividing the Balkans into two zones of influence, Britain and the USSR having various interests in controlling the South–East European countries such as Bulgaria, Hungary, Romania, Yugoslavia and Greece. With hindsight, Churchill may have been right, as, one year later, the Yalta and Potsdam agreements led to a *de facto* division of Europe into two camps. But he nevertheless violated the principle of self–determination cherished by Wilson and Roosevelt. Indeed, when Churchill agreed to start negotiations with Stalin, Roosevelt did not contemplate the possibility of such a division in the Balkans or anywhere else.

25 The Baruch Plan, which aimed at establishing an international atomic authority – the UN Atomic Energy Commission which adjourned indefinitely in 1949 – implementing control of atomic energy to the extent necessary to ensure its use only for peaceful purposes, would also have permitted the US to have access to the Soviet Union's nuclear plans, all the more so as the US was supposed to hand over its own weapons on the condition that all other countries pledge not to produce them and accept an adequate system of inspection.

26 John Ruggie offers a very convincing counterfactual argumentation. Had the USSR, Nazi Germany, or even Great Britain, emerged as the dominating power after 1945, the world order promoted by either of them would have been quite different from the one proposed by the United States (Ruggie, 1994).

27 According to Nicholas Spykman, *America's Strategy in World Politics: the United States and the Balance of Power* (New York: Harcourt Brace, 1942), p. 124, the United States was geopolitically positioned in regard to Europe as Great Britain was positioned in regard to the Eurasian continent, the only difference being a difference in scale: 'We have an interest in the European balance as the British have an interest in the continental balance.'

28 See his article, signed Mr. X., 'The Sources of Soviet Conduct', *Foreign Affairs*, 25, N°4 (July 1947), pp. 566–582. In this article, G. Kennan details the ideas expressed in his Long Telegram sent to Washington on 22nd February, 1946. 'The United States must expect that Soviet policies will reflect … a cautious persistent pressure toward the disruption and weakening of all rival influence and rival power. Balanced against this are the facts that Russia, as opposed to the Western world in general, is by far the weaker party … and that Soviet society may well contain deficiencies which will eventually weaken its own total potential. This would of itself warrant the United States entering with reasonable confidence upon a policy of firm containment, designed to confront the Russians with unalterable counter–force at every point where they show signs of encroaching upon the interests of a peaceful and stable world'.

29 Roger Kanet & Edward Kolodziej (eds), *The Cold War as Co–operation: Superpower Co–operation in Regional Conflict Management* (Baltimore: Johns Hopkins University

Press, 1991), analyse the working of the Russian–American co–management in the Third World.

30 Even if there was arguably some equilibrium between the two superpowers, the behaviour of the Western European countries as well as of Japan decisively tipped the scales in favour of the US. Whether this behaviour is explained by Walt's balance of threat theory or by power cycle theorists' satisfied power concept, it always consisted in one and the same band-wagon strategy detrimental to the USSR.

31 Waltz, of course, never uses the expression 'international society', but talks about stability. Compared to Waltz, J. Gaddis, *The Long Peace, op. cit.*, ascribes the stability of the Cold War to the specificity of the balance of nuclear terror, beyond the mere bipolar distribution of power.

32 To assert that during the Cold War the US had the initiative in proposing arms control pro-posals does not mean that the USSR did not want to control the arms race. However, accord-ing to G.H. Soutou, *La guerre de cinquante ans: Les relations Est–Ouest 1943–1990* (Paris: Fayard, 2001), pp. 11–12, the Soviet attitude had always been ambiguous. For instance, Khrushchev certainly admitted that a nuclear war would make no difference between class-es, but a nuclear strike nevertheless remained an option in the Red Army's battle plans.

33 One question still remains. Why did the Soviets agree to co–operate if this co–operation, at best, reproduced a *status quo* which was not favourable for them? A tentative answer is that the Soviets agreed to co–operate because they hoped they would be able to cheat while expecting that the Americans would abide by their promises. On the cheating problem in international co–operation, which would be invoked by the US during the crisis leading to Operation Iraqi Freedom, see the various contributions in Baldwin, 1993, and in S. Krasner (ed.), *International Regimes* (Ithaca: Cornell University Press, 1983).

34 On Gorbachev's crucial role in the last stage of the Cold War, see Richard N. Lebow & Thomas Risse–Kappen (eds), *International Relations Theory and the End of the Cold War* (New York: Columbia University Press, 1995).

35 John Ruggie emphasises the parallel between the speech Gorbachev made in May 1990 at Stanford University and Wilson's 'Peace without Victory' speech to the US Senate in January 1917. Gorbachev declared 'that we stand at the threshold of revising the concept of alliance building. Until now, alliances have been built on a selective, and in fact discrimina-tory, basis. They were based on setting countries against each other. ... But we are approach-ing a time when the very principle of alliance building should become different. It should mean unity to create conditions for a life worthy of human beings'. In other words, he adopt-ed the Wilsonian project of replacing traditional alliance politics by a collective security approach (Ruggie, 1994: 567).

36 Western Germany also practised self–restraint, of course.

37 These institutions also reassured Prime Minister Margaret Thatcher and President François Mitterrand who feared Germany's unification. Needless to say, the risks of a German *Sonderweg* were quite negligible.

38 On this long term continuity, see Jean Bérenger & Georges–Henri Soutou (eds), *L'Ordre européen du XVIé au XXé siècle* (Paris: Presses de l'Université de Paris–Sorbonne, 1998).

part two | from lockean to hobbesian anarchy

Anarchy is what states make of it.
(Alexander Wendt[1])

In Part II, I argue that Operation Iraqi Freedom was a clear break in the maturing process which I have postulated as a typical feature of international anarchy. I do not assert that this is due to the immediate impact this military operation had on the current international system. Indeed the unipolar structure has only been marginally affected, that is reinforced, by the transformation of a minor trouble–making power into a 'protectorate'[2] of the US.[3] My main argument hinges on the idea that the US will to impose democracy at bayonet point actually reflects an evolution of the values and identities underpinning America's foreign behaviour, and that this very evolution may well call into question the consolidation process of international society.

In Part I, I analysed the progressive transformation of the international system into an international society through the establishment of norms and institutions aiming at regulating interstate violence. I have shown that the creation of these institutions was mainly spurred on by the hegemonic powers, the United Kingdom, in the first place, and then the United States. I have implicitly explained this process from a rationalist perspective and made a link between the powers' behaviour and their interests. For instance, it was definitely in the interest of Britain in 1815, and of the US in 1945, to try to establish a long–term peaceful order rather than take advantage of their preponderant position; it was also in the vital interest of the majority of satisfied secondary powers – and definitely not in the national interest of a minority of revisionist states – to act in accordance with those norms and institutions. In Part II, I will complement this rationalist perspective with a constructivist approach of the origins of the powers' national interests.

According to constructivists, interests – i.e. what actors want – cannot exist without identities – i.e. who, or what, actors are. According to Alexander Wendt, 'an actor cannot know what it wants until it knows who it is' (Wendt, 1999: 231). In more concrete terms, before states start contemplating the prospect of some form of decentralised regulation of their interactions despite the absence of any central authority; before they search for the most appropriate means to contain violence inherent in their relations; before they consider whether it is in their interest, or not, to establish common institutions and share in their functioning, they have first and foremost to acknowledge their respective legitimate right to exist as autonomous units. In other words, they must stop perceiving the other entities as potential parts of a larger empire under their own domination. The existence of an international, or anarchical, society, presupposes that political entities have internalised the very notion of an international system and, consequently, relinquished the idea of an empire composed of hierarchically integrated and dominated units.

In Wendt's own words, the maturing process of international anarchy – the emergence of an international society – depends on the existence of a Lockean culture shared by states which are guided by the 'live–and–let–live' principle, and conceive of themselves as sovereign entities. Indeed, as long as states abide by the 'kill–not–to–be–killed' principle, typical of a Hobbesian culture, as long as they do not recognise the other states' right to sovereignty, as long as they are not ready to restrict the use of violence in their interactions, the question of the best means of regulating such latent violence cannot be raised, inasmuch as the resort to armed force is precisely the normal behaviour in Hobbesian anarchy.

Drawing his inspiration from Martin Wight and Hedley Bull (Wight, 1992; Bull, 1995, 2002),[4] Wendt upholds the idea that Lockean culture has prevailed since the Westphalian Peace, with the final triumph of the sovereignty principle, as evidenced by the high survival rate of states since the end of the Thirty Years War. Once a state has been recognised by the other states, it will most probably survive as a state. Before 1648, throughout Antiquity and the Middle Ages, Hobbesian anarchy was the internalized culture. Throughout that period – marked by a high death rate of political entities and the triumph of empire as the privileged form of political organization of human societies –, might was right. A state or community which was not powerful enough to defeat its adversaries was eliminated, subdued and eventually integrated into the conqueror's empire. After 1648, the Hobbesian culture periodically re–surfaced at the systemic level – during the Napoleonic Wars and World War Two. Napoleon and Hitler indeed aimed at denying vanquished states the right to be sovereign units. From their standpoint, the problem of regulating interstate violence was irrelevant.

The key claim of the argument in Part II will be that Operation Iraqi Freedom marks the return of such Hobbesian values – not at the systemic level, at least not yet, but at the actor level, on account of America's behaviour before, during, and after this military operation. Throughout the crisis, this behaviour has been significantly at odds with the general practices and beliefs shared by the vast majority of states matching their conduct and behaviour to internalised Lockean values.

In a Lockean culture, states see themselves as rivals, i.e. as sovereign units that have the right to be independent and autonomous, rather than as enemies, that is, as entities which are denied such rights. The acknowledgement of the right of each state to live implicitly entails the rejection of the preventive–war doctrine. Indeed, accepting the right to resort to a first strike would, in all logic, be inconsistent with the rivalry principle. In the Lockean anarchical culture, resorting to armed force is thus envisaged solely from a defensive, just–war perspective, after all other means of peaceful conflict resolution have failed. The belief in the illegitimacy of a preventive use of violence finally leads to the adoption of common rules, with a view to favouring pacific solutions to existing interstate conflicts. In other words, Lockean anarchy is also conducive to multilateral, instead of unilateral, conflict resolution.

In the forthcoming chapters, I propose to show that the principles of rivalry, just war and multilateralism, which the hegemonic US contributed to consolidating during the second half of the twentieth century, have been abandoned by the US during Operation Iraqi Freedom, and replaced by the enmity principle, the preventive–war doctrine, and unilateral policy–making.

NOTES

1   Wendt, 1992: 391.

2   I have borrowed this expression from Ralph Wilde & Barbara Delcourt, 'Le retour des "protectorats". L'irrésistible attrait de l'administration de territoires étrangers', in B. Delcourt *et al*, 2004: 210–47.

3   Contrararily, Bertrand Badie, *L'impuissance de la puissance* (Paris: Fayard, 2004), asserts that Operation Iraqi Freedom has not increased American power, but rather revealed the growing impotence of traditional power politics.

4   Martin Wight makes a distinction between three types of interpretations of international politics in the history of political thought: the realist tradition, mainly inspired by Machiavelli, Hobbes, and Clausewitz, according to which international relations are an anarchy; the rationalist tradition, proposed by Grotius, Locke, and Smith, which holds that international relations form an institutionalised intercourse; the revolutionary tradition, associated to Kant and Marx who contend that international relations are constitutive of a family of nations. Though influenced by Wight, Hedley Bull uses the three traditions to describe the concrete state international configurations can take. He distinguishes between a Hobbesian system, tantamount to a state of war; a Lockean system, synonymous with a state of co–operation; and a Kantian system, equivalent to a state of peace. Wendt sums up Bull's typology but gives it a more constructivist turn.

chapter four | from rivalry to enmity

The Pagans have sin and the Christians have right.
(The Song of Roland[1])

Wendt's concept of Hobbesian anarchy rests on *Leviathan's* depiction of the state of nature as a state of war. Hobbes referred to the 'time of war, where every man is enemy to every man' and asserted that 'in such condition there is no place for industry ..., no propriety, no dominion, no mine and thine distinct'. (Hobbes, 1651: 13) He contended that 'competition of riches, honour, command, or other power inclines to contention, enmity, and war, because the way of one competitor to the attaining of his desire is to kill, subdue, supplant, or repel the other'. (Hobbes, 1651: 13) He ascribed the origins of such competition to a perpetual and restless thirst for power, which ceases only in death, and explained such *animus dominandi* at once by the search for a 'more intensive delight', and by the impossibility for man to be satisfied with a 'moderate power ... because he cannot assure the power and means to live well, which he has present, without the acquisition of more' (Hobbes, 1651: 11).

According to Hedley Bull, Hobbes's description of the beliefs and practices constitutive of a state of war among men – inspired as it were by the idea the European societies of the time had of the 'primitive' life of the 'savages' they had just 'discovered' in America[2] and other places – is hardly relevant to interstate relations. Bull declares that 'states do not as a rule invest resources in war and military preparations to such an extent that their economic fabric is ruined'. Furthermore, statesmen acknowledge the existence of legal and moral rules', 'traditions of positive law and morality have been a continuous feature of international life', as exemplified by the legal and moral pretexts states tentatively find to justify their immoral or illegal undertakings. Finally, war between states cannot be compared to violence among individuals, because states are not vulnerable to violent attacks to the same degree as individuals are, inasmuch as interstate war is rarely absolute in its results and does not take the form of a single, instantaneous blow as may be the case with men. 'If, then, we were tempted to compare international relations with a pre–contractual state of nature among individual men', Bull says, 'we should choose not Hobbes's description of that condition, but Locke's (Bull, 1995: 82–83, 85). Bull's view is very convincing but lacks nuance.

Hobbes's description may not be relevant to the way contemporary states generally conceive of themselves – a conception which is indeed more inspired by Lockean than by Hobbesian values – but it is more than appropriate not only for understanding the working of inter–'national' politics before the emergence of the Westphalian system but also – and above all – to account for the permanence of Hobbesian values in some limited areas, despite the overall spread of Lockean anarchy in the contemporary international system, and the sudden emergence of Hobbesian practices at specific moments in history.

Conflicts, limited either in time – such as the Napoleonic Wars or World War Two, for example – or in space – such as the Israeli–Palestinian conflict, are evidence of the propensity of Hobbesian moments to continue to emerge sporadically, disrupting the Lockean anarchy. The persistence of Hobbesian values also characterises contacts between members of the international society and entities not regarded as belonging to this society. That was the case with non–European or non–'white' entities until World War Two; it has been, and is still, the case with entities excluded from international society by its dominant members, the 'brigand powers' during the interwar period[3] and the so–called rogue states of the current post–Cold–War period.[4]

After its decision to take an active part in the international system, instead of merely focusing on the Western hemisphere, in 1945, the US first acted in accordance with Lockean values, thus contributing, thanks to its hegemonic position, to consolidating the rivalry principle. For instance, the Cold War exemplified Lockean ideological rivalry, rather than Hobbesian existential enmity. Likewise, the rivalry principle prevailed during Operation Desert Storm and America's interventions in Bosnia and Kosovo.

Conversely, American policymakers revived a Hobbesian logic during the crisis that led to Operation Iraqi Freedom. In matters of sovereignty – the central institution of Lockean anarchy – Operation Iraqi Freedom put an end to Iraq's political independence, although Iraq's national independence was preserved. In terms of rhetoric, the Bush administration stigmatised the Iraqi regime, describing it as an enemy and denying it the status of a rival, more on account of its supposed intentions than its actions. In other words, the United States adopted a behaviour that was both pre– and extra–Westphalian. It passed judgment on and condemned Iraq not on the basis of the policies Baghdad had actually undertaken but on what this country represented or, more precisely, on what it was accused of representing.[5]

* * *

According to Wendt, Hobbesian anarchy exists when political actors, be they states or non–state actors, see themselves as enemies. The posture of enemies 'is one of threatening adversaries who observe no limits in their violence toward each other'. Enmity prevails when a political unit does not recognise the right of another entity 'to exist as an autonomous being and therefore will not willingly limit its violence' toward the adversary (Wendt, 1999: 258, 260).

As a set of shared beliefs and corresponding political practices, Hobbesian anarchy marked the relations between political units throughout antiquity and the Middle Ages. Rampant violence, typical of these times, and a high death rate among political units,[6] evidence the fact that resorting to offensive power politics was internalised as normal, appropriate behaviour. Every actor sought to kill in order not to be killed and everybody expected everybody else to adopt the same behaviour.

Machtpolitik characterised the first encounters between political units. If both survived, their relations were then guided by the enmity principle. There are countless historical examples. Suffice it to mention the interactions between Sumerians and Hittites, Egyptians and Assyrians, Greeks and Medean or Persian barbarians, Romans and German or Hun barbarians, Chinese and Mongols, Christians and Muslims – not only during the Crusades – or Spanish Conquistadores and the Aztecs, Incas and other indigenous peoples of the New World. The internalisation of Hobbesian values entailed the vision of a world divided into two zones, separated by a dividing line both material and symbolic, such as the Roman *limes* border fortifications or the Great Wall of China. This material border epitomised a clear distinction between internal domesticated order and the external violent disorder; between the well known interior cosmos and the unknown exterior chaos, as typically evidenced by the opposition between *Dar–el–Islam*, 'the house of peace', and '*Dar–el–Harb*', the territory of war (Schmitt, 2001: 57).[7]

Hobbesian culture also characterised the interactions taking place between distinct units within the same imperial entities, defended from the outside world – a fact confirmed by numerous eyewitness accounts. For instance, in his *Arthashastra* or *Book of the State*, a body of political recommendations dedicated to Chandragupta, emperor of the ancient Indian empire of Maurya, Kautilya wrote that 'the king who is possessed of good character and whose elements of sovereignty are at their best ... is called the conqueror'; 'the king who is situated anywhere on the circumference of the conqueror's territory is called the enemy'; and 'any neighbour of considerable power must be considered an enemy [...who ...] becomes assailable when he is involved in difficulties, ... destructible when he has little or no help, [...and ...] should be harassed otherwise' (quoted in Watson, 1992: 79). Similarly, in his account of the Peloponnesian War, Thucydides evoked the prevalence of the law of the strongest over interactions between Greek city–states, despite their common struggle against the Persian threat. In the Melian Dialogue, the Athenian generals reminded the Melians they were just about to attack that 'you know as well as we do that ... the standard of justice depends on the equality to compel and that, in fact, the strong do what they have the power to do and the weak accept what they have to accept'. That Thucydides wrote 'you know as well as we do' clearly shows that the law of the jungle was commonly considered to be the normal principle guiding political relationships at that time. We may also quote the more recent example of stone hieroglyphs discovered on the stairs of a pyramid in the Maya ruins of Dos Pilas in Guatemala after a hurricane in 2002. They clearly describe some sort of unceasing state of belligerence between two Maya city–states respectively heading the Tikal and Calakmul alliances. For a period of approximately a hundred years spanning over the ninth and tenth centuries, these two major powers craving for hegemony were involved in a permanent state of war that probably caused the final collapse of the Maya civilisation, as neither power succeeded in establishing lasting domination over the other.[8] Finally, in medieval Europe, *Respublica Christiana* was not devoid of conflicting interactions either. Saint Thomas Aquinas laid down the principles of the just–war doctrine in order to determine which wars waged between Christians were justified and thus legitimate. There would have been no need for such a doctrine had there not been armed conflict in the Christian world.

In view of the ubiquitous Hobbesian logic that prevailed until the Thirty Years War, 1648 was a real turning point. After the Westphalian Peace, Lockean anarchy increasingly came to be internalised as the new legitimate anarchical culture at the systemic level between the members of the then exclusively European international society, though occasional Hobbesian moments continued to occur. Until the emergence of a globalised international society after 1945, however, Hobbesian values continued to govern relationships between European international society and the entities beyond Europe.

Before the creation of the United Nations and the ensuing emergence of a universal international society,[9] Hobbesian culture continued to underpin the behaviour of the members of the international society towards its non–members.[10] Those entities were considered to be 'beyond the line' of international society, to quote Carl Schmitt (Schmitt, 2001: 95 *sqq*). They were perceived as belonging to an area within which the right of the conqueror and the unscrupulous use of force were the norm.[11] Britain's 'white man's burden', France's *mission civilisatrice*, America's 'manifest destiny' and Germany's *Am deutschen Wesen soll die Welt genesen* [German weal the world shall heal'] evidenced the idea that the territories outside Europe – and North America after the American War of Independence – were up for grabs, so to speak, a hard fact that Native Americans, the vast majority of Africans and many Asian peoples were to learn to their cost. In contrast to the true Hobbesian anarchy prevailing among empires and their component entities before the emergence of international society, only two out of the 'three principal causes of quarrel' considered by Hobbes to be at the origin of violence – 'competition (which) makes men invade for gain, diffidence (which) makes men invade for safety, and glory (which) makes men invade for reputation' (Hobbes, 1651: 13) – need be evoked to explain the aggressive behaviour of European powers towards the non–European world. The European powers attacked, conquered and occupied these territories in order to exploit their resources and convert their populations and not because they faced any threat from the existing political entities.

The fear a state feels vis–à–vis another state because of its actual or possible aggression explains the brief outbreaks of Hobbesian behaviour within international society. During the Napoleonic Wars and World War Two, a number of states, attacked by Napoleon and Hitler, both of whom wanted to put an end to European states as sovereign independent political units, adopted the posture of enmity. They were forced to fight back until the unconditional surrender of Napoleonic France and Nazi Germany – with the help of the US in the latter case. Indeed, the political elimination of Napoleon's and Hitler's regimes was the only way to eliminate the existential threat faced by European states. The adoption of this Hobbesian attitude as a reaction to the bellicose behaviour of Napoleon's France and Hitler's Germany, however, clearly underlines that the Hobbesian culture was no longer internalised as a norm. The Napoleonic and Hitlerian episodes were extraordinary moments, caused by the abnormal behaviour of Napoleon and Hitler in an environment dominated by Lockean culture, which heralded the progressive substitution of defensive *Realpolitik* for offensive *Machtpolitik*.

The Wendtian concept of Lockean anarchy draws on the description of the state of nature among men detailed by the English liberal philosopher John Locke in his *Second Treatise of Government* (Locke, 1690). Locke implicitly criticised Hobbes for having 'confounded' the state of nature and the state of war. In his view, the state of war was tantamount to 'a state of enmity, malice, violence and mutual destruction', whereas the state of nature was a 'state of peace, good–will, mutual assistance and preservation' (Locke, 1690: 3, §19). Locke explained that the state of nature was anything but a 'state of licence'. Indeed, in the state of nature, man, while enjoying 'an uncontrollable liberty to dispose of his person or possessions', was nonetheless constrained by the law of nature, which restrains him 'from invading others' rights, and from doing hurt to one another' (Locke, 1690: 2, §§6–7).

In the Lockean state of nature, everyone has a natural right to freedom and secure enjoyment of property and it is forbidden 'to harm another in his life, health, liberty or possessions'. For the emergence of a state of war, someone has to declare, 'by word or action, … a settled design upon another man's life' or upon his liberty, by attempting to 'enslave' him. As such words or actions 'put him in a state of war with him against whom he has declared such an intention, and so has exposed his life to the other's power to be taken away by him' (Locke, 1690: 2, §6; 3, §§16–7), there exists a natural law to punish those trespassing on somebody else's property. The execution of this law is the responsibility of every individual, and not merely the victim of the aggression.

> The execution of the law of nature is, in that state, put into every man's hands …: for the law of nature would, as all other laws that concern men in this world, be in vain, if there were nobody that in the state of nature had a power to execute that law, and thereby preserve the innocent and restrain offenders. And if any one in the state of nature may punish another for any evil he has done, every one may do so: for in that state of perfect equality, where naturally there is no superiority or jurisdiction of one over another, what any may do in prosecution of that law, every one must have a right to do (Locke, 1690: 2 §7).

Obviously, Locke acknowledged the existence of a natural right and duty to punish those who broke the laws of nature because he admitted the possibility that men might not always live according 'to the right rule of reason' which told them to respect other people's property. Thus the Lockean state of nature was a kind of intermittent state of peace interrupted by outbreaks of armed force i.e. a precarious state of peace rather than a mere truce as in Hobbes's analysis. In the Lockean state of nature, the Hobbesian 'will to contend' was sufficiently strong to prevent a will not to contend by battle from emerging.[12]

In his application of Locke's analysis to international politics, Wendt has adopted such a nuanced approach. According to Wendt, Lockean anarchy exists when a group of states see themselves as rivals, that is political entities mutually expecting one another to respect their own claim to be sovereign units. Nowadays, the survival of small states shows that the Lockean culture has been internalised to the 'third degree'. Great powers recognise the legitimacy of the small states' independence, not because they are forced to, or because it is in their interest to do so, but because they accept sovereignty as the central institution in the current international system. Wendt states for instance that 'the Bahamas has a right to life and liberty that the US would not even think of violating' because the US has 'internalised sovereignty norms so deeply … and regulates its own behaviour accordingly' (Wendt, 1999: 289–90). Nobody can force Washington to recognise the sovereignty of the Bahamas and it would be improbable to see American leaders undertake a cost–benefit calculation in order to know whether it is in their interest or not to recognise the Bahamas.

Wendt's example shows that Lockean sovereignty has nothing to do with Jean Bodin's 'perpetual and absolute power' of a Commonwealth.[13] It simply corresponds to a state's national independence and territorial integrity, which are the two elements of sovereignty explicitly established by the UN Charter.[14] This is exactly the meaning adopted by Wendt when he says that sovereignty has been established by positive contemporary international law (Wendt, 1999: 280).[15]

Consequently, rival states which share a Lockean culture expect they will be free of any aggressive action or attempt at integrating them within another entity; but they nevertheless do not envisage their reciprocal relations as totally peaceful, that is, devoid of violence. In other words, in Lockean anarchy, 'the right to some property, enough to 'live', is acknowledged, but which property may be disputed, sometimes by force', and rivals are thus 'competitors who will use violence to advance their interests but who will refrain from killing each other' (Wendt, 1999: 280, 258). The distinction between enemies and rivals is relative to the intentions states reciprocally ascribe to one another, as the threat a state perceives from a rival state is less intense than the threat from a hostile state. A state considering another state as an enemy will deny it the right to exist as an autonomous entity. It will be bent on eliminating it, either by destroying it or by exerting political sway over it. It strives to rob essential parts of its property, its 'life' and 'liberty' – to use Locke's words – i.e. its national or political independence, its right to political self–determination. A state considering another state as its rival will only try to defeat it militarily, or steal less vital components of its property, parts of its territory – Locke's 'health' – or economic resources – Locke's 'possessions'.

The Lockean culture which emerged in 1648 and was consolidated from 1815 onwards (see Part I) was extended in 1945 – when the US joined the international system for good – during the Cold War period and over the first ten post–Cold–War years. Washington's adoption of defensive *Realpolitik*, instead of offensive *Machtpolitik*, reflected in its diplomacy the internalised Lockean values that would henceforth guide US behaviour in foreign affairs. This is best exemplified by two key speeches respectively delivered by George Kennan and Ronald Reagan.

In his Long Telegram sent from Moscow to Washington on 22nd February, 1946, Kennan emphasised that Soviet Russia perceived the US as an enemy that had to be eliminated for the eventual success of the socialist model.

> We have here a political force committed fanatically to the belief that with the US there can be no permanent *modus vivendi*, that it is desirable and necessary that the internal harmony of our society be disrupted, our traditional way of life be destroyed, the international authority of our state be broken, if Soviet power is to be secure.

However, he did not recommend that American authorities should adopt in their turn the posture of enmity by paying the Soviets back in their own coin.

> Please note that … experience has shown that peaceful and mutually profitable coexistence of capitalist and socialist states is entirely possible. … To speak of a possibility of intervention against the USSR today, after the elimination of Germany and Japan and after the example of recent war, is sheerest nonsense. If not provoked by forces of intolerance and subversion the 'capitalist' world of today is quite capable of living at peace with itself and with Russia.[16]

In other words, at the outset of the Cold War, the US refused to opt for a Hobbesian logic. The fact that their adversary was ideologically different did not incite Washington's policy–makers to adopt a policy of seeking to get rid of the USSR or of transforming the nature of its regime. Quite on the contrary, they chose a containment strategy, betting on the adoption of the same self–restraint by their adversary in order to avoid escalation of hostilities due to a self–fulfilling logic of mutual existential threat.

Things were not much different two generations later, when Reagan took office in the White House in the early eighties. Relations between the US and the USSR cooled after Moscow's decisions to invade Afghanistan and deploy inter-mediate–range SS–20 missiles that could strike America's allies in Western Europe. Reagan resorted to expressions such as 'the evil empire'[17] in referring to the USSR but he intended to 'strengthen NATO' in order to cope with the Soviets, and counted on the future 'decay of the Soviet experiment' to get rid of Soviet Russia for good. Though he proclaimed that the Western states' 'military strength is a prerequisite to peace', he hopefully believed that this strength 'will never be used', betting on the fact that 'the ultimate determinant in the struggle that's now going on in the world will not be bombs and rockets but a test of wills and ideas, a trial of spiritual resolve, the values we hold, the beliefs we cherish, the ideals to which we are dedicated.'[18] To put it briefly, America's policy toward the USSR did not depend on the Soviet Union's totalitarian domestic regime or on its official ideology but on Russia's actual foreign policy undertakings, which were to be contained as they occurred, by force if necessary.

To tell the truth, it is impossible to isolate America's Lockean relation with the USSR from the overall Soviet–American power ratio. In other words, we cannot help thinking that the US internalised the Lockean norms not because of their persuasive legitimacy but because it was in America's interest to respect them, when considering the destructive potential consequences of a Hobbesian behaviour towards the other superpower. There is, of course, no definitive interpretation of what might be called the 'sincerity' of America's foreign–policy values throughout the Cold War. However, we should analyse America's post–1989 behaviour in order to determine whether Washington continued to act according to Lockean values after the end of the Cold War. If such is the case, the hypothesis that American policy–makers had internalised Lockean norms to the 'third degree' will be corroborated. Indeed, if the US really conformed to the values constitutive of Lockean anarchy, despite the absence of an adversary with roughly equal military force, the respect shown to Lockean values can no longer be attributed to an interested cost–benefit calculation.

Just after the fall of the Berlin Wall, the first Gulf crisis provoked by Saddam Hussein's invasion and annexation of Kuwait put America's internalisation of Lockean values to the test. The US clearly passed the test. By proclaiming that 'out of these troubled times, a new world order can emerge, … a world where the rule of law supplants the rule of the jungle', George H. Bush initiated a foreign policy in accordance with Lockean values, thus following in Wilson's and Roosevelt's steps – the most striking proponents of Lockean anarchy earlier in the twentieth century.

Operation Desert Storm was decided in conformity with Chapter VII of the United Nations Charter. The Security Council first 'determined' that there was indeed an 'act of aggression' tantamount to a 'breach of peace' on the part of Iraq (Chapter VII, art. 39). It then decided to take 'measures not involving the use of armed force' (Chapter VII, art. 41) by imposing an economic embargo and allowing the deployment of Operation Desert Shield, in hopes that these measures would force Baghdad to withdraw its army. In resolution 678 adopted on 29th November, 1990, the Council finally considered that these measures 'have proved to be inadequate'. It consequently decided to allow UN member–states to resort to armed force in order to help Kuwait recover its sovereignty, and declared that they were free to take 'such action by air, sea, or land forces as may be necessary to maintain or restore international peace and security'. Furthermore, Operation Desert Storm was limited to re–establishing the status quo ante. The US army was not commissioned to destroy or eliminate Iraq; its mission was to force Iraqi troops to withdraw from Kuwait. Iraq's sovereignty was respected, as the coalition's objective was not to overthrow Saddam Hussein's regime.

As evidenced by the speeches in which George H. Bush presented and justified America's decisions and actions against Iraq, the US remained faithful to the central institutions of the Lockean international society, in its dealings with Iraq, a state that had revived Hobbesian values by invading and annexing its neighbour. Not only did the US resort to a defensive use of force (see Chapter five) in order to put an end to an aggressive war, giving full respect of multilateral conflict–resolution procedures (see Chapter six) but, by asserting that 'no peaceful international order is possible if larger states can devour their smaller neighbours', the US president adhered to the sovereignty principle.

When George H. Bush proclaimed that the aim of Operation Desert Storm 'is not the conquest of Iraq; it is the liberation of Kuwait', he implicitly recognised that, once Kuwait's sovereignty had been restored, Iraq's sovereignty would also be respected. In other words, the US acted in accordance with Locke's conception of natural law. According to Locke, the power anyone may use to punish anyone else violating the natural laws

> is no absolute or arbitrary power, to use a criminal … according to the passionate heats, or boundless extravagancy of its own will, but only to retribute to him, so far as calm reason and conscience dictate, what is proportionate to his transgression, which is so much as may serve for reparation and restraint. For these are the two only reasons, why one man may lawfully do harm to another, which is that we call punishment (Locke, 1690: 2 §8).

Washington did not succumb to the 'passionate heats' of taking advantage of the window of opportunity offered by Iraq's aggression against Kuwait for the US to get rid of Saddam Hussein and/or to create a Kurdish or a Shi'a state with a view to reshaping the Middle East. American policymakers just 'repaired' the 'transgression', by restoring the former status quo and driving Iraq out of Kuwait. After the end of Operation Desert Storm and the adoption by the Security Council of resolutions forbidding Iraq from rearming, the US merely undertook the necessary actions to 'deter' Iraq from being tempted to invade Kuwait again in the future.

Admittedly, Washington's self–restraint could also be explained by its well understood interest in the Middle–East region. It was essential that Iraq should remain an independent state within its existing frontiers in order to preserve the regional balance between America's allies – Israel, Turkey, Egypt, Saudi Arabia – and adversaries – Iraq and Iran. Indeed this balance would have been upset with the creation of a Kurdish state, which would have destabilised Turkey, or the creation of a Shi'a state, a favourable configuration for Iran and a potential threat to Saudi Arabia. However, this line of argument is not incompatible with an explanation hinging on the central role of Lockean guidelines. Lockean anarchy is not tantamount to international harmony. It merely means promotion, respect and defence of common rules to regulate international violence by the members of the international society, in the absence of a central authority above states. Obviously, states do not relinquish their interests when they promote and defend these rules. According to Bull, the enforcement of such rules 'is crude and uncertain'. However, if states, such as the US, which 'judge and enforce international law' (Bull, 1995: 85), are indeed not merely guided by altruistic motivations, their will to advance their own national interests is not a form of *sacro egoismo* as in the past (see Chapter one) but rather pertains to some moderate egoism, compatible with the common interests of the members of the international society.

Were these common interests still prevalent when the Western allies sent troops to Bosnia and Kosovo some years after Operation Desert Storm? The Yugoslavian wars were the second test of America's conformity to Lockean values in the post–Cold–War period.

The militarised humanitarian intervention against Milosevic's Yugoslavia could be seen as a possible infringement of Lockean anarchy. Indeed, humanitarian intervention is *a priori* a violation of the non–interference principle, which is the domestic dimension of the sovereignty principle. This is an essential point as NATO's Allied Force bombing campaign against Yugoslavia during the Kosovo War in 1999 was not legally authorised by a resolution of the UN Security Council[19] but decided only by the members of the Atlantic Alliance, fearing a probable veto by Russia and China. However, a lack of legality does not necessarily mean a lack of legitimacy.

As a matter of fact, both episodes of armed force, in 1995 and in 1999, were undertaken on the basis of an explicit international law principle – human rights. Indeed in the preamble to the UN Charter 'faith in fundamental human rights, in the dignity and worth of the human person, in the equal rights of men and women and of nations large and small' is clearly reaffirmed. Article 1 stipulates that the achievement of 'international co–operation in solving international problems of an economic, social, cultural, or humanitarian character, and in promoting and encouraging respect for human rights and for fundamental freedoms for all without distinction as to race, sex, language, or religion' is one of the United Nations' purposes. In a way, then, NATO's interventions for the defence of Bosnia and Kosovo could be interpreted as the application of the UN Charter values, which were sacrificed throughout the Cold War in the name of the prevailing non–interference and sovereignty principles. Obviously, international law is characterised by the co–existence of potentially contradictory, even incompatible, norms. Either the non–interference principle prevails, which makes it impossible for the UN to protect human rights violated within the national jurisdiction of a sovereign state; or it is the defence of human rights that is the norm, which means that individuals have logically to be considered as holders of international rights. In that case the principle of non–interference cannot be invoked by a state violating fundamental human rights. During the Cold War, the first interpretation prevailed. From the late eighties onwards[20] the second interpretation has triumphed as, for instance, in Iraq's Kurdistan (Operation Provide Comfort), Somalia (Operation Restore Hope), or Rwanda (Operation Turquoise), in addition to the interventions in Bosnia and Kosovo.

In other words, NATO's interventions in Yugoslavia may represent less a betrayal of Lockean norms than the substitution of one of the Lockean values – human rights – for another one – sovereignty.[21] Lockean culture is not given once and for all. It is an evolving and changing culture depending on the values shared by states or, at least, by the majority of the most influential ones. It may then be asserted that in the 1990s the human–rights principle competed, at least temporarily and partially, with the sovereignty principle.

Anyway, there can hardly be any doubt that America's behaviour during the 2002–3 Iraqi crisis, which was the third test of America's internalisation of Lockean values after the end of the Cold War, clearly broke with the Lockean culture, for two main reasons.

First, if we consider the definition of Lockean culture as an anarchy based on sovereignty as the central institution and on the mutual respect of property – life, liberty, health and possessions – Operation Iraqi Freedom took more from Iraq than its possessions (i.e. its oil resources, which passed into the control of American companies). Admittedly, neither Iraq's health, that is its territorial integrity – there was no Kurdish or Shi'a secession – nor Iraq's life, i.e. its national independence, were affected, as Iraq remained a *de jure* sovereign state. However, although Operation Iraqi Freedom was not a 'policide'[22] it nevertheless 'enslaved' Iraq by depriving it of its political 'liberty'. As the American 'conqueror' imposed the new political regime in Baghdad, Iraq lost its right to self–determination.[23]

Secondly, Washington considered Baghdad to be an enemy and not a rival. In the State of the Union Address delivered by George W. Bush on 29th January, 2002, Iraq was stigmatised as a member of the 'axis of evil'.

> North Korea is a regime arming with missiles and weapons of mass destruction, while starving its citizens. Iran aggressively pursues these weapons and exports terror, while an unelected few repress the Iranian people's hope for freedom. Iraq continues to flaunt its hostility toward America and to support terror. ... States like these, and their terrorist allies, constitute an axis of evil, arming to threaten the peace of the world.[24]

Iraq became the prime target of George W. Bush's attacks. In a speech delivered in Cincinnati on 7th October, 2002, he declared that Iraq was 'unique', because of 'its past and present actions, its technological capabilities, the merciless nature of its regime'. Above all, Iraq was accused of threatening the US. In his Address to the United Nations General Assembly, on 12th September, 2002, the US president stated that

> the United Nations was born in the hope that survived a world war – the hope of a world moving toward justice, escaping old patterns of conflict and fear. ... After generations of deceitful dictators and broken treaties and squandered lives, we dedicated ourselves to standards of human dignity shared by all, and to a system of security defended by all. ... Today, these standards, and this

> security, are challenged ... above all ... by outlaw groups and regimes that accept no law of morality and have no limit to their violent ambitions. In the attacks on America a year ago, we saw the destructive intentions of our enemies. ... And our greatest fear is that terrorists will find a shortcut to their mad ambitions when an outlaw regime supplies them with the technologies to kill on a massive scale. In one place – in one regime – we find all these dangers, in their most lethal and aggressive forms.

This regime, this place, was Iraq.

Why Iraq? Because, according to American authorities, the failed diplomatic efforts to force Saddam Hussein to respect the various UN resolutions that banned Iraq's rearmament showed

> that there can be no peace if our security depends on the will and whims of a ruthless and aggressive dictator ..., a student of Stalin, using murder as a tool of terror and control, within his own cabinet, within his own army, and even within his own family.

Let us focus on the very interesting analogy with Stalin. The US policy toward the USSR had never been dictated by Stalin's domestic behaviour but rather by his foreign initiatives. In the case of Saddam Hussein, on the contrary, Washington evoked the very nature of Iraq's internal regime, with a view to justifying America's policy towards Baghdad.

> America believes that all people are entitled to hope and human rights, to the non–negotiable demands of human dignity. People everywhere prefer freedom to slavery; prosperity to squalor; self–government to the rule of terror and torture. America is a friend to the people of Iraq. Our demands are directed only at the regime that enslaves them and threatens us.

The last point perfectly sums up the image of Iraq in the mind of the Bush administration – Iraq was an enemy because it threatened the US and it threatened the US because it was a dictatorship, thus compelling the US to eliminate this dictatorship in order to put an end to the threat. The Bush doctrine implied that '(a) state's foreign policy is shaped, if not determined, by its domestic political system' (Jervis, 2003b: 371) and US behaviour towards Iraq was the direct consequence of the threatening intentions ascribed to Baghdad on the basis of its domestic regime. In that respect, the link between domestic and foreign policy is particularly revealing of the return of a Hobbesian vision. Even more than Wendt's concept of enmity, it is Carl Schmitt's conception of hostility that is most relevant here, if we want to understand the deep changes initiated by Operation Iraqi Freedom.

According to Schmitt, the concept of enemy generally refers to 'the other, the stranger; and it sufficient for his nature that he is, in a specially intense way, existentially something different and alien, so that in an extreme case conflicts with him are possible'[25] and cannot be solved either by a set of pre–established general norms or by the sentence of an impartial third party. Within this general category, a distinction is made between the 'quasi–theological enemy', who corresponds to Wendt's concept of enemy, he who will be fought until elimination, and the *justus hostis* or 'just foe' who corresponds to Wendt's rival, defined as the adversary who 'ceases to be someone who must be annihilated'. In Schmitt's view,

> the elimination or the avoidance of the war of annihilation is possible on the condition that the adversary is recognized as an equal, as a *justus hostis*.

This is what happened with the emergence of the Westphalian system. Up to the Middle Ages, *Respublica Christiana* conceived of the territories of non–Christian, pagan peoples, as a territory to be converted, and of the territories of Muslims as an enemy territory to be conquered and annexed by the Crusades.

Likewise, after the emergence of the Westphalian system in Europe, the non–European territories continued to be perceived as 'land free to be occupied', while in the European international society of the time war had become a 'resort to arms among *personae morales*', i.e. between entities recognising each other's right to exist independently as sovereign units.

By denying Saddam Hussein the status of a *justus hostis* on account of the nature of Iraq's domestic regime, the US excluded Iraq from contemporary global international society. Washington revived the 'brutality' of both religious wars – 'annihilation wars' by necessity as protagonists 'are discriminated as criminals or pirates' – and 'colonial wars' fought against 'savage peoples' (Schmitt, 2001: 143, 186, 148, 62, 143, 144, 143). In a word, Operation Iraqi Freedom can be seen as an annihilation war made against a hostile political unit. It is a war waged against an enemy in the double sense of Carl Schmitt, i.e. against an enemy stigmatised as 'quasi–theological' and 'savage' because of his dictatorial regime, which must be transformed into a democracy, and as a 'pirate' or 'criminal' whose aggressive outlaw behaviour, bent on acquiring weapons of mass destruction in order to use them or to supply them to state or non–state allies, must be stopped by all means.

* * *

To put it briefly, the only possible way for the Bush administration to deal with rogue states was to resort to hard–power resources, as rogue states 'have no rights', because they are outlaws, on a par with the savages, the barbarians, the only good Indians who were dead Indians (Wight, 1992: 49 *sqq*). Operation Iraqi Freedom means the return of a pre– and extra–Westphalian conception of international politics, the renaissance of an ideology dividing the world between Us and Them, the good and the evil, because of the Manichean conviction shared by the American leaders of the legitimate right and irresistible force of their civilisation to expand 'beyond the line'.[26]

It matters little, then, that the Iraqi threat might have been ineffective or imaginary, as fallacious perceptions are also objective realities. Following Wendt, it is important to emphasise the fact that the Hobbesian conception of enmity 'implies nothing about whether enemy images are justified. Some enemies are "real"', as in the case of the Nazis with the Jews, 'and others are "chimeras"', as in the case of the Jews for the Nazis. But 'this difference', which may affect the dynamics of enmity and influence the possibility of overcoming it, 'does not affect the reality of Hobbesian cultures. Real or imagined, if actors think enemies are real then they are real in their consequences' (Wendt, 1999: 261–2).

Above all, a state seeing another state as an enemy will respond by 'acting like a deep revisionist' (262). This is exactly what happened during the second Gulf crisis. Admittedly, it was not the first time that America had adopted 'a Manichean approach to the definition of their enemy, a global interpretation of threat, and an ideological conception of challenge' (Haine, 2003). It was not the first time either that the spread of the liberal model was considered to be the necessary condition of America's national security. But it was the first time that, after the end of WWII and outside their Latin–American backyard, Americans actually put their threats into practice and resorted to a massive amount of military force in order to bring about a change of regime.[27]

During the Cold War, George Kennan and Ronald Reagan had opted for a containment strategy in order to cope with the Soviet Union's effective capacities and objective initiatives, such as the occupation of East and Central Europe and the deployment of intermediate–range missiles. During the first Gulf crisis, George H. Bush resorted to arms in order to restore a status quo violated, by international agreement: the invasion and annexation of Kuwait by Saddam Hussein. George W. Bush's policy stands in stark contrast to this tradition. It consists of unilaterally deciding on and implementing a strategy based neither on containment or co–operation but on preventive warfare with the purpose of eliminating a political regime, despite the absence of any concrete aggressive action or evidence of possession of weapons of mass destruction on that regime's part.

NOTES

1   *The Song of Roland* is an epic French poem composed at the end of the eleventh century. It tells the story of the ambush at Roncesvalles in the Pyrenees in 788, where Charlemagne's retreating Franks headed by Roland, were attacked by Basques. In this *chanson de geste*, the Basques are transformed into Saracens. Quoted in Wight, 1992: 52.

2   After describing the life of men before the social contract as 'solitary, poor, nasty, brutish, and short', Hobbes wrote that 'savage people in many places of America ... live at this day in that brutish manner' (1651: 13).

3   During the interwar period, British liberal internationalists such as John M. Keynes considered the League of Nations to be an instrument that could enable the 'pacific powers' (i.e. democracies) to punish the 'brigand powers' (Nazi Germany, fascist Italy, militarist Japan)

accused of violating established international norms. See D. Markwell, J. M. Keynes, 'Idealism and the Economic Bases of Peace', in P. Wilson & D. Long, *Thinkers of the Twenty Years' Crisis: Inter-war Idealism Reassessed* (Oxford: Clarendon, 1995), pp. 189–313.

4   The notion of 'rogue state' is not specific to George W. Bush's administration. The term was coined under Clinton's Presidency – see Robert Litwak, *Rogue States and US Foreign Policy: Containment after the Cold War* (Washington: Woodrow Wilson Center Press, 1995). It was officially abandoned by the Democrats in spring 2000.

5   See Jack Donnelly, 'Sovereign Inequalities and Hierarchy in Anarchy: American Power and International Society', *European Journal of International Relations*, 12, N°2 (June 2006), pp. 139–170, published after the French edition of this book. Donnelly describes the states which are treated as outlaw states, 'more for who they are than for what they have done', as 'ontological outlaws', as opposed to 'behavioural outlaws'. In the specific case of Iraq, such a distinction amounts to considering Iraq as a behavioural outlaw in 1990 – when it violated the sovereignty principle by attacking and annexing Kuwait – and as an ontological outlaw in 2002–2003: Washington saw Iraq as a *de facto* outlaw state whatever its actions were.

6   Alexander Wendt refers to a research work by R. Carneiro, published in 1978, in which he states that 'the world has gone from 600,000 autonomous political units in 1,000 BC to about 200 today' (Wendt, 1999: 266).

7   Needless to say, the description of 'inter–imperial' relations as Hobbesian relations is an ideal–type description. There were also examples of non–violent interactions. For instance, the first known peace treaty was signed in the year 1279 BC by the Egyptian Pharaoh Ramses II and Hattousil, King of the Hittites. Likewise, the opposition between *Dar–el–Islam* and *Dar–el–Harb* did not prevent the Abbasid Caliph Harun al–Rachid from forming an informal coalition with the Frankish Emperor Charlemagne, on account of their joint opposition to their common adversaries, the Umayyad Emir of Cordoba and the Emperor of Byzantium. The fact is that when empires decided not to ignore one another, peaceful relations between them were the exception, and not the rule.

8   See John Wilford, 'Maya Carvings Tell of Two Superpowers', *New York Times*, 19th September, 2002.

9   See the contributions of Hedley Bull, 'The Emergence of a Universal International Society' and 'The Revolt against the West', in Bull & Watson, 1984: 117–26 and 217–228.

10 Needless to say, Hobbesian culture also prevailed in the relationships between units outside the international society.

11 Carl Schmitt differentiates between three types of dividing lines. The first type is the Spanish–Portuguese '*raya*' established by the Pope in the late fifteenth century and delimiting the zones open to Spanish conquests and those reserved to Portuguese discoveries. The second type is the 'amity lines' jointly acknowledged by the British, the French and the Dutch from the mid sixteenth century onwards. Seas were considered to be zones of free navigation and the non–European territories, open spaces. The third type is the 'Western Hemisphere Line' as established by the Monroe Doctrine in 1823, according to which the European colonial powers would no longer interfere in the affairs of the American Continent which was subsequently submitted to the domination of the United States. I will not dwell specifically on Schmitt's typology but rather focus on the idea he develops of a world divided into two zones

characterised by different norms of appropriate behaviour – the zone of the international society and its Lockean culture; the zone beyond the line of this international society, where great powers regard the political units they encounter as enemies.

12 The emergence of what Hobbes might have called 'a sufficiently known will not to contend by battle' would actually mean the triumph of Kantian anarchy.

13 This is the definition of sovereignty proposed by the French jurist and political thinker Jean Bodin in Book 1 of his *Six Books of the Commonwealth* (1576).

14 This amounts to saying that Wendt's conception of sovereignty is not open to criticisms recently made against the idea of the central role of the sovereignty norm since the Peace of Westphalia. See Stephen Krasner, *Sovereignty: Organized Hypocrisy* (Princeton: Princeton University Press, 1999). See also Bertrand Badie, *Un monde sans souveraineté: Les Etats entre ruse et responsabilité* (Paris: Fayard, 1999).

15 Contemporary international law establishes the internal and external dimensions of the sovereignty principle. In Article 2 §1 of the UN Charter, the external dimension is emphasised, by invoking the 'sovereign equality' of all the member states; in Article 2 §7, the internal dimension is highlighted, by invoking the 'domestic jurisdiction' of any member state. As early as the mid eighteenth century, Emer de Vattel, *The Law of Nations*, had claimed the right of all states to be sovereign. 'Nations composed of men, and considered as so many free persons living together in a state of nature, are naturally equal, and inherit from nature the same obligations and rights. Power or weakness does not in this respect produce any difference. A dwarf is as much a man as a giant; a small republic is no less a sovereign state than the most powerful kingdom.' (de Vattel, 1758: Prelims §xviii).

16 George Kennan, 22 February 1946. Source: http://en.wikisource.org/wiki/The Long Telegram

17 Ronald Reagan, Speech to the House of Commons, London, 8th June, 1982. Source: http://www.heritage.org/Research/Europe/WM106.cfm

18 Obviously, the priority given to the ideological struggle, for instance in favour of *Solidarnosc* in Poland or Charter 77 in Czechoslovakia, did not prevent America from providing military aid to other anti–communist 'freedom fighters', from Central America and Southern Africa to Afghanistan.

19 Contrary to Operation *Allied Force*, Operation *Deliberate Force* in Bosnia–Herzegovina in 1995 was decided after the violation of various UN Security Council resolutions by the Bosnian Serb Army, which had attacked UN–designated 'safe areas' in Bosnia.

20 The concept of humanitarian intervention was developed theoretically at the end of the 1980s, notably by French law professor Maro Bettati and former Director of Médicins Sans Frontières Bernard Kouchner. See *Le devoir d'ingérence* (Paris: Denoël, 1987). On the initiative of France, humanitarian intervention was codified by UN's General Assembly's resolutions 43/131, voted on 8th December, 1988, and 45/100, voted on 14th December, 1990.

21 This opposition is an illustration of the various contradictions which co–exist within international liberalism – liberal doctrine or liberal practice. See James Richardson, *Contending Liberalisms in World Politics: Ideology and Power* (Boulder: Lynne Rienner, 2001), as well as S. Hoffmann, 'The Crisis of Liberal Internationalism', *Foreign Policy*, N° 98 (Spring 1995), pp. 159–77.

22 This expression which was used by Abba Eban, Israel's Foreign Secretary, in 1967, is quoted by Michael Walzer in *Just and Unjust Wars* (Walzer 1991(1977): 52). According to

Eban, a policide is the suppression of a state's independence by another state, and should not be confused with the replacement of a state's political regime through the intervention of another state.

23   Post–Saddam Iraq is without any doubt more democratic than Saddam Hussein's Iraq. However, the fact remains that Iraq has lost its right of self–determination through Operation Iraqi Freedom – the right of self–determination is the collective right of a nation to decide through its own means upon its political organisation. The distinction was made by I. Kant, in the fifth preliminary article of his *Perpetual Peace*, in which he emphasised the idea that the absence of freedom in a state is not a sufficient reason to justify the interference of another state in its domestic affairs. 'Such an interference on the part of external powers would be a violation of the rights of an independent people ... struggling with an internal evil. It would, therefore, itself be a cause of offence, and would make the autonomy of all other states insecure' (Kant, 1795). John Stuart Mill shared the same idea in his essay called 'A Few Words on Non–Intervention' published in 1859. 'I know it may be argued that the virtues of freemen cannot be learned in the school of slavery, and that if people are not fit for freedom, to have any chance of becoming so they must first be free. ... But the evil is that if they have not sufficient love of liberty to be able to wrest it from merely domestic oppressors, the liberty which is bestowed on them by other hands than their own, will have nothing real, nothing permanent'.

24   All the statements of George W. Bush I quote can be found on the White House website http://www.whitehouse.gov.

25   Carl Schmitt, *The Concept of the Political* (1932), Chicago, University of Chicago Press, 1996, p. 26.

26   Many recent essays written since the end of the Cold War have shared, sometimes unconsciously, this vision of a world divided between a zone of peaceful industrialised democracies and a zone of aggressive autocratic 'barbarians'. See F. Fukuyama, 'The End of History?', *The National Interest*, N°16 (Summer 1989), pp. 3–18; *The End of History and the Last Man* (New York: The Free Press, 1992); Jean–Christophe Rufin, *L'Empire et les nouveaux barbares* (Paris: Hachette, 1991); Max Singer & Aaron Wildawsky, *The Real World Order: Zones of Peace, Zones of Turmoil*, (Chatham: Chatham Publishers, 1992); Samuel Huntington, *The Clash of Civilisations and the Remaking of World Order* (New York: Simon & Schuster, 1997); Robert Cooper, *The Breaking of Nations: Order and Chaos in the Twenty–First Century* (London: Atlantic Books, 2003). Needless to say, these essays do not necessarily call for the use of armed force as a good means of overcoming this divide.

27   See Denis Duez, 'Le changement de régime: Nouveauté ou constante de la politique étrangère des Etats–Unis?', in B. Delcourt *et al.*, 2004: 165–88. Duez, p. 182, recalls Clinton's position on Iraq, akin to George W. Bush's attitude as regards objectives but completely different as for the necessary means to achieve these objectives. Indeed, while the 1998 Iraq Liberation Act asserted that 'it should be the policy of the United States to support efforts to remove the regime headed by Saddam Hussein from power in Iraq and to promote the emergence of a democratic government to replace that regime', the policy adopted aimed at bringing assistance to support a transition to democracy in Iraq. In other words, Bush's strategy of imposing democracy has succeeded Clinton's enlargement doctrine.

chapter five | from just war to preventive war

Carthage must be destroyed
(Cato the Elder[1])

After stigmatising Saddam Hussein as an enemy, the US resorted to armed force in order to get rid of this so–called rogue state. If we refer to the National Security Strategy adopted in September 2002, Operation Iraqi Freedom was a pre–emptive war.

> The US has long maintained the option of pre–emptive actions to counter a sufficient threat to our national security. ... To forestall or prevent ... hostile acts by our adversaries, the US will, if necessary, act pre–emptively (National Security Strategy, 2002).

In the present chapter I contend that the choice of the qualifying adjective 'pre–emptive' was anything but fortuitous, as part of George W. Bush's attempt to legitimate Operation Iraqi Freedom. Indeed, unlike the concept of a preventive war, a pre–emptive war pertains to the just–war doctrine.

The concepts of pre–emptive and preventive war cannot easily be dissociated (Levy, 1997). Both relate to the same 'better–now–than–later' logic and refer to the idea of an anticipatory war waged by a state at the point in time 't', in order to avoid the risks implied by having to wage a war at the point in time 't+1', under less favourable circumstances. The first difference lies in the temporality of the threat: a pre–emptive war, strike, or action, is undertaken in order to cope with a threat considered to be imminent; whereas a preventive war, or strike, or action, aims at coping with a threat considered to be potential but likely to materialise at some point in the future. In other words, a pre–emptive action is a tactical riposte to a short–term threat, while a preventive action is a strategic reply to a long–term threat. The second difference, which is complementary to the first one, relates to the source of the threat. In a pre–emptive war, a state A attacks at the point in time 't' the actual military capacities an adversary B is just about to mobilise against A; whereas the objective of a preventive war launched by a state A is to prevent, at the point in time 't', state B from building up military capacities which might be mobilised against A at points in time 't+1', 't+2', 't+n', etc. In other words, a pre–emptive war aims at countering a real threat, whereas a preventive war seeks to forestall a hypothetical or potential threat.

The normative difference is just as important as the above–mentioned differences and it is this difference that explains why George W. Bush has resorted to the concept of pre–emptive war. Indeed, pre–emptive war is the only type of anticipatory war to be regarded as legitimate, because it obeys strictly defined conditions, such as the presence of an imminent threat that leaves no alternative than the armed option. Conversely, resorting to preventive war is viewed as illegitimate. If we compare the various different reactions in the world to Israel's air strikes against Iraq's Osirak nuclear plant in June 1981 and against Egyptian and Syrian military airports in June 1967, there are conspicuous differences. The 1967 attack was considered to be a legitimate pre–emptive strike. The Israeli government knew with certainty that the Egyptian and Syrian military air forces were about to bomb Israel's territory and the only possible option was to destroy the bombers on the ground before they could take off. The situation was totally different on 19th June, 1981, when the Security Council of the United Nations in its resolution 487 'strongly condemn(ed) the military attack by Israel in clear violation of the Charter of the United Nations and the norms of international conduct'. Though Iraq was allegedly building a nuclear facility that might one day be used to produce nuclear weapons and thus threaten Israel's security, such a threat was neither imminent nor effective, and could not justify any pre–emptive strike against the Osirak nuclear plant by Israel.

In the contemporary international system, Israel's preventive action against the Osirak nuclear reactor in June 1981 can be seen as the Hobbesian exception that proves the Lockean rule. Preventive war was legitimate throughout the periods in history marked by prevailing Hobbesian anarchy. Political entities resorted to offensive preventive wars in order to profit from a window of opportunity arising from their temporary military resource advantage. They also resorted to defensive preventive wars in order to prevent the emergence of vulnerability due to a resource gap detrimental to them and potentially favourable to their adversaries (Schweller, 1992). To put it briefly, preventive wars waged for defensive reasons were fought in order to avert the relative decline of the preventive–war initiators; whereas preventive wars fought for offensive reasons aimed at consolidating the imbalance of power already existing in favour of the preventive–war initiators.

After the end of the Thirty Years War, which led to the spreading of Lockean values, the offensive version of preventive war was progressively abandoned in international society. Only the defensive version of preventive war survived but with the emerging prevalence and diffusion of the norms of the just–war doctrine, this also lost legitimacy, all the more so since the balance of power norm in practice turned out to be power politics in disguise.

The pre–emptive war doctrine is part of this just–war doctrine. After being largely ignored by the major European powers, it was endorsed by the United States during the first half of the nineteenth century, on the occasion of a dispute with its former colonial master, Great Britain. Since 1945, the pre–emptive war norm has been established by the UN Charter and confirmed by various Security Council resolutions and decisions made by the International Court of Justice, thus becoming a linchpin of today's international conflict–resolution regimes.

I will show in this chapter that Operation Iraqi Freedom marks a break with this norm. The US has taken up 'the sword in place of the pen' (Clausewitz 1809–30: Book 8, VI), thus rehabilitating preventive war as a means of conflict resolution.

* * *

The Hobbesian conception of the conduct of war is founded on two fundamental postulates – 'the acceptance of unlimited war, of the maximum exercise of strength', and of the exclusion of any compromise with the enemy during the battle, as 'the destruction of the enemy (is) the goal of war'; and 'the belief in preventive war', equivalent to the absence of any rule concerning the launching of a war (Wight, 1992: 220–1). According to Hobbes, every state has the absolute liberty and right to do anything it is convinced is in its interest. In concrete terms, 'augmentation of dominion' is a perfectly acceptable means, 'allowed' in order for a state to preserve its existence, which means that the annihilation of an enemy is part of the legitimate objectives of a foreign policy. Moreover, a state should not hesitate to launch an anticipatory war in order to guarantee its safety.

> There is no way for any man to secure himself so reasonable as anticipation; that is, by force, or wiles, to master the persons of all men he can so long till he see no other power great enough to endanger him: and this is no more than his own conservation requires, and is generally allowed (Hobbes, 1651: 13).

In the Hobbesian conception of anarchy, war is a world in itself, a world of necessity and of constraint, where no holds are barred. Hobbes wrote that 'where there is no common power, there is no law; where no law, no injustice'. Consequently, 'force and fraud are ... the two cardinal virtues'. The expansion of one's empire is allowed because in the state of nature there is 'no propriety, no dominion, no mine and thine distinct, but only that to be every man's that he can get, and for so long as he can keep it'. Launching preventive attacks is self–evidently necessary as 'the will to contend by battle' is permanent among states unable to feel secure except on the condition that they 'see no other power great enough to endanger (them)' (Hobbes, 1651: 13).

The Hobbesian conception of warfare was internalised by all the major powers throughout antiquity and the Middle Ages and later temporarily revived by Napoleon's France and Hitler's Germany. In its preventive dimension,[2] this conception led to the acceptance of preventive war as 'normal, even common tools of statecraft' (Paul Schroeder, quoted in Levy, 1987: 84). For instance, the Spartans felt compelled to launch a preventive war because of the fear inspired in them by Athens's growth. The French Revolutionaries decided to attack the Austrians in 1792 as their leader, Brissot, was convinced that 'time only improves their position and makes ours deteriorate'. Hitler also believed in 1939 that the 'favourable circumstances' profitable to Germany would 'no longer prevail in two or three year's time'.[3]

It is only retrospectively that preventive wars can be perceived as a characteristic feature of past Hobbesian periods. From a strictly conceptual standpoint, the concept of preventive war is indeed tautological with the concept of Hobbesian anarchy. As, in a Hobbesian culture, states are by definition permanently afraid of 'being attacked, subjected, dominated, or annihilated' (Herz, 1950: 157) by other states, a state which does not resort to war before being attacked, runs the risk of being eliminated. In Hobbesian anarchy, any war is a preventive one and, to a certain extent, a war is a preventive war or it is not a war. The logical conclusion that may be drawn is that the concept of 'preventive war' presupposes the idea that there are wars other than preventive ones and that resorting to armed force is not *per se* the normal, appropriate, and legitimate behaviour of a state confronting another state. In other words, the concept of 'preventive war' presupposes the existence of Lockean anarchy. It is on the very condition that there exist non–Hobbesian norms of international conduct that states have to justify their decisions to launch armed attacks which are considered to be normal as long as Hobbesian values and perceptions prevail.

I argue that states have felt such a need to justify their military actions since the end of the Thirty Years War. Following the Westphalian Peace, states mutually recognised each other's right to be independent entities. War was still considered to be a legitimate means in as much as it allowed a state to guarantee its security; but not when it made it possible for a state to increase its power to the detriment of another state.

In all logic then, the offensive version of the preventive war – the opportunity of exploiting a window of opportunity, procured by a resource advantage, in order to wage a war aiming at increasing this advantage – was no longer perceived to be legitimate after 1648. More precisely, since the advent of the contemporary international system, the concept of preventive war has been closely associated with the balance of power doctrine. A preventive war no longer designates any type of war waged according to the 'better–now–than–later' logic, whatever the motivation may be at its origin, but a war provoked by the fear felt by the initiator state faced with the actual or potential rise of the power resources of another state is perceived as a future adversary.

The idea was expressed at the end of the sixteenth century by Francis Bacon. In his essay called 'Of Empire', published in 1597, Bacon asserted that every state had the right to resort to armed force in order to prevent any other state from increasing its power resources.

> Twice is he blessed who had his quarrel just, and thrice is he who gets his blow in first.

According to Bacon, striking first was the only means for states to be sure that

> none of their neighbours do overgrow so (by increase of territory, by embracing of trade, by approaches, or the like) as they become more able to annoy them, than they were.[4]

Throughout the period of Westphalian equilibrium, the major powers of the time conformed their behaviour to the idea according to which

> cities and kingdoms ... enlarge their dominions upon all pretences of danger, and fear of invasion, or assistance that may be given to invaders; endeavour as much as they can to subdue or weaken their neighbours by open force, and secret arts, for want of other caution, justly; and are remembered for it in after ages with honour (Hobbes, 1651: 17).

They alternately launched defensive preventive wars. That was the case of the War of the Spanish Succession in 1701, a war waged by Great Britain and the Low Countries against France in order to thwart any potential imbalance that would have been favourable for Louis XIV. Indeed the mere prospect of a Franco–Spanish union, or alliance, or axis, was enough to imagine the rise of a future threat to the interests of the initiator states. Thus it was no surprise that the Westphalian competitive equilibrium should have implied a never–ending succession of preventive wars – as power dynamics in equilibrium consists in the continuous rise of some powers and decline of others.

Ferdinand Galiani, an Italian contemporary observer and analyst of the prevailing practices of his time, considered preventive wars to be the fundamental causes of

> the misfortunes of mankind. .... Because one foresees that the House of the Habsburg will increase, because the French, a hundred years from now, will do such a thing, we begin to cut one another's throat right now (quoted in Schweller, 1992: 236).

But policy–makers' mentalities and political practices did not change until the nineteenth century, when, for the first time, the concept of preventive war was successfully challenged by the pre–emptive war norm stemming from the broader just–war doctrine.

The just–war doctrine denied the conception of war as the reign of necessity, the idea that resorting to war was the appropriate behaviour of states in their interactions, the justification of the principle *inter arma, silent leges* ['in wartime, law is silent']. The just–war doctrine focused on the question of morality in the use of military force. It addressed both the causes of the decision to go to war – *jus ad bellum*: are these causes just? – and the way war was conducted once it had broken out – *jus in bello*: do the combatants behave justly? In other words, the just–war doctrine posited two general principles: a just war necessarily has to be 'undertaken for the sake of peace', 'for the obtaining of right' (Grotius, 1625: Preliminary Discourse); a just war must not to be carried on 'beyond the bounds of justice and fidelity' once it is undertaken.[5]

There were, of course, Roman and, above all, Christian foundations to the just–war doctrine, developed first by Saint Augustine in reaction to the absolutely pacifist strain of Christian ethics, based on Christ's injunction to 'turn the other cheek', and then by Saint Thomas Aquinas, who acknowledged the right of the crusaders to resort to armed force in order to recover the Holy Land, which had been occupied by Muslims. If we leave aside these origins, however, the basic assumptions of contemporary just–war doctrine could be said to be rooted in the Lockean conception of anarchy. According to this conception, 'peace is the norm, and war the violation or exception; peace is logically prior to war' (Wight, 1992: 206). Consequently, the objective pursued by the developers of just–war doctrine was to define the criteria pertaining to the use of force so that war remained exceptional. Beyond Locke, it was above all the jurists of the seventeenth and eighteenth centuries, such as Hugo Grotius and Emer de Vattel, who set out these criteria, on the basis of their conception of international anarchy.

This conception was inspired both by their conception of the state of nature among men and by the Spanish neo–scholastics. In their philosophical perspective, Grotius and de Vattel rejected Hobbes's pessimistic outlook on human nature. According to Grotius,

> among the things peculiar to men is his desire of society, that is, a certain inclination to live with those of his own kind, not in any manner whatever, but peaceably, and in a community regulated to the best of his understanding (Grotius, 1625: Preliminary Discourse).

In a kind of anticipatory reply to Hobbes's adoption of the common–sense wisdom 'man is a wolf to another man', Grotius quoted an old proverb, 'a dog will not eat a dog's flesh'. De Vattel also criticised Hobbes.

> Hobbes has had the boldness to assert that war is the natural state of man. But if, by 'the natural state of man', we understand (as reason requires that we should) that state to which he is destined and called by his nature, peace should rather be termed his natural state. For, it is the part of a rational being to terminate his differences by rational methods; whereas, it is the characteristic of the brute creation to decide theirs by force. Man … stands in need of the intercourse and assistance of his species, in order to enjoy the sweets of life, to develop his faculties, and live in a manner suitable to his nature. Now, it is in peace alone that all these advantages are to be found: it is in peace that men respect, assist, and love each other (de Vattel, 1758: Book IV, §1).

If we now turn to the influence of the neo–scholastic school of thinkers, Grotius and de Vattel were inspired by authors such as Francisco de Vitoria and Francisco Suarez of Spain, who upheld the idea of the existence of a universal community of mankind.

> However divided into different peoples and kingdoms it may be, mankind has nevertheless always possessed a certain unity, not only as a species, but also, as it were, as a moral and political unity, called for by the natural precept of mutual love and mercy, which applies to all, even to the foreigners of any nation. Therefore, although a given Sovereign State, Commonwealth, or Kingdom, may constitute a perfect community in itself, nevertheless, each of these states is also, in a certain sense ... a member of that universal society; for never are these states, when standing alone, so self–sufficient that they do not require some mutual assistance, association and intercourse, at times for their greater welfare and advantage, but at other times because of some moral necessity or lack, as is clear from experience (Suarez, quoted by Mesnard, 1977: 654).

Grotius, and, more particularly de Vattel, lived in periods that saw the consolidation of the first territorial states, which contradicted the claim of the existence of universal mankind. Consequently they tried to reconcile the political realities of their time with their own convictions. The result was a kind of compromise. Admittedly, they accepted the fact that every 'society has her affairs and her interests', that every state 'remains absolutely free and independent' with respect to all other states (de Vattel, 1758). But as they progressively came to abandon the concept of universal mankind, they chose to replace it not by the concept of the state of war but by the concept of international society. According to Grotius, 'among all or most states there ... are some laws agreed on by common consent which respect the advantage not of anybody in particular, but of all in general' (Grotius, 1625: Preliminary Discourse). Logically, these 'laws' included those criteria which aimed at defining the reasons for resorting to armed conflicts.[6]

The first criterion was a formal one. A just war could only be a 'solemn war', i.e. a war 'made by the authority of those that have the sovereign power in the state' (Grotius, 1625: Book 1, III).[7] The idea was to further the domestic political stability of the emerging states, by delegitimising civil wars, waged by at least one protagonist who by definition could not claim this sovereign authority. Called 'private wars' by Grotius, these civil wars were at once due to religious quarrels and to the conflicts generated by emerging states' efforts to gain a monopoly over fiscal imposition and coercive means. They contributed to what he called the 'licentiousness in regard to war which even barbarous nations ought to be ashamed of'. Grotius, as well as Machiavelli and Bodin before him and Hobbes after him, was of course eager to defend the necessity of internal stability.

There is, however, a link between the claim that only 'public wars' could be just wars and the substantive criteria defining such just wars. Indeed, as states are tempted to intervene in civil wars in order to support one of the fighting factions, civil wars can turn into interstate wars, as happened, for instance, during the Thirty Years War. In Carl Schmitt's words, by claiming that a just war is a 'formal war' opposing states seen as *personae morales publicae ... recognizing one another as justi hostes*' (Schmitt, 2001: 143)[8], the just–war doctrine has contributed to dissociating domestic and foreign policy. If states see themselves as equal sovereigns, they logically agree to refrain from interfering in one another's internal affairs, such as religious quarrels, which are no longer considered to be public affairs. After the Westphalian treaties, one of the past causes of previous interstate wars, i.e. states supporting domestic factions engaged in civil conflicts within other states, was no longer accepted as a just cause of war. What then were the just causes of war in the eyes of the jurists?

In order to appreciate the answer given to this question, it is interesting to recall the causes of dispute among men as acknowledged by Hobbes. According to Hobbes, there are three major causes of quarrels and these are just by definition, as there is neither society nor rule in a state of anarchy.

> First, competition; secondly, diffidence; thirdly, glory. The first makes men invade for gain; the second, for safety; and the third, for reputation. The first use violence, to make themselves masters of other men's persons, wives, children, and cattle; the second, to defend them; the third, for trifles, as a word, a smile, a different opinion, and any other sign of undervalue, either direct in their persons or by reflection in their kindred, their friends, their nation, their profession, or their name (Hobbes, 1651: 13).

In comparison, Grotius and de Vattel did not perceive 'competition' and 'glory' as just causes of war. Wars of conquest, waged for the control of other states' territories or resources, as well as wars of conversion, conducted with a view to imposing one's values on other societies, could not be just, as these two types of offensive wars violated the property principle, in the Lockean meaning of the word.[9] Only defensive wars waged for security reasons could be just, because the 'first duty of everyone (is) to preserve himself in his natural state … and to avert those things which are repugnant … to Nature', in accordance with the 'law of nations' which allows us 'to repel force by force', and with 'natural reason' which 'allows us to defend ourselves against danger' (Grotius, 1625: Book 1, III).

What specific meaning was given to the concept of danger by the jurists? They actually acknowledged two different types of danger. First there is danger when a state is attacked, a hypothesis already considered a century before by de Vitoria, who claimed that 'there is a single and only just cause for commencing a war, namely a wrong received' (quoted in Walzer, 1991(1977): 62). According to Grotius and de Vattel, resorting to armed force is legitimate for the sake of self–defence. 'There is no other reasonable cause of making war than an injury received', wrote Grotius. De Vattel held a similar opinion when he declared that

> the right of employing force, or making war, belongs to nations no farther than is necessary for their own defence, and for the maintenance of their rights. Now, if any one attacks a nation, or violates her perfect rights, he does her an injury. Then, and not till then, that nation has a right to repel the aggressor, and reduce him to reason (de Vattel, 1758: Book III, §26).

Secondly, there is danger when an attack is imminent, or ongoing. In the just–war doctrine, a state can legitimately resort to armed force when another state is set to attack. Resorting to arms is thus the only means to guarantee security. Grotius emphasised both that a war is 'just and lawful' when the danger is 'present' and that 'if a man takes arms, and his intentions are visible to destroy another, the other may very lawfully prevent his intentions' (Grotius, 1625: Book 2, I). This hypothesis was shared by de Vattel, who thought that a nation was allowed to resort to arms in order to cope with an aggression and specified that

> further, she has a right to prevent the intended injury, when she sees herself threatened with it. Let us then say in general, that the foundation, or cause, of every just war is injury, either already done or threatened. The justificatory reasons for war show that an injury has been received, or so far threatened as to authorize a prevention of it by arms (de Vattel, 1758: Book III, §26).

To put it briefly, the just–war doctrine admits the possibility that an anticipatory war may be just. But this kind of anticipatory war is fundamentally different from the Hobbesian preventive war, albeit a defensive preventive war. In the Hobbesian conception of international politics, the danger, and the ensuing right to prevent this danger, exist as soon as there is a real, or perceived increase, or even the mere fear of a potential increase, in another state's power capacities. This idea was rejected by the jurists. According to Grotius,

> the dread of our neighbour's increasing strength is not a warrantable ground for making war upon him. ... I can by no means approve what some authors have advanced, that by the law of nations it is permitted to take up arms to reduce the growing power of a prince or a state which, if too much augmented, may possibly injure us. ... To pretend to have a right to injure another merely from the possibility that he may injure me is repugnant to all the justice in the world. For such is the condition of the present life that we can never be in perfect security. It is not in the way of force, but in ... innocent precautions that we are to seek relief against uncertain fear (Grotius, 1625: Book 2, XXII).

De Vattel took up the same idea, and used the example of the War of the Spanish Succession to demonstrate it. In his analysis of the kingdom of France under Louis XIV, he wrote that

> when once a state has given proofs of injustice, rapacity, pride, ambition, or an imperious thirst of rule, she becomes an object of suspicion to her neighbours, whose duty it is to stand on their guard against her. They may come upon her at the moment when she is on the point of acquiring a formidable accession of power – may demand securities – and if she hesitates to give them, may prevent her designs by force of arms (De Vattel, 1758: Book III, §44).

Commenting on the decision of Great Britain and the Low Countries to launch a preventive war against France, which they accused of seeking to establish too close a union with Spain, he nevertheless declared that this reaction had been 'too suspicious'. Why? Because the prospective imbalance of power, despite France's record of avowed ambitions and repeated acts of treachery, might have successfully been checked by a closer and stronger alliance between Great Britain and Austria. Such a strategy would have prevented the eruption of a war which was actually an unjust war, launched as it was by Great Britain on account of a future, hypothetical danger that represented neither an actual nor an imminent threat to Britain's national–security interests.

> It is safest to prevent the evil when it can be prevented. A nation has a right to resist an injurious attempt, and to make use of force and every honourable expedient against whosoever is actually engaged in opposition to her, and even to anticipate his machinations, observing, however, not to attack him upon vague and uncertain suspicions, lest she should incur the imputation of becoming herself an unjust aggressor (de Vattel, 1758).

To sum up, in the just–war tradition, an anticipatory war is legitimate when there is objective evidence of present, instead of past, appetites for conquest, when a state is about to be attacked – and not when there are mere suspicions about another state's increasing power, when there is escalation of existing threats – and not merely when there are anticipations of future dangers.

The just–war doctrine was ignored both by Great Britain and the Continental European powers. Before 1789, London acted according to the Hobbesian conception of the preventive war in its competition with France. The War of the Spanish Succession was a defensive preventive war and the Seven Years War was an offensive preventive war. From 1792 to 1815, Britain's decisions to go to war against France partook of the collective self–defence principle, as it was the right not only of the states attacked but also of every member of the international society to punish those who acted in violation of the international norms – Revolutionary and Napoleonic France (see Chapter four). From 1815 onwards, Great Britain was able to stabilise the European order thanks to its pre–eminence, first through the Vienna Concert established at its behest, then through its deterrent supremacy.[10] Outside Europe, London pursued traditional power politics without any consideration for the just–war doctrine. And it was precisely on the occasion of a conflict opposing Great Britain and the US on the Canadian border that the concept of just anticipatory war, henceforth called pre–emptive war, was specified by Britain's adversary, the United States of America. The event is known as the *Caroline* affair.

In 1837, an anti–British rebellion broke out in Canada, a British dominion at peace with the US – the last war opposing the two nations had been in 1812–14. American citizens supported the rebels and supplied them with money, provisions, and arms sent on board the steamboat SS *Caroline* on the Niagara River. As a response, Canadian loyalists headed by a Royal Navy Captain crossed the international boundary and seized the *Caroline*, towed her into the current, set her afire, cast her adrift over Niagara Falls, and killed a US citizen. In 1840, a British citizen named Alexander McLeod, who had declared that he had killed this US citizen, was arrested in the US. Britain protested and invoked the self–defence principle. According to London, the attack on the *Caroline* was justified by Canada's security interests. The US government, however, rejected this argument. Secretary of State Daniel Webster asked Her Majesty's government to prove that there was 'a necessity of self–defence, instant, overwhelming, leaving no choice of means, and no moment for deliberation', and 'that the local authorities of Canada, even supposing the necessity of the moment authorized them to enter the territories of the United States at all, did nothing unreasonable or excessive; since the act justified by the necessity of self–defence, must be limited by that necessity, and kept clearly within it.'[11]

The crisis was finally settled by the Webster–Ashburton Treaty. From the perspective of the just–war doctrine, the *Caroline* affair was a crucial turning point. After 1840, preventive war was no longer considered to be a legitimate means of foreign policy. Such normative rejection was so universal that even Chancellor Bismarck felt compelled to assert his clear refusal to resort to preventive wars.

> Preventive war is like suicide from fear of death. … The idea of undertaking a war because it might be inevitable later on and might then have to be fought under more unfavourable conditions has always remained foreign to me and I have always fought against it. … For I cannot look into Providence's cards in such a manner that I would know things beforehand (quoted in Levy, 1987: 103).

The only form of force considered to be in accordance with the just–war doctrine was thus the pre–emptive war, or strike, or action, which had to meet two necessary conditions. The first condition was relative to the degree of necessity of such an anticipatory action. A state invoking the right to act by anticipation had to prove that any action other than the use of armed force would jeopardise its national security. In other words, a state had to show that there was a real danger for its own security if it chose a deterring posture, or opted for diplomatic negotiations. There was also the proportionality criterion. Once a state had shown that it could not but act in an anticipatory way, it also had to prove that its anticipatory action was proportionate to this necessity, and did not go beyond the requirements of its immediate national–security needs.

The concept of pre–emptive war was thus the crowning achievement of the just–war tradition, called the 'legalist paradigm' by Michael Walzer, who explicitly refers to Hedley Bull. The 'legalist paradigm' hinges on the following points: there exists an international society of independent states, no state being allowed to challenge any other state; international law establishes the rights of the members of international society, especially in matters of territorial integrity and political sovereignty; any use of force or any imminent threat of force by one state against the rights of another is constitutive of an aggression, as soon as there are boundary crossings, be they effective or imminent; such an aggression justifies two kinds of armed response – a war of individual self–defence waged by the victim of the aggression and a war of collective–self–defence led by the victim and any other member of the international society bent on enforcing international law; there is no other just war than when a state is confronted with an unjust aggression, and never in the case of political or religious differences, domestic heresy or injustice; the aggressor state can be punished once it has been repulsed, in order to prevent any repetition of such an aggressive act (Walzer, 1991 (1977): 58 *sqq*).

The UN Charter, spurred on by Franklin Roosevelt who had taken up Wilson's failed plans, has definitely institutionalised this tradition. In Article 2 (4) is reaffirmed the prohibition in principle of the use of armed force.

> All Members shall refrain in their international relations from the threat or use of force against the territorial integrity or political independence of any state, or in any other manner inconsistent with the Purposes of the United Nations.

Admittedly, Article 51 acknowledges the principle of individual and collective self–defence as the one and only exception, while at the same time limiting the scope of this exception.

> Nothing in the present Charter shall impair the inherent right of individual or collective self–defence if an armed attack occurs against a Member of the United Nations, until the Security Council has taken measures necessary to maintain international peace and security.

There is, however, no contradiction between these two articles. In that respect, Rousseau's well known criticism according to which international law

> has never been passed or sanctioned by common agreement …, is not based upon any general principles …, varies incessantly from time to time and from place to place … and … is therefore a mass of contradictory rules which nothing but the right of the stronger can reduce to order (Rousseau, 1760)

is not relevant in the case of the UN Charter. The combination of Articles 2 (4) and 51 with the spirit of the Charter shows that the interpretation of Article 51 must be restrictive. On account of the general principle which posits that any state has to refrain from the use or the threat of force in any manner inconsistent with the purposes of the United Nations, and since the first purpose of the United Nations is 'to save succeeding generations from the scourge of war', it is logical to think that the use of force by a state before 'the Security Council has taken measures necessary to maintain international peace and security' is only possible, in the case of an ongoing attack, when there is evidence convincing enough of the existence of an instant, overwhelming threat, leaving no choice of means and no time for deliberation.

Moreover, the tradition of the right of self–defence is superseded by the restrictions as specified in the second sentence of Article 51:

> Measures taken by members in the exercise of this right of self–defence shall be immediately reported to the Security Council and shall not in any way affect the authority and responsibility of the Security Council under the present Charter to take at any time such action as it deems necessary in order to maintain or restore international peace and security.

Obviously and briefly stated, there exists a hierarchy of values which opposes the use of armed force, albeit for the sake of self–defence.[12]

America's behaviour throughout the post–WWII period corroborates this analysis. Until the second Gulf Crisis, it acted in accordance with the tradition inaugurated by Webster. During the Cold War,[13] Washington voted, for instance, the UN Security Council's resolution 487 condemning Israel's bombing of the Osirak nuclear facility. Jeane Kirkpatrick, US ambassador to the United Nations, went as far as to compare the Israeli attack to the Soviet Union's aggression against Afghanistan and accused Israel of having violated the UN Charter because it did not explore all the existing possibilities for a peaceful settlement before resorting to armed force. In other words, the US ambassador based her argument on Webster's requirement – to be legitimate, an anticipatory strike has to correspond to an imperative necessity for the initiator state. She agreed with the other members of the Security Council in considering that Iraq's developing a nuclear plant that potentially threatened Israel's security was not a justification of Israel's preventive bombing.

Above all, the US explicitly excluded any resort whatsoever to a preventive strike against the USSR during the Cold War – even during the first ten years of this period, when the US benefited from a *de facto* monopoly of nuclear weapons, which would have made it possible for the US army to launch a preventive strike without triggering massive retaliation on the part of the Red Army.[14] For instance, the National Security Council Report 68, issued on 14th April 1950, during the presidency of Harry Truman, admitted the possibility of a pre–emptive nuclear strike in the case of an imminent Soviet attack but explicitly excluded the hypothesis of a preventive war, although Washington expected the USSR to launch a war as early as 1955, in the absence of any significant build–up of America's own armaments.

> It goes without saying that the idea of 'preventive' war – in the sense of a military attack not provoked by a military attack upon us or our allies – is generally unacceptable to Americans. ... A surprise attack upon the Soviet Union, despite the provocativeness of recent Soviet behaviour, would be repugnant to many Americans. Although the American people would probably rally in support of the war effort, the shock of responsibility for a surprise attack would be morally corrosive. Many would doubt that it was a 'just war' and that all rea-

sonable possibilities for a peaceful settlement had been explored in good faith (quoted in Schweller, 1992: 261–2).

Dean Acheson's comment, made during the Korean War, expressed the same idea.

> We seek to build forces adequate to deter aggression or to meet it. We do not seek to create greater strength than we need for this purpose, we do not desire military forces great enough to launch a preventive war (quoted in Schweller, 1992: 263).

Lastly, in autumn 1954, though it was generally admitted that the Soviet nuclear capacity would soon represent an effective threat to America's security, the Basic National Security Policy Paper clearly reaffirmed that 'the US and its allies must reject the concept of preventive war or acts intended to provoke war' (quoted in Schweller, 1992: 263).

During the first post–Cold–War years, George H. Bush remained faithful to the just–war tradition. Operation Desert Storm conformed to the self–defence principle. First, resolution 660 (1990), adopted on 2nd August, 1990, determined 'that there is a breach of international peace and security as regards the Iraqi invasion of Kuwait' and demanded 'that Iraq withdraw immediately and unconditionally all its forces'. A few days later, resolution 661 (1990), adopted on 6th August, 1990, affirmed 'the inherent right of individual or collective self–defence, in response to the armed attack by Iraq against Kuwait, in accordance with Article 51 of the Charter' and decided to impose an economic embargo. Finally resolution 678 (1990), adopted on 29th November, 1990, 'noting that ... Iraq refuses to comply with its obligation to implement resolution 660,' and 'acting under Chapter VII of the UN Charter', 'authorizes member–states cooperating with the Government of Kuwait, unless Iraq on or before 15 January 1991 fully implements ... the above mentioned resolutions, to use all necessary means to uphold and implement resolution 660 (1990) and all subsequent relevant resolutions and to restore international peace and security in the area'. In other words, from a legal (see Chapter six) and a substantial standpoint alike, Operation Desert Storm respected the just–war principle. By combining 'economic blockade, military threat, and diplomatic deadline', the US and their allies tried to convince Saddam Hussein to withdraw his armed forces from Kuwait. But as 'that did not happen, war was, though not a 'last', surely a legitimate resort'.[15]

Operation Enduring Freedom, which was launched against the Taliban in Afghanistan after the 9/11 terrorist attacks, also conformed to the self–defence principle, although the Afghan state was not considered to be the initiator of the attacks against the World Trade Center and the Pentagon. As early as 13th August, 1998, after the terrorist attacks in Nairobi and Dar–Es–Salaam, the Security Council adopted resolution 1189 (1998) 'convinced that the suppression of acts of international terrorism is essential for the maintenance of international peace and security'. The Security Council stressed 'that every member state has the duty to refrain from organizing, instigating, assisting or participating in terrorist acts in another state or acquiescing in organized activities within its territory directed towards the commission of such acts', and called upon 'all states to adopt … effective and practical measures for security cooperation, for the prevention of such acts of terrorism, and for the prosecution and punishment of their perpetrators'. In its resolution 1368 (2001), adopted on 12th September, 2001, the Security Council not only unequivocally condemned 'in the strongest terms the horrifying attacks which took place on September 11' and regarded 'such acts … as a threat to international peace and security', but also recognised 'the inherent right of individual or collective self–defence in accordance with the Charter'. Lastly, resolution 1373 adopted on 28th September, 2001, decided 'that all states … shall refrain from providing any form of support, active or passive, to entities or persons involved in terrorist acts', called on 'states to work together urgently to prevent and suppress terrorist acts', and acknowledged 'the need for states to complement international cooperation by taking additional measures to suppress, in their territories through all lawful means, the financing and preparation of any acts of terrorism'. Certainly, these resolutions were not explicit authorisations of the use of force but, by recognising the right of self–defence against terrorist attacks perpetrated by non–state actors, they indirectly legalised Operation Enduring Freedom. Indeed, Al'Qaeda members were to be found on Afghan territory and the Taliban did not 'take additional measures' to suppress terrorist activities, nor did they 'ensure that any person who participates in the financing, planning, preparation or perpetration of terrorist attacks … is brought to justice'.

The change then occurred during the second Gulf crisis. America's official statements and documents admittedly referred to the pre–emptive war doctrine.

> The US has long maintained the option of pre–emptive actions to counter a sufficient threat to our national security. The greater the threat, the greater is the risk of inaction – and the more compelling the case for taking anticipatory action to defend ourselves, even if uncertainty remains as to the time and place of the enemy's attack. To forestall or prevent such hostile acts by our adversaries, the US will, if necessary, act pre–emptively. … In an age where the enemies of civilization openly and actively seek the world's most destructive technologies, the United States cannot remain idle while dangers gather (National Security Strategy, 2002).

Obviously, the problem with that statement is that it was made by the US authorities at a time when there was no imminent or effective threat from Iraq, either against the US or against its allies in the Middle East or anywhere else. Does that mean that George W. Bush's administration ignored the criteria defining a legitimate pre–emptive war and differentiating it from an illegitimate preventive war? Of course not. American policy–makers did try to propose a new doctrine of pre–emptive war, arguing that Iraq was a completely new, original threat, either directly because of the nature of the weapons of mass destruction it possessed or tried to acquire, or indirectly through its support of non–state terrorist networks.

> Given the goals of rogue states and terrorists, the United States can no longer solely rely on a reactive posture as we have in the past. ... We cannot let our enemies strike first. ... The overlap between states that sponsor terror and those that pursue WMD compels us to action. ... Rogue states and terrorists do not seek to attack us using conventional means. Instead, they rely on acts of terror and, potentially, the use of weapons of mass destruction – weapons that can be easily concealed, delivered covertly, and used without warning (*Ibid.*).

The key point of Washington's argument was the following one – the traditional pre–emptive war doctrine recognised by international law, and conditioning the anticipatory use of force in the face of 'an imminent threat, most often a visible mobilization of armies, navies, and air forces preparing to attack' was no longer relevant to cope with the new threats, 'shadowy networks of individuals (that) can bring chaos and suffering to our shores for less than it costs to purchase a single tank'. According to Washington, 'the struggle against global terrorism is different from any other war in our history' and that was the reason why the 'best defence is a good offence'. In its fight against its enemies, in its resolute search for weapons of mass destruction, confronted as it was with terrorists trying to penetrate open societies by using modern technological devices to harm them, America, 'as a matter of common sense and self–defence, will act against such emerging threats before they are fully formed' (*Ibid.*).

* * *

It is not easy to refute Washington's argument, at least if one accepts the idea of the existence of terrorist networks and/or rogue states that can indeed be suspected of not 'seek(ing) to attack using conventional means' and are likely to employ 'weapons of mass destruction that can be easily concealed, delivered covertly, and used without warning' (*Ibid.*). It remains nonetheless true that the political conclusion, according to which the concept of imminent threat has to be adapted to the capacities, intentions and objectives of today's enemies, is tantamount to rehabilitating the type of argument which was precisely at the origin of the rejection of the preventive war, i.e. the uncertainty felt by a state because of its incapacity to work out an adversary state's intentions. Let me refer again to the opinion of Grotius, mentioned earlier in this chapter, that 'to pretend to have a right to injure another merely from the possibility that he may injure me is repugnant to all the justice in the world' because 'such is the condition of the present life that we can never be in perfect security' (Grotius, 1625, Book II, I).

By attacking 'upon vague and uncertain suspicions', the US turned into an 'unjust aggressor' (de Vattel, 1758: Book III, §35), all the more so as 'aggression most often takes the form of an attack by a powerful state upon a weak one' (Walzer, 1991 (1977): 67). Among other reasons, Israel's air raids against Arab airports in 1967 were considered to be a pre–emptive strike because 'the asymmetry in the structure of forces set a time limit on diplomatic efforts' (85). Asymmetry was also a characteristic feature of Operation Iraqi Freedom but it was in favour of the attacker, i.e. the US, and not the target, i.e. Iraq. Moreover, America's decision–makers were far from being confronted with the 'necessity of self–defence, instant, overwhelming, leaving no choice of means, and no moment for deliberation', to recall Daniel Webster's conditions. Few crises were the subject of such intense international deliberation (see Roberts, 2003) and numerous allies of the US were convinced that the pursuit of negotiations would eventually force Iraq to yield.

This last argument however did not count for much in Washington. Convinced that a war could not be avoided 'and that to defer it would only be an advantage to others',[16] the American authorities were determined to act unilaterally.

NOTES

1   Eager as he was to forestall Carthage's possible renaissance after the Second Punic War, the Roman Senator Cato the Elder repeatedly ended his speeches with the following sentence: '*Ceterum censeo Carthaginem esse delendam*' (the common quote '*delenda (est) carthago*' is the short version of the original quote).

2   In the present chapter I will focus on this feature of the Hobbesian conception of warfare, the necessity of preventive warfare, and not dwell on its other aspect, the unlimited character of warfare. Needless to say, Operation Iraqi Freedom perfectly corresponds to this definition, as exemplified by the speech made by George W. Bush a few hours after the start of America's attack. 'Now that conflict has come, the only way to limit its duration is to apply decisive force. And I assure you, this will not be a campaign of half measures, and we will accept no outcome but victory.' This statement, which was corroborated three weeks later by the final result of the military operation, illustrates Washington's acceptance of the Hobbesian logic. In a Lockean culture, war is limited, in the sense that it does not aim at eliminating the adversary, although it may be severe in terms of human victims and material destruction. Operation Iraqi Freedom was unlimited in the Hobbesian sense. Thanks to new technological devices the US could successfully annihilate its enemy, the Iraqi regime, without eliminating the Iraqi people.

3   These Historical examples are given by Stephen Van Evera in *The Causes of War* (Van Evera, 1999: 76–7). See also Dale Copeland, *The Origins of Major War* (Ithaca: Cornell University Press, 2000), who proposes a general theory of all the major historical wars in terms of preventive wars, from the Peloponnesian Wars to the Second World War.

4   I borrow the first half of the quote from Martin Wight, *International Theory. The Three Traditions*, (Wight, 1992: 220) and the second from Michael Walzer, *Just and Unjust Wars*, (Walzer 1991 (1977): 77). Bacon's first idea directly relates to the just–war doctrine held at that time by the Spanish neo–scholastics. Bacon alludes to them when writing that 'the opinion of some of the schoolmen (is not) to be received that a war cannot justly be made but upon a precedent injury or provocation. For there is no question that a just fear of an imminent danger,

though no blow be given, is a lawful case of war'. This statement proves that the concept of preventive war implies the existence of the alternative rhetoric of the just–war doctrine.

5   In this essay I will focus on the principle of *jus ad bellum*, relative to the causes of war, and not on *jus in bello*, relative to the conduct of war.

6   The just–war doctrine merely seeks to define the use of arms, and not to forbid it. According to Grotius, 'right reason and the nature of society ... do not prohibit all manner of violence, but only that which is repugnant to society, that which invades another's right ... The use of force which does not invade the right of another is not unjust' (Grotius, 1625: Book I, 2). In other words, the just–war doctrine should not be confused with a pacifist doctrine. As part of the Lockean tradition, it is not founded on the amity principle but on the rivalry principle, which accepts limited war.

7   In this chapter I will not dwell on details concerning this formal criterion, since, in the contemporary world, it refers to the authorization to go to war granted by the UN Security Council. See Chapter six.

8   If I use Carl Schmitt's analysis of the importance of the formal criterion in the definition of a just war, I do not approve his assertion that it is the only criterion, an assertion probably due to the broader context of his essay and to his desire to rationalise, if not justify, Germany's foreign–policy behaviour during the first half of the twentieth century. In fact, Grotius never agreed with the idea that the presence of two states, or two public authorities – *personae morales* conceiving of themselves as rivals, or *justi hostes* – was sufficient to legitimise a war. Quite on the contrary, he emphasised that 'those wars that are commenced by public authority ... are not less criminal, if begun without a just foundation.' (Grotius, 1625: Book III, 1) And the just foundation exclusively refers to defensive objectives. A war waged by a state in order to attack another state, though it is a 'solemn war', is nonetheless an unjust war, an aggression, contrary to Schmitt's interpretation of the evolution of European international law.

9   One century before Grotius, the University of Salamanca had already voted a resolution condemning the Spanish conquest of America as an unjust war, whatever the aim of this conquest may have been – the conversion of the natives or the search for silver and gold as a means to finance the wars fought by Spain against the Ottoman Muslims. This criticism of the Hobbesian conception of war thus emerged at a time when the 'might–is–right'–principle was most deeply internalised in Europe. This is a very important point if we consider the context in which this criticism was made, i.e. European behaviour 'beyond the line'.

10   The Crimean War launched by Great Britain and France against Russia in 1854 was an exception to this general pattern, as it was indeed a preventive war. By attacking Russia, Britain and France tried to prevent the emergence in South–East Europe of a prospective imbalance in favour of Russia, which tentatively took advantage of the ongoing irreversible decline of the Turkish Empire.

11   For the details of the *Caroline* affair, see Roberts, 2003.

12   For a contradictory opinion to mine, see Anthony Arend, 'International Law and the Pre–emptive Use of Force', *The Washington Quarterly*, 26, N° 2 (Spring, 2003), pp. 89–103. Other references relative to the difference between preventive and pre–emptive war include David Luban, 'Preventive War', *Philosophy and Public Affairs*, 32, N° 3 (July 2004), pp. 207–48; Walter Slocombe, 'Force, Pre–emption and Legitimacy', *Survival*, 45, N° 1 (Spring

2003), pp. 117–30; Barbara Delcourt, 'De la sécurité collective à la sécurité selective', in B. Delcourt *et al.*, 2003: 21–39.

13 There are of course exceptions to this general rule. The best known is the so–called 'Nicaragua' affair, which can be considered to be a kind of reverse *Caroline* affair. In the eighties, American soldiers penetrated into Nicaragua which was ruled by the progressive Sandinista regime, killing Nicaraguan soldiers accused by the US of supplying arms to the Salvadorean communist guerrillas who were fighting against the US–sponsored Salvadorean regime. The International Court of Justice of The Hague, to which the Nicaraguan government referred the case, rejected America's argument. Even if proved, the fact of providing arms could not justify the actions performed by American troops which, actually, were constitutive of an aggressive action taking place on the territory of a state whose sovereignty had been violated.

14 See Schweller, 1992, and Richard N. Lebow, 'Windows of Opportunity? Do States Jump Through Them?', *International Security*, 9, N° 1 (Summer 1984), pp. 147–86. President Johnson pursued the same strategy concerning America's attitude toward the Chinese nuclear programme. See William Burr & Jeffrey Richelson, 'Whether to Strangle the Baby in the Cradle: The United States and the Chinese Nuclear Program 1960–1964', *International Security*, 25, N°3 (Winter 2000–2001), pp. 54–99.

15 Michael Walzer, *Arguing about War*, New Haven, Yale University Press, 2004, pp. 88–9. This book includes Walzer's reflections, written in 2002–3, about the Iraqi crisis and war, pp. 143–68, in which he applies the just–war criteria developed in *Just and Unjust Wars*. In a comment written in September 2002, he concludes that a military operation based on the arguments advanced by the Bush administration would be a 'preventive', not a 'pre–emptive', operation, p. 146; in a comment written in March 2003, he calls Operation Iraqi Freedom an 'unjust' war' (p. 160).

16 Niccolo Machiavelli, in *The Prince*, ascribed to the Romans a belief in the inevitability of war and the advantages of preventive war.

chapter six | from multilateralism to unilateralism

Thank God for the Death of the United Nations.
(Richard Perle[1])

The US was convinced that a preventive war was the only possible and effective option to force Saddam Hussein to disarm. For that purpose, America was determined to resort to whatever means it considered to be adequate to get rid of a regime accused of threatening its security. In his Address to the Nation delivered on 12th March, 2003, George W. Bush asked Saddam Hussein to leave power within the next forty–eight hours and explicitly proclaimed the will of the US to pursue its policy, in spite of the avowed opposition of many states.

> For more than a decade, the United States and other nations have pursued patient and honourable efforts to disarm the Iraqi regime without war. ... Our good faith has not been returned. ... The United States of America has the sovereign authority to use force in assuring its own national security. ... Some permanent members of the Security Council have publicly announced they will veto any resolution that compels the disarmament of Iraq. These governments share our assessment of the danger, but not our resolve to meet it. ... The United Nations Security Council has not lived up to its responsibilities, so we will rise to ours.

The rhetoric adopted by the US president perfectly reflected Washington's choice of a behaviour based on the Hobbesian self–help principle – in the state of nature, everybody has

> the liberty ... to use his own power as he will himself for the preservation of his own nature; that is to say, of his own life; and consequently, of doing anything which, *in his own judgement and reason*, he shall conceive to be the aptest means thereunto (Hobbes, 1651: 14 emphasis added).

In matters of international security, the self–help principle concretely means acting unilaterally. Confronted with a serious problem, expected or unexpected, a state will act in accordance with its own analysis of the situation and for the best defence of its national interests in such a specific context.

The self–help principle prevailed throughout antiquity and the Middle Ages, up to the two World Wars. The normal behaviour of a state was to resort to unilateral action. For instance, in 1701 Great Britain launched a preventive war against Louis XIV, accusing him of trying to upset the existing order by imposing his nephew on the Spanish throne. Likewise, during the Revolutionary and Napoleonic Wars, the consecutive coalitions which opposed France united and broke up commensurately with the successive victories and defeats of the different protagonists. On the eve of 1914, European powers polarised into two rigid alliances having abandoned their flexible alliances and alignments. In the 1930s, buck–passing was the preferred strategy adopted by the three Continental powers confronted with the threat of Hitler and so on.

Contrary to a unilateral self–help policy,

> multilateralism is an institutional form which coordinates relations among three or more states on the basis of generalized principles of conduct, that is, principles which specify appropriate conduct for classes of actions, without regard to the particularistic interests of the parties or the strategic exigencies that may exist in any specific occurrence (Ruggie, 1998: 109).

In international security matters, multilateralism aims at increasing predictability in international politics, under the form of collective security, i.e. 'security for all states, by the action of all states', by exposing 'all states which might challenge the existing order by the arbitrary unleashing of their power' to the prospect of collective sanctions being imposed (Claude, 1962: 110).

The idea that making peace rests on an association of states can be traced back to the first peace projects proposed by European irenic thinkers as early as the seventeenth century. It was institutionalised after the two World Wars and the failure of unilateralist policies to maintain peace, which gave more credibility to the alternative of collective security devices. The US played a crucial role in this institutionalisation process. Born free and 'lucky',[2] the US adopted a unilateral isolationist strategy in the first century of its existence, for both objective and subjective reasons. The only means for the young Republic to consolidate its national security and territorial integrity was indeed to take advantage of its geopolitical position and avoid the risks attached to its potential involvement in the international system dominated by European powers. The US – which had gained independence after successfully waging a war of decolonisation – refused to form entangling alliances that might have constrained its freedom of action. However, in the early twentieth century, when the country significantly increased its material resources and was thus tempted to abandon the isolationist policy it had pursued so far, American policy–makers had to choose between various options for the content and form of their foreign policy. Should they adopt a liberal foreign policy aiming at the promotion of democratic and free–market values; or should they convert to a realist foreign policy, guided by the mere defence of the national interest, defined as security and power? Should they remain faithful to their isolationist practices and go on acting unilaterally, as in the past, or should they act multilaterally, within the institutional framework of international institutions?

After two short–lived parentheses – Theodore Roosevelt's unilateral realism and Woodrow Wilson's multilateral liberalism – the US opted for the post–WWII compromise in 1945. It implied combining a form of multilateral realism within the UN framework in its relations with its adversaries – the USSR during the Cold War and Iraq during the first Gulf crisis – and multilateral liberalism within the Atlantic Alliance in its relations with its European allies.

In this chapter, I contend that the US has relinquished these two forms of multilateralism in Operation Iraqi Freedom and adopted a new and original strategy – unilateral liberalism.

* * *

In the Hobbesian conception of international politics, unilateralism refers to the principle of national interest as the main guideline for the states' foreign behaviour. In the specific domain of international security, to act unilaterally means to rely upon one's own resources in order to maintain one's security. First, since the anarchic structure and violent nature of the international milieu implies an unceasing state of war, a state cannot exclude the possibility of being attacked by another state and being thus forced to resort to arms. Consequently, whatever other aims states may have, 'security is their most important objective' (Mearsheimer, 2001: 31), because 'only if survival is assured can states safely seek such other goals as tranquillity, profit and power' (Waltz, 1979: 126). Secondly, states which strive to guarantee their own security must rely on their own resources, because all other states are potential threats by definition. Applying to states Hobbes' view that 'men live without other security than what *their own strength and their own invention* shall furnish them' (Hobbes, 1651: 13, emphasis added), Kenneth Waltz emphasises that 'to achieve their objectives and maintain their security, units in a condition of anarchy ... must rely on the means and the arrangements they can make for themselves. Self–help is necessarily the principle of action in an anarchic order' (Waltz, 1979: 111).

To take up Waltz's own words, to act in accordance with the self–help principle concretely means to adopt a balancing behaviour aiming either at preventing any other state from becoming the preponderant unit of the international system, or at re–establishing a balance of power in the case of an already upset balance. 'A self–help system is one in which those who do not help themselves, or who do so less effectively than others, will fail to prosper, will lay themselves open to dangers, will suffer. Fear of such unwanted consequences stimulates states to behave in ways that tend toward the creation of balances of power' (118).

Empirical reality, however, hardly confirms Waltz's analysis. Besides the use of preventive war (see Chapter five), balancing is merely one possible strategy chosen by states in order to establish their security.[3] 'Strategies for checking aggressors'[4] may indeed take various forms.

Waltz is right when he asserts that the deterrence strategy is the first strategy adopted by states in order to prevent other states from gaining power at their expense. Such a strategy consists in exhibiting one's force, flexing one's muscles so to speak, in order not to have to use it. For that purpose, states either opt for a form of internal balancing – building up their own power capacities – or external balancing – forming alliances with other states and even sometimes adopting a chain–ganging strategy. 'Internal balancing is self–help in the purest sense of the term' (Mearsheimer, 2001: 157). In the history of international politics, this strategy was successfully practised by the two off–shore balancers – Great Britain in the second half of the nineteenth century and the US in the second half of the twentieth century. As they were both preponderant powers, they could choose to devote only a relatively limited part of their resources to the defence budget during non–crisis periods and to wait for the outbreak of crises before substantially increasing their military expenditure. For instance, from the American standpoint, the arms race between the US and the Soviet Union throughout the Cold War was an illustration of such internal balancing.

Predominant powers, whether they are confronted with one major adversary, as in the case of the US with the USSR, or with a plurality of potential rivals, such as the United Kingdom from the beginning of its decline onwards, tend to complement this internal balancing strategy with an external balancing strategy behaviour. They do not hesitate to form alliances with secondary satisfied states in order to forestall a common threat from a third–party power. For instance, on the eve of the First World War, the declining preponderant British power formed a rigid alliance with France and Tsarist Russia in a tentative opposition to the rising German contender. In the same vein, Western European states joined the US in the post–1945 Atlantic Alliance, with a view to preserving their security, which they felt was threatened by Soviet Russia. In the Second World War, the various satisfied powers threatened by Hitler's expansionism had already chosen a chain–ganging strategy that had led them to accept a coalition with their former adversary, the USSR, despite their conflicting interests and aspirations, because Nazi Germany was perceived as an even greater threat. That move echoed the attitude adopted by Great Britain, which had combined its forces with Russia's during the French Revolutionary and Napoleonic Wars.

The chain–ganging strategy with the USSR during the Second World War was chosen by Britain after the failure of the buck–passing strategy it had jointly adopted with the USSR and France in the 1930s.

> Between 1933 and March 1939, ... the United Kingdom passed the buck to France, which tried to push Hitler eastward against the smaller states of Eastern Europe and possibly the Soviet Union, which in turn tried to pass the buck to the United Kingdom and France. In March 1939, the United Kingdom finally joined forces with France against the Third Reich, but the Soviet Union did not join with its former allies. ... Stalin continued to pursue a buck–passing

strategy, hoping that the United Kingdom and Nazi Germany would become involved in a long and costly war. That approach failed, however, when the *Wehrmacht* invaded the Soviet Union on June 22, 1941. Only then did the British and the Soviets become allies against the Third Reich (Mearsheimer, 2001: 308–9 and 315–316).[5]

The USSR had even adopted a bandwagon strategy when it signed the Molotov–Ribbentrop Pact in 1939. Instead of choosing to balance the rising threat from Germany, Stalin hoped to profit from Hitler's expansionism by accepting Hitler's grip on the Western half of Poland in exchange for his own control over the Eastern half, the Baltic States and Finland. There were secret protocols in the pact that explicitly stipulated some 'territorial and political rearrangements'. The same revisionist strategy was pursued by various intermediate powers of Central Europe – Hungary, Romania, and Bulgaria. Though London was never tempted by such a policy, it nevertheless completed its buck–passing strategy in the 1930s with an appeasement policy towards Hitler. This strategy was grounded on the – fallacious – analysis that Hitler's expansionism was a classical form of nationalism and that Germany could become a satisfied power if its demands were met.

To put it briefly, states adopt eclectic options. In their desire to guarantee their security, they resort to a vast range of unilateral strategies. Such a pragmatic behaviour is perfectly rational from an individual standpoint. According to the existing power distribution, it is sometimes in the interest of a state to rely on its own power resources. It may sometimes be more logical to count on its allies' capacities; balance an adversary's objective capacities or its perceived intentions; bandwagon with a threatening power or try to appease it; remain faithful to an ally or let him bear the burden of fighting the common adversary, or even let him down, either by leaving the alliance or by signing a separate peace in the hope that both the former ally and the former adversary will be exhausted by their fight.[6]

The fact is that such individual rationality eventually ends up in some form of collective irrationality or, to say the least, in a collectively sub–optimum outcome, with the regular irruption of the wars that individual rationality is precisely supposed to prevent. According to realists, states regularly resort to war in order to guarantee their security because of their subjective uncertainty about the behaviour of other states. In all logics there are uncertainties only when states behave in an unpredictable, ambiguous, or changing way – which is exactly the case when a state alternately balances, bandwagons, or passes the buck. From a strictly logical perspective, unilateralism could mean stability if states permanently adopted a balancing strategy. Let us take the example of a state tempted to increase its capacities or attack its neighbours. If such a state knew that another state would increase its own capacities and/or form a coalition with a third–party state in order to match its resource build–up or check its aggressive intentions, it would refrain from trying to augment its power or exhibiting its hostile intentions, as such decisions might well prove to be counterproductive. However, as states do not adopt a single behaviour, i.e. a balancing strategy, but prefer to choose between a variety of tactics, the recurrence of war is the logical outcome of self–help in international politics.

Some four centuries ago, irenic thinkers had already come to the same conclusion. In 1623, while Grotius was considering his just–war principles within the framework of an exclusively European international law, the French irenist Emeric Crucé, in his essay called 'The New Cyneas',[7] imagined a project that could ensure a perpetual and universal peace.

Crucé was a pacifist. He rejected the idea that the value of a state was degenerated by peace. He asserted that wars, which in his views pertained to barbarian mores, were due to the fact that states acted unilaterally, 'went their own way' and 'did not communicate'. In order to eschew the triumph of this self–help principle, Crucé wanted the Princes – or their delegates – of all countries to convene in one place and debate so as to avoid war. The chosen place for this permanent assembly was Venice, a 'neutral and indifferent locus for all the Princes' conveniently situated in between Christian entities and remote lands – Muscovy, the Ottoman Empire, Japan, India, China, Africa, and Ethiopia.[8] Gathering 'the ambassadors of all the monarchies and sovereign republics' with the idea of a 'perfect reconciliation', this assembly would aim to pacify international politics. Each ambassador would expound his state's claims and complaints and the assembly would arbitrate international disputes by the majority of the monarchies' votes.[9] The assembly's decision would be considered as an 'inviolable law', thanks to the dynamics of collective involvement – 'which Prince would be foolhardy enough to defy the company of all the monarchs of the world?' – and to the collective use of force in the case of one member of the assembly refusing to submit to the chosen arbitration. In order to make a refractory member see reason, all the other members would promise to 'punish by arms' those tempted to violate the majority's decisions, thus inciting everyone to abide by them.

By emphasising that the assembly 'would judge on all disputes, keep one and all in good terms, anticipate and appease discontent by gentle dissuasion, if possible, or by use of force, if necessary' (Crucé, 2004: 88–93), Crucé anticipated the multilateral collective security regime that was developed three centuries after by the UN Security Council, whose main objective – to eschew war as a means of conflict resolution – is also inspired by a mix of *Realpolitik* and *Liberalpolitik*. In Crucé's views, international stability was based on the limitation of the external dimension of the states' sovereignty, as states did indeed meet and negotiate on a permanent basis, thus agreeing to drop unilateral interest promotion; it also rested upon the common interests of some great powers, satisfied enough with the existing order to agree upon the identification of the threat and the use of force in the case of a violation of the decision by dissatisfied members. In other words, Crucé was well ahead of his time and it took three hundred years before his idea of a collective security system took shape,[10] after the two World Wars, on the initiative of the US.[11]

When the US proclaimed its independence, its founding fathers, who were inspired by John Locke's liberal philosophy, were torn between the contending and diverging diplomatic guidelines recommended by Alexander Hamilton and Thomas Jefferson.

Hamilton was a realist. He posited that international politics was tantamount to a state of war and believed that the US would sooner or later get involved in the quarrels opposing European powers. According to him, it was useless to try to escape these conflicts. The US had to consolidate its own power base in order to cope successfully with the lack of moderation shown by the other powers. Moreover, in its relations with the two great powers of the period – Great Britain, which 'frequently engaged in war' despite its predominant interest in commerce, and France, which was guided by a 'spirit of universal domination', it was in the interest of the US to opt for an alliance with Britain, this being 'a lesser evil'.[12] Jefferson was an isolationist. Even if he despaired of abolishing war, he was nevertheless convinced that the 'disposition to war' could be lessened 'by improving the mind and morals of society'. According to him, the US had the capacity to favour the diffusion of peace, on the condition that it pursued a foreign policy guided by national interests defined in accordance with 'moral duties'. For that purpose, the US had to remain aloof from European affairs thanks to 'the wide ocean' separating the United States from the European powers.[13]

George Washington found a compromise. In his *Farewell Address*, he recommended that his fellow citizens should have 'as little political connection as possible' with foreign nations while at the same time 'extending ... commercial relations'.

> Europe has a set of primary interests which to us have none, or a very remote, relation. Hence ... it must be unwise in us to implicate ourselves by artificial ties in the ordinary vicissitudes of her politics, or the ordinary combinations and collisions of her friendships or enmities. Our detached and distant situation invites and enables us to pursue a different course. ... Why forego the advantages of so peculiar a situation? Why quit our own to stand upon foreign ground? Why, by interweaving our destiny with that of any part of Europe, entangle our peace and prosperity in the toils of European ambition, rivalship, interest, humour or caprice? It is our true policy to steer clear of permanent alliances with any portion of the foreign world, so far, I mean, as we are now at liberty to do it. ... We may safely trust to temporary alliances for extraordinary emergencies.[14]

By warning future American policy–makers against the constraints implied by peacetime alliances, Washington's message extolled the unilateralist policy adopted by the US during the first century of its existence. The US chose to follow its own course by deciding to remain aloof from the European international system. The question is to determine if this unilateralism actually pertained to the logic of interest as cherished by Hamilton – it was in the interest of the US to consolidate its own power resources and not expose its security and integrity, which could be threatened if it decided to intervene in a system dominated by the much more powerful European powers – or to the ethics of identity as privileged by Jefferson – the refusal to intervene in international conflicts as the only way for the US to protect the manifest destiny of an exceptional people guided by liberal values and entrusted with the providential mission of contributing to improving life on earth. In fact, the US indeed acted unilaterally but it was, at least partially, a unilateralism by default, as a reaction to the type of unilateralism practised by the great European powers of the time.

The US remained faithful to this posture throughout the nineteenth century, even after the adoption of the Monroe Doctrine. In 1823, Spain had to face up to the rebellion of its Latin–American colonies and was tempted to appeal to the Holy Alliance in order to crush the rebels. The Monroe Doctrine was, above all, a defensive doctrine that epitomised the New World's desire to put an end to the eurocentric view prevalent since Christopher Columbus that American territories were open to conquest and colonisation.

> Our policy, in regard to Europe, … is not to interfere in the internal concerns of any of its powers. … But, in regard to these continents, circumstances are eminently and conspicuously different. It is impossible that the allied powers should extend their political system to any portion of either continent, without endangering our peace and happiness.[15]

Things started to change in the late nineteenth century. Increasing resources provided the US with the opportunity to intervene successfully in extra–hemispheric affairs. American elites eventually decided to drop their proclaimed isolationism in favour of a form of assumed internationalism. This change initiated several debates on the American diplomatic doctrines that would, from then on, shape American foreign policy.

The first debate hinged on the very nature of America's internationalism and the question whether American foreign policy should privilege the promotion of ideas and values embodying American identity, such as freedom, democracy, the triumph of law and human rights, or the defence of America's material interests in terms of prosperity and security. The liberals, who defended the idea that America was the beacon of a new, democratic world order, opposed the realists, who saw the US as a traditional power (on this opposition see Kissinger, 1994). The second debate related to ways and means of implementing this newly chosen internationalism. According to the unilateralists, the US could and should pursue its unilateral policy as it had done during the nineteenth century, relying exclusively upon itself and not tying its hands by alliances. Conversely, the multilateralists claimed that the US could not but act jointly with the other powers, as its nineteenth century isolation was at an end. Four combinations were then possible[16] – realist unilateralism, tantamount to offensive power politics or *Machtpolitik*; liberal unilateralism, initiating messianic crusades; liberal multilateralism, leading to benign leadership; and multilateral realism, akin to defensive power politics or *Realpolitik*.

At the very beginning of American internationalism, Theodore Roosevelt's big–stick policy and his Corollary to the Monroe Doctrine – which turned Latin America into Washington's backyard – heralded America's conversion to the realist unilateralism prevailing in traditional European power politics. But Roosevelt's politics of conquest – the expression of a thirst for power and a desire to carve out a colonial empire – was short–lived, not just in time, since this 'imperial moment' was followed by a return to isolationism, but also substantially. America's expansionism was exclusively focused against Spanish colonial power, in Cuba and the Philippines. In the rest of the world, it merely concerned small territories, some Pacific islands or the Panama Canal Zone. This 'imperial under–stretch', to use the expression coined by Fareed Zakaria,[17] was due to the specific constraints imposed by the defence and promotion of human values and liberal ideas on American foreign behaviour, at odds with a purely materialist definition of national interests.

It was precisely America's identity that was at the origin of America's second temporary internationalist moment, promoted by Wilson during the years 1917–20. Woodrow Wilson called for the promotion of America's proclaimed ethical standards instead of the defence of America's interests defined as power. He did not hesitate to criticise the decisions and actions taken by his predecessors in foreign–policy matters.

> I believe that America ... should be ready in every point of policy and of action to vindicate at whatever cost the principles of liberty, of justice, and of humanity to which we have been devoted from the first. ... We shall ... never again take another foot of territory by conquest. We shall never in any circumstances seek to make an independent people subject to our dominion; because we believe, we passionately believe, in the right of every people to choose their own allegiance and be free of masters altogether.[18]

As he wanted to build peace 'upon the tested foundations of political liberty',[19] he relied on multilateralism and an institutionalised co–operation with other nations to extend liberal democracy, the free market, and the triumph of law, as, in his view, there would have been a contradiction in terms to seek to impose liberal values upon anybody without their consent. However, by agreeing to get involved in permanent institutions that would potentially tie America's hands, the Wilsonian project put an end to the freedom of action that had characterised America's diplomacy throughout the first century of its existence. This was why the US Senate refused to ratify the Treaty of Versailles and the creation of the League of Nations, thus turning America's second internationalist moment and multilateral liberalism into a dead letter.

This option just held for a while, as liberal multilateralism rose from its ashes with Franklin Roosevelt who initiated America's third – and irreversible – internationalist moment. Opposed as he was to unilateralism and alliance politics, Roosevelt favoured the creation of the multilateral collective security system of Chapter VII of the UN Charter, which he saw as the only means to put an end to the vicious circle implied by the 'security–through–self–help' policy. Decisions to resort to sanctions, armed or unarmed, against an aggressor state, were to be taken by the concert of the great powers with a permanent membership status within the

Security Council. As the USSR rejected America's projects, their subsequent and regular use of the veto paralysed the working of the institution.[20] America's multi-lateralism was thus two–fold during the Cold War – liberal with its allies and realist with its adversaries.

With its European and Canadian allies, the US formed the Atlantic Alliance, which was an *ersatz* form of collective security.[21] The NATO treaty, as proved in Article 5, was complementary to Chapter VII of the UN Charter, both in its formal reference to the UN system and to the principles of indivisibility and common response to an aggressor.

> The Parties agree that an armed attack against one or more of them in Europe or North America shall be considered an attack against them all and consequently they agree that, if such an armed attack occurs, each of them, in exercise of the right of individual or collective self–defence recognised by Article '51 of the Charter of the United Nations, will assist the Party or Parties so attacked by taking forthwith, individually and in concert with the other Parties, such action as it deems necessary, including the use of armed force, to restore and maintain the security of the North Atlantic area. Any such armed attack and all measures taken as a result thereof shall immediately be reported to the Security Council. Such measures shall be terminated when the Security Council has taken the measures necessary to restore and maintain international peace and security.[22]

For the American authorities, who had refused any entangling alliance since George Washington, the compatibility of the NATO Treaty with the UN Charter was both the necessary condition for, and the evidence of, their involvement. It implied that they abandoned the unilateralist policy that had marked their past diplomacy. Considering that, after Pearl Harbour, any form of political isolationism in the Western Hemisphere, coupled with a purely commercial internationalism, was no longer possible, the strict adherence to the self–help principle would have led the US to create a traditional alliance, characterised by discretionary and authoritative decisions on its part, and limited sovereignty for its partners as the logical complement of America's absolute control over the coalition, on a par with the structure of the Warsaw Pact imposed by the USSR on its satellites. In fact, the US only imposed the model of the Rio Treaty which, in accordance with the UN Charter, was directed against nobody in particular. The US conceived of NATO not as 'an alliance, but as the expression of an association of likeminded nations' (Haine, 2004: 192). American policy–makers not only accepted the fact that an institutionalised alliance with Europe could increase America's own insecurity; as such, an alliance implied equal sacrifice for an unequal cause, should one of its allies be attacked. They also agreed to reduce their own autonomy. According to Article 4, the Atlantic Alliance was characterised by a multilateral management of the policy undertaken by the protector in favour of its allies; by decisions open to consultations, which could be modified, and were ratified by consensus; by a loose definition of authority shared out between all the members with the same rights. 'The Parties will consult together whenever, in the opinion of any of them, the territorial integrity, political independence or security of any of the Parties is threatened.' This rule implied more than the exchange of information. It established the principle of collective consultation between all the members on all issues before any decision was made. Member states were thus encouraged to refrain from undertaking unilateral initiatives. They were invited to take into consideration the other members' interests in the definition of their own national interest.

Throughout the Cold War, this liberal multilateralism prevailed, even during the periods of heightened tension. For instance, in the Cuban missile crisis, the US paid heed to its allies' potential reactions as, according to Dean Rusk,

> an unannounced, quick action on our part could well lead to a kind of allied disunity that the Soviet attack will capitalize upon very strongly. ... We are the central bone structure of the alliance ...; (any) action has to be thought about in connection with alliance solidarity (quoted in Haine, 2004: 212–13).

American leaders refused to undertake any unilateral action. George Ball declared that a surprise attack on behalf of the US, comparable to the Pearl Harbour attack, would be 'the kind of conduct one might expect of the Soviet Union', but not of America. He was conscious of 'the kind of sense of a funk' such an action would provoke in the allied countries, and warned that 'far from establishing our moral strength' it 'would in fact alienate a great part of the civilized world by behaving in a manner wholly contrary to our traditions (quoted in Haine, 2004: 215).

To sum up, American ethical values and liberal identity guided America's relations with its allies throughout the Cold War and up to the allied operations in Bosnia and Kosovo in the 1990s, which were decided and executed within the framework of the Atlantic institutions. At the same time, multilateralism, in its realist version, also prevailed in America's relations with its adversaries, the USSR during the Cold War (see Chapter three) or Iraq during the first Gulf crisis. As regards the first American intervention against Saddam Hussein, George H. Bush declared that 'this is not, as Saddam Hussein would have it, the United States against Iraq. It is Iraq against the world', thus underlining the multilateral nature of Operations Desert Shield and Desert Storm. America's reaction to Iraq's invasion and annexation of Kuwait was an integral part of the collective self–defence norm established by the multilateral institutions aiming at promoting the indivisible security of all the members of the international society.

It was thus before and during Operation Iraqi Freedom that the US abandoned its decade–old multilateral posture[23] and substituted, in its relations with both its allies and adversaries, the traditional 'multilateral if we can, unilateral if we must' principle with the new motto 'Unilateral all the time, multilateral if the rest of the world wants to tag along'.[24]

First, unilateralism supplanted America's traditional realist multilateralism in the attitude the Bush administration adopted towards the collective security system of the UN. In his Address to the United Nations General Assembly, delivered on 12th September, 2002, George W. Bush declared that 'my nation will work with the UN Security Council to meet our common challenge. ... We will work with the UN Security Council for the necessary resolutions. But the purposes of the United States should not be doubted. The Security Council resolutions will be enforced – the just demands of peace and security will be met – or action will be unavoidable'. He repeated the same idea in his State of the Union Address on 28th January, 2003.

> We have called on the United Nations to fulfil its charter and stand by its demand that Iraq disarm. We're strongly supporting the International Atomic Energy Agency in its mission to track and control nuclear materials around the world. We're working with other governments to secure nuclear materials in the former Soviet Union, and to strengthen global treaties banning the production and shipment of missile technologies and weapons of mass destruction. In all these efforts, however, America's purpose is more than to follow a process – it is to achieve a result: the end of terrible threats to the civilized world. All free nations have a stake in preventing sudden and catastrophic attacks. And we're asking them to join us, and many are doing so. Yet the course of this nation does not depend on the decisions of others. Whatever action is required, whenever action is necessary, I will defend the freedom and security of the American people. ... We will consult. But let there be no misunderstanding: if Saddam Hussein does not fully disarm, for the safety of our people and for the peace of the world, we will lead a coalition to disarm him.

Through his claim that 'the Iraqi dictator is not disarming; on the contrary, he is deceiving' and his evocation of Saddam Hussein's various prevarications over the previous twelve years, George W. Bush contended that 'trusting in the sanity and restraint of Saddam Hussein is not a strategy, and it is not an option'. This is the logic of Hobbes, who upheld the idea that 'it is a precept, or general rule of reason: that every man ought to endeavour peace, *as far as* he has hope of obtaining it; and when he cannot obtain it, that he may seek and use all helps and advantages of war' (Hobbes, 1651: 14, emphasis added). Washington's refusal to allow the UN inspectors to carry on with their investigations and its decision to launch an armed attack against Iraq, regardless of the positions of the other states, complied with the Hobbesian conception of international action, unilateral by necessity as indeed, in the state of nature, states 'live without other security than what their own strength and their own invention shall furnish them'. In Hobbes's views, if everyone is 'commanded to endeavour peace', one is forced to lay down one's right to guarantee one's security by all means on the condition that 'others are willing too' (Hobbes, 1651: 14). Conversely, 'if other men will not lay down their right, as well as he, then there is no reason for anyone to divest himself of his: for that were to expose himself to prey, which no man is bound to, rather than to dispose himself to peace' (Hobbes: 1651: 14). That was exactly the analysis made by the Bush administration. As Iraq did not respect the UN resolutions, there was no obligation for America to pass on its individual self–defence right to the society of states acting within the framework of Chapter VII of the UN Charter. As Iraq, by refusing to open its territory to the UN inspectors, did not give up its freedom to act unilaterally, the US was forced to act unilaterally, for fear of losing the possibility of preventing Iraq from jeopardising America's own security.

However, such assumed unilateralism did not stop the US from trying to persuade its critics that Operation Iraqi Freedom fully respected the rules of multilateralism, precisely because of Iraq's unwillingness to comply with the UN resolutions adopted since the end of Operation Desert Storm. In his letter addressed to the Security Council on 20th March, 2003, the US Ambassador to the UN, John Negroponte, declared that 'the actions being taken are authorized under existing Council resolutions, including its resolutions 678 (1990) and 687 (1991)' (quoted in Roberts, 2003). Unfortunately for the US, a careful reading of these resolutions shows that Negroponte's argument was fallacious and unfounded.

In its resolution 678 (1990), adopted on 29th November, 1990, the UN Security Council, after noting that Iraq had refused to comply with its obligation to implement resolution 660 (1990) and the subsequent resolutions asking Baghdad to restore Kuwait's sovereignty, had authorised 'member states cooperating with the government of Kuwait ... to use all necessary means to uphold and implement resolution 660 (1990) and all subsequent relevant resolutions and to restore international peace and security in the area'.[25] In its resolution 687 (1991), adopted on 3rd April, 1991, the Security Council had declared that the signature of the ceasefire depended on Baghdad's 'unconditional acceptance' of the obligations imposed by the Non–Proliferation Treaty, on its renouncing committing any terrorist attack or supporting any terrorist organisation, and on the on–site inspection of the elimination of its weapons of mass destruction by agents of the International Atomic Energy Agency.

There is of course no doubt that Iraq persistently violated this last resolution throughout the years 1991–2002. As early as 15th August, 1991, the Security Council's resolution 707 (1991) 'condemn(ed) Iraq's serious violation of a number of its obligations ... of resolution 687 (707) ... to cooperate with the Special Commission and the IAEA', and 'require(d) the government of Iraq forthwith to comply fully and without delay with all its international obligations'. Resolution 1205 (1998), adopted on 15th November, 1998, 'condemn(ed) the decision by Iraq of 31 October 1998 to cease co–operation with the Special Commission as a flagrant violation of resolution 687 (1991)', and 'demand(ed) that Iraq ... provide immediate, complete and unconditional cooperation with the Special Commission and the IAEA'. Finally, the Security Council in its resolution 1441 (2002), adopted on 8th November, 2002, after recalling its resolutions 660 (1990) and 678 (1990), 'deploring the absence, since December 1998, of international monitoring, inspection, and verification ... of weapons of mass destruction and ballistic missiles', and 'deploring also that the Government of Iraq has failed to comply with its commitments with regard to terrorism', 'decide(d) that Iraq ha(d) been and remain(ed) in material breach of its obligations, ... in particular through (its) failure to cooperate with United Nations' inspectors and the IAEA'.

However, resolution 1441 (2002), which recalled that the Security Council 'has repeatedly warned Iraq that it will face serious consequences as a result of a continued violation of its obligations', decided 'to afford Iraq ... a final opportunity to comply with its disarmament obligations' and 'to convene immediately' upon a report by the UN inspectors of 'any interference by Iraq with inspection activities' or of 'any failure by Iraq to comply with its disarmament obligations'. Such a report was never written and transmitted by the inspection commission headed by Hans Blix and Mohamed El Baradei.[26] The Security Council thus had no reason to 'convene', which meant that the legal requirement for the use of arms against Iraq, namely an explicit authorisation for such an armed sanction given by the majority of the Security Council members without a veto by any permanent member, was not met.

Moreover, the fact that Iraq had repeatedly violated the various resolutions with which it should have complied did not legitimise the use of armed force against this country, as proved by the analysis *a contrario* of Resolution 678 (1990), which authorised Operation Desert Storm. In this resolution it was specified that the use of 'all necessary means' was authorised not only in order 'to uphold and implement resolution 660 (1990) and all subsequent relevant resolutions', but also 'to restore international peace and security in the area'. In other words, the proven existence of 'a threat to the peace', of a 'breach of the peace', or an 'act of aggression' was the necessary condition for legally resorting to arms according to Article 39 of the UN Charter. The mere violation of UN resolutions was not enough. As there was neither a breach of the peace nor a threat to the peace on the part of Saddam Hussein in 2002 and 2003, the US decision to launch Operation Iraqi Freedom clearly violated the prevailing multilateral standards.

Lastly, the US was not the only country that could refer to Iraq's violation of UN resolutions. Indeed, resolution 678 (1990), recalled by John Negroponte, mentioned the 'member states cooperating with the government of Kuwait'. The US was not the only state that could justify its policy on this resolution. Other states could do so, notably the states which, like France for instance, proposed an alternative political approach.

Actually, the fact that the US did not share, and did not even take into consideration the French or German analysis of the situation shows that American unilateralism also prevailed in its relations with some of its traditionally closest allies.

The end of the liberal multilateral approach that had so far prevailed in transatlantic relations can be traced back to the immediate aftermath of 9/11. Whereas for the first time in its history, NATO, through the voice of its Secretary–General Lord Robertson, was getting ready to appeal to Article 5 – a collective consultation with a view to a collective action – America preferred to launch Operation Enduring Freedom at the head of an *ad hoc* coalition, in the name of the freedom of action indispensable to defeat global terrorism.

Inspired by American chiefs of staff who considered that the 1999 bombing campaign during the Kosovo War had been affected by the absence of such a freedom of action, as decisions had had to be taken unanimously by the nineteen member states of NATO, the Bush administration resorted to 'a coalition of the willing', in the name of a new strategy thus summarised by Paul Wolfowitz – in an allusion to Donald Rumsfeld in a speech delivered at the *Wehrkunde* Conference in Munich on 4th February, 2002. 'The mission has to determine the coalition, not the other way around. … Otherwise, as the Secretary says, the mission will be reduced to "the lowest common denominator". As a corollary of that, there will not be a single coalition but rather different coalitions for different missions, what the Secretary calls "flexible" coalitions.' Consequently, there was hardly any mention of NATO in the National Security Strategy adopted in September 2002; the organisation was only referred to through its contribution to 'mission–based coalitions'.[27] The victim of a polite indifference on behalf of the US during Operation Enduring Freedom against the Taliban regime,[28] the Atlantic Alliance was consciously excluded from the launching and conducting of Operation Iraqi Freedom, which indirectly evidenced the fact that this intervention was more a messianic crusade than a defensive operation aiming at protecting the security of a member state of the Alliance. All the more so as George W. Bush not only dropped the traditional tendency of past administrations to consult their allies. He also tried to divide what American neo–conservatives called Old Europe, i.e. France and Germany, from New Europe, i.e. Great Britain and the other European member states which supported his policy. In a clear warning delivered on 20th September, 2001, he declared 'either you are with us, or you are with the terrorists'.

* * *

Jean–Yves Haine's analysis of America's abandonment of the Western liberal multilateralism perfectly sums up America's return to Hobbesian values.

> By marginalizing NATO in Afghanistan, the White House decision makers have clearly favoured the formation of an *ad hoc* coalition decidedly incompatible with the Alliance's cohesion. By dividing it over the Iraq crisis, they turn their back on a diplomatic practice grounded on consensus which had characterized America's involvement in Europe ever since its start. As a matter of fact, the specificity of the Atlantic Alliance rests upon its multilateral principles, whose most important pillars were consultation and consensus. In such a framework, persuasion supplanted constraint, and perseverance forged influence. By advocating cohesion while authorizing dissension, the Atlantic regime symbolized this liberal paradox characteristic of America's policy towards its allies. The new American strategy, based on quite diverse coalitions of the willing, as well as on the blackmail or bribing of recalcitrant allies, reflects an instrumental conception of the Alliance at odds with the Atlantic practice. This conception did all the more trouble Europe as the American rhetoric became at once more radical towards its adversaries, merged into an axis of evil, and more Manichean towards its allies, placed in the tricky position of being either an unconditional supporter of, or an inevitable traitor to, the US (Haine, 2004: 286).

To put it briefly, the US has proclaimed itself 'more equal than others'[29] by choosing a deliberately unilateral stance in order to promote its values. By opting for a form of 'Wilsonianism with boots',[30] which has placed it above the rules of appropriate behaviour within international society that the US had contributed to consolidating, America has turned into a revisionist power as, indeed, multilateralism is by definition favourable to the existing status quo in its realist version, and favourable to progressive changes within the existing stability in its liberal version.

The question is to know whether the return of Hobbesian anarchy implied by this liberal unilateralism will be durable or short–lived. To try to give a tentative answer to this question, given that, since the end of World War Two, expansionist episodes of American foreign policy behaviour have been mere parentheses of 'arrogance',[31] I will, in Part III, analyse the possible causes of Operation Iraqi Freedom.

NOTES

1   Richard Perle, 'Thank God for the Death of the United Nations. Its abject failure gave us only anarchy. The world needs order', *The Guardian*, 21st March, 2003. Perle refers to anarchy in its most common sense – disorder and troubles.

2   Expression due to Robert Keohane, quoted by John G. Ruggie, 'Interests, Identity and American Foreign Policy', in Ruggie, 1988: 203–28. The same idea had been expressed by de Tocqueville, *Democracy in America*, vol. 2. 'Fortune, which has conferred so many peculiar benefits upon the inhabitants of the United States, has placed them in the midst of a wilderness, where they have, so to speak, no neighbours: a few thousand soldiers are sufficient for their wants' (de Tocqueville, 1831: Volume 2, XXII).

3   The empirical examples of unilateral behaviour I refer to date back to the post–1648 and even post–1815 events. Nevertheless they do not contradict my – i.e. Wendt's – overall hypothesis according to which Lockean anarchy has replaced the formerly prevailing Hobbesian culture since 1648. Such a replacement has necessarily been a progressive process, for two main reasons. First there is a time–lag between the emergence of new ideas and their adoption in the political practice; secondly some values develop more rapidly than others as norms are more or less quickly shared by a more or less high number of states. Thus, whereas the enmity structure was replaced by the rivalry principle as early as 1648, it was only in the second half of the nineteenth century that the pre–emptive war norm became prevalent and supplanted the preventive war practice. Multilateralism only became the norm after the two World Wars.

4   Cf. J. Mearsheimer's typology in *The Tragedy of Great Power Politics* (Mearsheimer, 2001: 155 *sqq*).

5   J. Mearsheimer, (2001: 139–140), compares the balancing and buck–passing strategies, and goes as far as to assert that states prefer to pass the buck when they feel threatened. This claim is incompatible with Waltz's theory, according to which states have to balance, and indeed do balance, in order to guarantee their security. Waltz's theory also runs counter to the analysis of Stephen Walt, who contends that states balance threats and not power resources (Walt, 1987). Since the publication of John Vasquez & Colin Elman (eds),

Realism and the Balance of Power: A New Debate (Upper Saddle River: Prentice Hall, 2003), two new concepts have emerged in the debate among the realist advocates of the balance of power theory – the concept of 'risk balancing' coined by Jeffrey Taliaferro, *Balancing Risks: Great Power Intervention in the Periphery* (Ithaca: Cornell University Press, 2004), in order to explain the military interventions of the great powers in regions where their vital interests are not at stake; and the concept of 'soft balancing' used to explain the behaviour of contemporary secondary states that cannot – yet – adopt a traditional balancing policy towards the unilateral action of the US administration. They resort to soft–balancing measures that do not directly challenge US military preponderance but use international institutions, economic statecraft, and diplomatic arrangements to delay, frustrate and undermine US policies. See the Summer 2005 issue of *International Security*, 31, N° 1.

6   On this bloodletting–strategy, see John Mearsheimer, *The Tragedy of Great Power Politics*, (2001: 155). Mearsheimer quotes Lenin's declaration in which he justified the separate peace of Brest–Litovsk. 'In concluding a separate peace now, we rid ourselves of both imperialistic groups fighting each other. We can take advantage of their strife, which makes it difficult for them to reach an agreement at our expense, and use that period when our hands are free to develop and strengthen the Socialist revolution'.

7   Emeric Crucé, *Le Nouveau Cynée ou Discours des occasions et moyens d'établir une paix générale et la liberté de commerce pour tout le monde* (1623), (Rennes: Presses Universitaires de Rennes, 2004). The title of Crucé's book is an allusion to the peace–making role of Cyneas, advisor to King Pyrrhus in the third century BC.

8   Whereas other perpetual peace projects, as expressed by Duc De Sully and Abbé de Saint–Pierre, were limited to the European/Christian international society of the time, and more or less explicitly directed against the Ottoman Empire, the scope and extension of Crucé's peace project were truly universal.

9   Crucé was favourable to the monarchical regime of divine law. He did not only suggest that the meetings of the assembly be presided by the Pope, but he also imagined that the votes of the Republics represented in the assembly should only be taken into account either to give more weight to the decisions made by the majority of the monarchies or to settle the voting of the monarchies in the assembly.

10   On the occasion of the Vienna Congress, Friedrich Gentz, quoted by Moorhead Wright (ed.), *Theory and Practice of the Balance of Power 1486–1914* (London: Dent, 1975), p. 97, interpreted the European Concert as a collective security system, by asserting 'that any European state attempted to attain power through unlawful activities, or that had indeed attained it, … should be treated as the common enemy of the *whole community*' (emphasis added). However, as Gentz implicitly referred to France as the state likely to threaten what he called the whole community, his analysis cannot be representative of the idea of collective security, by definition directed against no specific state.

11   I have not mentioned the activities of various English and American peace societies in the late nineteenth and early twentieth centuries, preceded by the analyses of some jurists, such as the Belgian Gustave de Molinari, the Scot James Lorimer or the Swiss Johann Bluntschli who, in the aftermath of the wars of the Italian and German unifications, spread the idea of peace by international arbitration and sanctions. See F. Hinsley, *Power and the Pursuit of Peace* (Cambridge: Cambridge University Press, 1963), pp. 133 *sqq.*

12 Alexander Hamilton, quoted in A. Wolfers & L. Martin (eds), *The Anglo–American Tradition in Foreign Affairs,* (New Haven, Connecticut: Yale University Press, 1956), pp. 139–154.

13 Thomas Jefferson, quoted in *ibid.*, pp. 155–165.

14 George Washington, *Farewell Address*, 1796. Source: http://www.yale.edu/lawweb/avalon/washing.htm.

15 The Monroe Doctrine, 1823. Source: http://www.yale.edu/lawweb/avalon/monroe.htm.

16 See Justin Vaïsse, 'Les Etats–Unis sans Wilson: L'internationalisme américain après la guerre froide', *Critique internationale*, N° 3 (Spring 1999), pp. 99–120, who refers to the typology proposed by Eugene Wittkopf, *Faces of Internationalism* (Durham: Duke University Press, 1990).

17 F. Zakaria, *From Wealth to Power: The Unusual Origins of America's World Role* (Princeton: Princeton University Press, 1998: 44sqq).

18 Woodrow Wilson, 4th November, 1915. Quoted in Arnold Wolfers & Lawrence Martin (eds), *The Anglo–American Tradition in Foreign Affairs: Readings from Thomas More to Woodrow Wilson* (New Haven: Yale University Press, 1956), pp. 265–6.

19 *Ibid.*

20 Brought into being by the Korean conflict, the Acheson resolution, adopted on 30th November, 1950, and acknowledging the right of the UN General Assembly to recommend and to adopt collective measures, including the use of armed force, if the Security Council is unable to adopt a decision because of the veto by one of its permanent members, constitutes a violation of Article 11.2 of the UN Charter: according to this article, if indeed 'the General Assembly may discuss any questions relating to the maintenance of international peace and security', it remains that 'any such question on which action is necessary shall be referred to the Security Council by the General Assembly either before or after discussion.'

21 See Frank Ninkovitch, *Modernity and Power: A History of the Domino Theory in the Twentieth Century* (Chicago: University of Chicago Press, 1994).

22 North Atlantic Treaty, 4th April, 1949. Source: http://www.nato.int/docu/basictxt/treaty.htm.

23 In addition to the armed intervention against Iraq, the behaviour of George W. Bush's administration was also marked by unilateralism in many other domains. On the arms control regimes, the US decided to launch the National Missile Defence programme despite the ABM treaty; in the domain of human rights promotion, it refused to adhere to the International Criminal Court; on the issue of environmental protection, it rejected the Kyoto Protocol signed by the Clinton administration. For an overview of the relationship of the US and multilateral institutions in general, see N. MacFarlane, M. Mastanduno, & R. Foot (eds), *US Hegemony and International Organizations: The United States and Multilateral Institutions* (Oxford: Oxford University Press, 2003).

24 This comparison was made by Richard Gephardt, in his speech 'American Engagement and the War against Terror' delivered in San Francisco on 22nd July, 2003. Quoted by Philip Zelikow, 'The Transformation of National Security', *The National Interest*, N° 71 (Spring 2003), pp. 24–5.

25 The texts of the various UN Security Council's resolutions I quote can be found at http://www.un.org/documents/scres.htm.

26 And for a very good reason, too: Iraq did not possess any weapons of mass destruction, as the British first, and the Americans, some time later, had to acknowledge, once their troops were in Iraq. See Hans Blix, *Disarming Iraq: The Search for Weapons of Mass Destruction* (London: Bloomsbury, 2004).

27 This option no longer exists in the National Security Strategy adopted in 2006. Source: http://www.whitehouse.gov/nsc/nss/2006/.

28 Once Operation Enduring Freedom was accomplished, the member states of NATO, including France, were invited to contribute to maintaining order in Afghanistan. They accepted NATO's new role in taking part in the International Security Assistance Force (ISAF).

29 Paul Schroeder, 'Iraq: The Case against Pre–emptive War', *The American Conservative*, 21st October, 2002, pp. 12–27.

30 This expression was first used by Pierre Hassner, 'Etats–Unis, la force de l'empire ou l'empire de la force', *Cahiers de Chaillot*, N° 54 (September 2002), p. 43.

31 See the book published during the Vietnam War by Senator William Fulbright, *The Arrogance of Power* (London: J. Cape, 1967).

part three | a proto–systemic war

The truest quarrel, though the least in speech,
I conceive to be the growth of the Athenian power
(Thucydides[1])

How can Operation Iraqi Freedom be explained? What causes should be studied? How should they be studied? These are the questions that have to be addressed by anyone trying to assess the future impact that America's decision to go to war against Saddam Hussein may have on the international order.

In social sciences, explaining and understanding are the two main conceptions which guide the scientific study of causes.[2] According to the first conception, which originates in the triumphant rise of natural science during the period of Renaissance humanism and the Enlightenment, social processes are comparable to natural processes. Objective causes determine social activity, whatever perception of the causes actors may have. In the discipline of international relations, Kenneth Waltz, for instance, claims that international politics can be the object of a nomological–causal explanation. Just as the movements of the planets can be explained by the law of universal gravitation, international politics can be accounted for by the anarchical structure of the international milieu and the relative position of the various states within the distribution of power capacities. The major causes of war are not to be found 'within man', or 'within the structure of the separate states' but rather 'within the state system' (Waltz, 1959: 12). There are wars because there is no supranational authority that can prevent them and their very frequency is inversely correlated to the bipolarisation of the international system.

Conversely, according to the second conception, inspired by nineteenth–century historical relativism, social activity is by definition embedded in a specific space–time context. It is thus radically different from natural phenomena. Social action cannot be explained – i.e. be ascribed to an objective cause – but merely understood – through the analysis of how the actors concerned apprehend its exterior causes. In the discipline of international relations the comprehensive conception of social sciences, defined by Max Weber as the interpretive understanding of social action with a view to finding a causal explanation of its course and effects, was first introduced by the French theorist Raymond Aron. Challenging the very idea of universal factors affecting states' behaviour, he aimed at addressing the question of

> the historical diversity of international systems by discriminating between the variables which have different meanings from one era to another and those which survive as such at least temporarily (Aron, 1967: §53–§54).

Admittedly, Aron contended that the causes of war were to be found in 'structural conditions of bellicosity due to the permanent features of international society', i.e. its anarchical structure and its homogeneous or heterogeneous nature, but he added that wars could also be caused by fundamentally undetermined goals of states' foreign policies – power, glory, and ideas (Aron, 2003: 71 *sqq*) – influenced by the way heads of states apprehended their environment (Aron, 1967).

In the Part III of the present essay, I propose to start my analysis from the second, comprehensive conception of causality and focus on how actors 'define(d) the issues and the alternatives, what they believe(d) about the situation and each other, what they aim(ed) to achieve and how'.[3] But I will go beyond this interpretative approach and adopt a more critical tone,[4] which is absent from Aron's research work. Actually, the meaning ascribed by actors to their own actions and to those of the others, though it may be inter–subjective and thus contribute to the social construction of reality, should nonetheless be de–constructed as regards its origins, and de–mystified as regards its social, political, or ideological functions. For that purpose I will draw my inspiration – making due allowance – from one example of an interpretative and critical analysis of a war in international relations literature, namely, Thucydides' account of the Peloponnesian War.

In his study of the causes of the Peloponnesian War, Thucydides summarises his method thus:

> This war ... began from that time when the Athenians and the Peloponnesians broke the league, which immediately after the conquest of Eubeoa had been concluded between them for thirty years. The causes why they broke the same, I have therefore set down first, because no man should have to seek from what ground so great a war amongst the Grecians could arise. And the truest quarrel, though least in speech, I conceive to be the growth of the Athenian power which, putting the Lacedaemonians into fear, necessitated war. But the causes of the breach of the league publicly voiced, were these ... (Thucydides, 411 BC: Book 1, §23).

This method is quite reminiscent of what Weber calls significant causality. Indeed Thucydides starts his analysis from the presentation of the war as given by the city–states of Corcyrea and Potidea, which appealed to Sparta, their strongest ally, to counter Athens' bellicose intentions. However, he is not satisfied with the official explanations, and insists on what he believes to be the fundamental, or structural, cause of the war, i.e. the growth of Athenian power. At last, he does not consider the crucial cause of the war to be Athens's growing power *per se* but rather the meaning ascribed to it by the Spartans, that is, the fear it inspired in them.

In an attempt to apply this method to the study of the causes of Operation Iraqi Freedom, I will start from the motivations to go to war as advanced by American official authorities. These pertain both to the threat Iraq represented in American eyes and to the US will to create democracy in Iraq as a response to this threat. In Chapters seven and eight I will adopt a critical approach to these 'publicly voiced' causes. In Chapter seven I propose to analyse whether the concept of the security dilemma may contribute to explaining America's decision to launch an armed intervention against Iraq; in Chapter eight I will look more deeply into the imperialist theory of war, in order to assess whether the causes of the US's will to expand democracy stem from the very functioning of the American domestic political regime.

Chapter nine, finally, will deal with what I hold to be the 'truest' cause of Operation Iraqi Freedom – a cause nobody has explicitly voiced – namely, the dynamics of the contemporary power cycle: I contend that the US leadership interprets this evolution as bound to be eventually unfavourable for America, which explains its choice to resort to arms in the hope of delaying America's relative decline.

NOTES

1   Thucydides, 411 BC, *The Peloponnesian Wars*, Book 1, §23.
2   See Martin Hollis & Steve Smith, *Explaining and Understanding International Relations* (Oxford: Clarendon, 1990).
3   M. Hollis & S. Smith, *Explaining and Understanding International Relations*, *op. cit.*, p. 2.
4   The origins of the modern critical tradition are to be found in Karl Marx & Friedrich Engels, *The German Ideology* (1845–46). In International Relations, despite the various post–positivist approaches that have flourished since the eighties, E.H. Carr's *Twenty Years' Crisis: 1919–1939* (1946, 2nd edition) (Basingstoke: Palgrave, 2001), is still the most convincing example of this critical tradition.

chapter seven | security dilemma and opportunistic expansionism

If the necessities of self–defence justified our interest in Cuba in the 1860s, they may justify a like interest in Hawaii today. Now or in a few years' time, a logical argument could be built to support a war of self–defence waged by the United States on the Yangtze or the Volga or the Congo.
(Philip Jessup[1])

'I have often wondered … how men could be foolish enough to put so much effort, money, and courage to cause their own mutual ruin'. In a letter sent to Abbé Antoine de Berghes in 1514, Erasmus of Rotterdam summed up the general feeling of helplessness overcoming, since the early beginning of political thought, anyone contemplating 'the multiple damage of war, and all the devastation, embarrassments and horrendous accidents it causes' (quoted in G. Livet, 1972: 102). It seems obvious that 'no man is so foolish to prefer war to peace' as indeed, to quote Herodotus, 'in peace children bury their fathers, while in war fathers bury their children'. However, anybody acknowledging that 'war is to be found throughout all history and all civilizations' (Aron, 2003: 150) cannot help referring to Heraclitus, for whom 'war is both father and king of all; some he has shown forth as gods and others as men, some he has made slaves and others free'.[2] How can we possibly refute the idea that human folly drives the world if 'war always finds a way', in Brecht's own words in Mother Courage,[3] though 'there is no man … who does not wish to have peace'[4] according to Saint Augustine in City of God?

In IR, there is an explanation of this apparent contradiction between the normative rejection of war by rational beings and 'war's dismal recurring through the millennia' (Waltz, 1989: 44). This explanation is relative to the realist description of international politics as an anarchical domain, states striving for their security and thus being forced to regularly resort to armed force. Aron gives a very apt description of this situation.

Let us start from the schema of international relations: the political units, proud of their independence, jealous of their capacity to make major decisions on their own, are rivals by the very fact that they are autonomous. Each, in the

> last analysis, can count only on itself. What then is the first objective which the political unit may logically seek? An answer is proposed by Hobbes in his analysis of the state of nature. Each political unit aspires to survive ... If we admit that war is not desired for its own sake, the belligerent power that dictates the peace at the end of hostilities seeks to create conditions guaranteeing that it need not fight in the immediate future and that it may keep the advantages gained through force. ... If we suppose that security is the final goal of state policy, the effective means will be to establish a new relation of forces or to modify the old one so that potential enemies, by reason of their inferiority, will not be tempted to take the initiative of an aggression (Aron, 2003: 72).[5]

According to the Bush administration, Operation Iraqi Freedom perfectly met the requirements of America's security. Iraq indeed posed a threat to the security of the US or its allies, either directly or indirectly, by providing weapons of mass destruction to terrorists who could then launch new attacks. As the Americans 'refuse to live in fear',[6] the US government was compelled to resort to war for fear of jeopardising America's survival.

If we combine the argument developed by the White House with the realist explanation of states' behaviour, there seems to be only one logical and compelling conclusion on the origins and nature of Operation Iraqi Freedom. Operation Iraqi Freedom was but an ordinary illustration of the 'ruthless and dangerous business' of international politics; America's decision to go to war against Iraq pertained to the 'genuinely tragic' essence of international politics as great powers 'have little choice but to pursue power and to seek to dominate the other states in the system' (Mearsheimer, 2001: 2–3).

Unfortunately for the Bush administration, American realists themselves have refused such an interpretation. If they have acknowledged that 'military force should be used ... when it advances US national interests' and gone as far as to recommend that the country should be ready to 'invade Iraq if it threatens to attack America or its allies', they have declared that 'war with Iraq does not meet this standard', thus concluding that 'war with Iraq is not in America's national interest'.[7] In order to understand the stance adopted by the realists,[8] we must analyse the necessary conditions which, according to realism, have to be met before the search for security may be regarded as a major cause of a war. The first condition refers to a geographical factor – the more territorially contiguous two political units are, the higher the risk of war between them is. The second condition is related to the type of armaments possessed by the contending units – there is a direct correlation between the risks of war or the chances of peace and the offence–defence balance defined as the 'the relative ease of aggression and defence against aggression' (Van Evera, 1999: 118).

In the following pages I will apply this theory to Operation Iraqi Freedom. I will argue that America's war against Iraq was not a war imposed on the US by the necessity of shutting the window of vulnerability represented by the alleged Iraqi threat but, quite on the contrary, a form of opportunistic expansionism due to the window of opportunity the US could take advantage of thanks to its military resource differential.

* * *

'The search for security is a pervasive motive for war' (Van Evera, 1999: 189). This sentence sums up the first major explanation given by realists of the regular recurrence of war between political units. By striving for security, states are regularly led to resort to arms. The causal mechanism is the well known concept of the 'security dilemma'.

In an anarchical setting marked by the absence of any supranational central authority, every single state is permanently exposed to the risk of being attacked by another state. It is in a permanent situation of insecurity, because of the potential 'threats to (its) acquired values'.[9] In response, it aims at guaranteeing its own security by all means and becoming 'free from threat' (Buzan, 2007: 37). 'In anarchy, security is the highest end. Only if survival is assured can states safely seek such other goals as tranquillity, profit and power. They cannot let power, a possibly useful means, become the end they pursue. The goal the system encourages them to seek is security' (Waltz, 1979: 126).

However, the fact that a state strives for security does not mean it is secure. Quite on the contrary, the decisions made by state A and the actions it undertakes in order to improve its military preparedness foster uncertainty and insecurity in all the other states, as they can never be sure that these military preparations are not directed against them. In fact, state B, when contemplating state A's military build–up, tends to see it as a threat, and will thus act accordingly, by improving its own military readiness. By doing so, state B heightens state A's uncertainty and, in its turn, state A will feel compelled to augment its capacities, and so on. To put it briefly, 'many of the means by which a state tries to increase its security decrease the security of others' (Jervis, 1978: 169), and states consequently face a security dilemma. Whatever they may do when confronted with another state's increasing military resources, whether they expect the worst or choose to keep a low profile, they are and remain in a state of insecurity.

According to realists,[10] states sometimes go to war in order precisely to break this 'vicious circle of security and power accumulation' (Herz, 1950: 157). Indeed, the only way for states to escape – at least temporarily – the security dilemma is to defeat their adversaries in order to impose their own will upon them, thus averting the threat they might represent. This is the explanation advanced by John Mearsheimer.

The great powers that shape the international system fear each other and compete for power as a result. Indeed, their ultimate aim is to gain a position of dominant power over others, because having dominant power is the best means to ensure one's own survival. Strength ensures safety, and the greatest strength is the greatest insurance of safety. ... All states are influenced by this logic ... of constant security competition ... reflected by the concept of ... the 'security dilemma'. ... The best way for a state to survive in anarchy is to take advantage of other states and gain power at their expense. The best defence is a good offence (Mearsheimer, 2001: XI–XII, 35–6).[11]

However, realists consider the security dilemma to be a cause of war only if states face a real security dilemma, and not an imaginary one. They assert that the reality of the security dilemma affecting states – its impact as a cause of armed conflicts in other words – depends on its intensity, which may vary according to two major factors – geographical proximity and the offensive vs. defensive nature of armaments.

Hobbes was among the first political thinkers to explicitly emphasise the role of territorial contiguity as a cause of war, in his description of sovereigns in 'the posture of war' because of their 'continual jealousies' having 'their forts, garrisons, and guns … and continual spies *upon their neighbours*' (Hobbes, 1651: 21, emphasis added).

Jean–Jacques Rousseau shared this view, though it stemmed from a very different view of man's condition in the state of nature from Hobbes'. Natural man leads a predominantly solitary life with hardly any contact with others. He thus does not mistrust his fellow creatures. 'Taught by experience that the love of well–being is the sole motive of human actions, he found himself in a position to distinguish the few cases, in which mutual interest might justify him in relying upon the assistance of his fellows; and also the still fewer cases in which a conflict of interest might give cause to suspect them' (Rousseau, 1754: Part II). Social relations only exist when there is an imperative need to co–operate in order to survive, and it is precisely in such temporary situations that competition and mistrust emerge. Rousseau epitomised the point with his stag–hunt metaphor (Rousseau, 1754: Part II), summed up by Kenneth Waltz who also refers to the general conclusion that realists draw from the application of this example to international politics.

> Assume that five men who have acquired a rudimentary ability to speak and to understand each other happen to come together at a time when all of them suffer from hunger. The hunger of each will be satisfied by the fifth part of a stag, so they 'agree' to cooperate to trap one. But also the hunger of any one of them will be satisfied by a hare, so, as a hare comes within reach, one of them grabs it. The defector obtains the means of satisfying his hunger but in doing so permits the stag to escape. His immediate interest prevails over considerations for his fellows … The application of Rousseau's theory to international politics is stated with eloquence and clarity in his commentaries on Saint–Pierre and in a short work entitled *The State of War*. … The states of Europe, he writes, 'touch each other at so many points that no one of them can move without giving a jar to all the rest; their variances are all the more deadly as their ties are more closely woven (Waltz, 1959: 167–8, 183).

To sum up, Rousseau also considered territorial contiguity to be a determining factor in the likelihood of armed conflicts between political units because conflicts presuppose the existence of social intercourse, as there can be no contending interests where there are no interactions at all. War is 'a permanent condition that requires constant relations' (Rousseau, 1760). All things being equal, a state obviously has more 'constant relations' with its immediate neighbours than with distant states and, as a result, it is with its neighbours that the state of war is likely to result in a 'war strictly so called'. Indeed, each state

> feels weak so long as there are others stronger than itself. Its safety and preservation demand that it makes itself stronger than *its neighbours*. It cannot increase, foster or exercise its strength than at their expense ... It is forced to compare itself in order to know itself; ... it becomes small or great, weak or strong depending on *its neighbour's* extending or shrinking, and strengthening or weakening (Rousseau, 1760, emphasis added).

Since Hobbes and Rousseau, empirical research has corroborated the hypothesis of a correlation between the frequency of wars and territorial contiguity. Lewis Richardson has shown that the more neighbours a state has, the more likely it is to get involved in an armed conflict.[12] Stuart Bremer has found that two states sharing land or sea contiguity are 35 times more likely to go to war against each other than two non–neighbouring states[13] and Paul Diehl has established that 92 per cent of the great–power wars of the period 1815–1980 were triggered by territorial disputes between two neighbouring initiator states.[14]

How can we explain why the frequency of wars should be correlated to geographical proximity? How can we understand that a scholar such as John Vasquez goes as far as to claim that territorial contiguity is the factor distinguishing those durable rivalries that result in armed conflicts from those that do not?[15] A first logical answer is given by Aron, who argues that the control of, the access to, and the sovereignty over a territory are often the immediate war aims pursued by contenders in an armed conflict.

> A collectivity occupies a certain territory. It can logically consider the surface of the earth at its disposal as too small. In rivalry among peoples, the possession of space was the original stake. Secondly, sovereigns have often estimated their greatness according to the number of their subjects: what they desired, beyond frontiers, was not territory, but men. Lastly, the armed prophet is sometimes less anxious to conquer than to convert: indifferent to the wealth of the earth and what it contains, he does not calculate the numbers of his workers or soldiers; he seeks to spread the true faith, he wants the organization corresponding to his interpretation of life and history to encompass gradually all of humanity (Aron, 2003: 74).

It seems reasonable to posit that the territories a state wants to conquer and the souls it would like to convert are those closest to its borders. Likewise, the material resources a state is led to defend, as well as the populations it wants to remain loyal are, first and foremost, coveted by its neighbours. So it is by no means surprising that territorial disputes should have been the major issue at stake in roughly half the wars since 1648. Suffice it to mention, among many other examples, the numerous wars that pitted Russia against Poland or Germany against France in the past, or between India and Pakistan, Iraq and Iran, Ethiopia and Eritrea, etc., in the second half of the twentieth century.[16]

But there is another explanation of the role of territorial contiguity as a cause of war, and this explanation is relative to the security dilemma. The intensity of the security dilemma increases proportionally to geographical proximity, because neighbour states form what Barry Buzan calls security complexes.

> A security complex is defined as a group of states whose primary security concerns link together sufficiently closely that their national securities cannot realistically be considered apart from one another. ... Because threats operate more potently over short distances, security interactions with neighbours will tend to have first priority ... Security complexes are generated by the interaction of anarchy and geography. The political structure of anarchy confronts all states with the security dilemma, but the otherwise seamless web of security interdependence is powerfully mediated by the effects of geography (Buzan, 2007: 160–1).

As a matter of fact, a contiguous state is perceived to be more threatening than a remote state, given what Kenneth Boulding calls the 'loss–of–strength–gradient', i.e. the fact that the further away the target of aggression, the less a state can influence another state through military strength.[17]

The territory of a neighbouring state is thus a significant war stake, not only in terms of space or population but also because of its impact on the security dilemma. Indeed the control by a state of a part of the neighbouring state's territory provides the conqueror with a strategic depth that can act as a buffer zone against any potential threat. Among other examples, we may quote the conquest and occupation by Israel of various neighbouring Arab territories – Sinai, the Golan Heights, South Lebanon – for security, and not territorial reasons. It would otherwise be difficult to explain why Israel did retrocede the Sinai Peninsula to Egypt once the peace treaty was signed, while Israeli forces still occupy the Syrian Golan Heights and launched two offensives in South Lebanon in 25 years – respectively in 1982 and 2006 – as part of their fight against Syria and Lebanon–based anti–Israel activists.

It is all the more interesting to analyse Tel Aviv's decisions to launch military operations in order to guarantee its security, as Israel has not only occupied contiguous territories but even bombed Iraq's Osirak nuclear plant in 1981. As Iraq is not an immediate neighbour of Israel, this decision clearly illustrates the fact that the intensity of the security dilemma does not depend only on geographical proximity but also on the nature of weapons,[18] a hypothesis that is at the origin of the offence–defence theory of war.

The offence–defence balance has been defined as 'the relative ease of aggression and defence against aggression' (Van Evera, 1999: 118).[19] It rests on the dialectic of the sword and the shield. In other words, some weapons can be considered to be offensive (such as bombers for instance), whereas others are more defensive (anti–aircraft batteries, among others). According to the offence–defence balance theory, when attackers and defenders clash, some specific combinations of weapon technologies, mobilisation plans and military doctrines are proportionally favourable to the attacker, whereas other combinations are likely to be proportionally favourable to the defender. In order to size up this advantage, the offence–defence balance is measured via a comparison of the amount of money a state has to invest in offensive weapons in order to compensate the amount of money spent by another state on defensive weapons, and vice versa. The balance is offence–dominant, i.e. favourable for the attacker, when the ratio of the cost of the necessary forces for the attacker to take control of a territory, to the cost of the defender's forces, is less than 1, and defence–dominant, i.e. favourable for the defender, when this ratio is more than 1. At the end of the Middle Ages, for instance, the invention and massive use of cannons gave a significant advantage to attackers, because cannons could destroy formerly invulnerable fortresses. Likewise, mass conscription during the French Revolution and the First Empire gave France an offensive edge on the defensive armies of its opponents mainly composed of mercenaries. Conversely, Vauban's new fortification techniques favoured defenders during the seventeenth and eighteenth centuries. So did the combined effects of machine guns, barbed wire, entrenchments and railway networks at the beginning of the twentieth century.

If we postulate the offence–defence balance concept, the problem is to determine if there is a correlation between the offence vs. defence balance and the risks of war vs. the chances of peace. Are wars more likely to break out when the offence–defence balance is offence–dominant and are defence–dominant periods more peace–prone? On that issue, Stephen Van Evera[20] has proposed the most comprehensive answers.

Van Evera begins by arguing that, when it is easier, or less costly, for an aggressor to conquer its adversary's territory than for the adversary to defend its territory, the risks of war are higher, because of an intensified security dilemma due to an offence–dominant balance. Indeed, if the defender state, confronted with potential attack by a state that is increasing its offence–dominant military means, does not respond accordingly, it exposes itself to a greater risk of being attacked. If it reacts by augmenting its own military capacities, it will launch an offensive arms race that may well escalate into a full–scale armed conflict. Conversely, when it is easier, or less costly, for a defender to defend its territory than for its aggressive adversary to attack its territory, the intensity of the security dilemma reduces as a result, because of a defence–dominant balance. In that case, the chances of peace are higher. Indeed, a state that does not respond to another state's military build–up by increasing its own military means is not exposed to a higher risk of being attacked, if the weapons acquired by its adversary are not potentially offensive weapons. Conversely, if it does react by developing its own military resources, the ensuing 'arms race' is in fact a de–escalation, because the defensive nature of the weapons consolidates both states' respective defensive capacities.

Van Evera details the various theoretical reasons that may explain why an offence–dominant balance is war–prone while a defence–dominant balance is peace–prone. When military technology favours offensive action, a revisionist state will be inclined to go to war. From a strictly military standpoint, opportunistic expansionism is encouraged, as conquest is easy – or perceived to be so – and aggression rewarding. Attack is by definition not costly and very likely to be successful. Moreover, the incentive to strike first is greater because a first strike will undoubtedly disrupt the defender's defensive positions. Successful surprise attacks favour anticipatory wars. From a diplomatic point of view, a dissatisfied state will not contemplate any peaceful conflict resolution, given the greater chances of obtaining satisfaction by adopting a *fait accompli*–strategy, i.e. going to war. Furthermore, offence–dominance is a self–reinforcing phenomenon because third–party states are tempted to adopt bandwagon behaviour, joining the revisionist state in order to share the expected gains of its aggression. Even a *status quo* state, though not war–prone, is encouraged to behave aggressively in the case of an offence–dominant balance. From a military perspective, self–defence is more risky as borders are hard to defend. Defensive expansionism that aims at extending a defence perimeter appears to be a rewarding strategy, in the name of the 'the best defence is a good offence' principle. From a diplomatic perspective, a satisfied state will not trust the peaceful agreements proposed by a revisionist adversary state. Indeed it is in the interest of the aggressive state to cheat and adopt a policy of secret military build–up, given the advantage conferred by secrecy in the case of an offence–dominant balance.

Conversely, when the balance is defence–dominant, peace is favoured. Conquest is difficult, and potential aggressors are deterred from going to war by its high cost and low probability of success. Borders are easier to defend, and there is thus no reason to choose the option of defensive expansionism. As every state knows that other states have no interest in attacking, an objective collective security logically results from increased subjective individual certainty, hinging on the expected rational behaviour of the actors. There is no advantage in striking first and preventive wars are all the less attractive as a state knows that it will be able to defend itself successfully, thanks to its second–strike capabilities. Windows of vulnerability, i.e. prospective gaps in force ratios, do not increase the security dilemma, while windows of opportunity, i.e. prospective shifts in power ratios, do not increase offensive capacities. States are incited to resort to peaceful means of conflict resolution because resorting to arms is hardly rewarding and possible cheating by an adversary is hardly harmful. No state is interested in jumping on the bandwagon with an aggressive state and potential military rivalries will thus not be accentuated by political alliances.

The next step in Van Evera's analysis is to ask how this theory performs in tests (Van Evera, 1998), which he answers through three case studies – Europe since the French Revolutionary Wars, the US since 1789, and ancient China during the Spring and Autumn and Warring States periods. His hypothesis is corroborated by the case studies. The study of Europe since the French Revolution, for instance, reveals a perfect correlation between the frequency of wars and shifts in the offence–defence balance. During the period 1792–1815, offence was strong, because of France's mass conscription, and wars very frequent. After 1815, the major European powers abandoned mass armies, because their conservative leaders were afraid of the revolutionary potential they represented. There was thus a return to a defence–dominant balance. As anticipated in the offence–defence theory, the nineteenth century was very peaceful. There was yet another change in the period spanning from 1890 to 1918, marked by a significant war–proneness, because political and military authorities mistakenly perceived the advantage of offence over defence.[21] A new shift occurred in the period 1918–45, when 'German *Blitzkrieg* doctrine [combined] armour and infantry in an effective offensive combination' (Van Evera, 1998: 18), which resulted in frequent wars. Finally, since 1945 and the adoption by major nuclear powers of the defensive deterrence doctrine, defence has been favoured and there has been a constant decrease in the number of interstate wars.

Van Evera finally comes to the conclusion that both theoretical hypotheses and empirical statements confirm that 'war will be more common in periods when conquest is easy, or is believed easy, than in other periods', because, among other reasons, 'a given state will initiate and fight more wars in periods when it has, or believes it has, larger offensive opportunities and defensive vulnerabilities' (Van Evera, 1999: 166).

Now if I combine Van Evera's approach to the offence–defence theory with the conclusion drawn from the geographical proximity hypothesis, I can posit the following hypothesis: two states are more likely to go to war against each other when they are territorially contiguous and when the offence–defence balance is offence–dominant. In other words, a state's search for security may be regarded as a convincing motive for its decision to launch an armed attack against another state when – and if – it suffers from a window of vulnerability in the case of a neighbouring state with offensive–dominant weapons at its disposal. Are these conditions fulfilled in the case of Operation Iraqi Freedom? Does America's war against Saddam Hussein correspond to a war fought by a state – the US – that 'can no longer guarantee its security by defensive means' and that 'is virtually forced to resort to force in order to assure its survival' (Lindemann, 2004: 41) against another state – Iraq?

If we focus on the first condition, relative to the territorial factor, geographic considerations as such can hardly be invoked. Indeed Iraq is some 10,000 kilometres away from American borders. However, reality is more complex than this commonsense conclusion might suggest. What is true for an 'ordinary' state is not necessarily valid in the case of the US. While most states are only affected by what may happen in their immediate neighbourhood, 'for a hegemon, the world is its neighbourhood' (Jervis, 2003a: 84). The security of a superpower such as the US is linked to the global international system, especially in some crucial regional security complexes such as the Near East and the Middle East, *a fortiori* after 9/11 and Operation Enduring Freedom against the Taliban regime in Afghanistan.

It was this very argument which was taken up by American authorities when they declared that they would not permit 'a brutal dictator, with a history of reckless aggression, with ties to terrorism, with great potential wealth, ... to dominate a vital region and threaten the United States'.[22] In their eyes, it was not only America's own security that was at stake in the confrontation with Iraq but also that of the US's regional allies, and even international security. In other words, the distance separating Iraq from the US is not *per se* an obstacle to considering the search for security as a valid motivation for the decision to launch Operation Iraqi Freedom. Can the same conclusion be drawn if we consider the second factor pertaining to the security dilemma, i.e. America's possible defensive vulnerability?

According to the Bush administration, the answer to this question is unquestionably positive. Iraq is a rogue state, a hitherto unknown threat, either directly or indirectly, through its ties to terrorist networks.

> The nature of the Cold War threat required the United States – with our friends and allies – to emphasize deterrence of the enemy's use of force, producing a grim strategy of mutually assured destruction. With the collapse of the Soviet Union and the end of the Cold War, ... new deadly challenges have emerged from rogue states and terrorists. None of these contemporary threats rival the sheer destructive power that was arrayed against us by the Soviet Union. However, the nature and motivations of these new adversaries, their determination to obtain destructive powers hitherto available only to the world's strongest states, and the greater likelihood that they will use weapons of mass destruction against us, make today's security environment more complex and dangerous. ... In the Cold War, especially following the Cuban missile crisis, we faced a generally *status–quo*, risk–averse adversary. Deterrence was an effective defence. But deterrence based only upon the threat of retaliation is less likely to work against leaders of rogue states more willing to take risks, gambling with the lives of their people, and the wealth of their nations. In the Cold War, weapons of mass destruction were considered weapons of last resort whose use risked the destruction of those who used them. Today, our enemies see weapons of mass destruction as weapons of choice. For rogue states, these weapons are tools of intimidation and military aggression against their neighbours. These weapons may also allow these states to attempt to blackmail the United States and our allies to prevent us from deterring or repelling the aggressive behaviour of rogue states. Such states also see these weapons as their best means of overcoming the conventional superiority of the United States. Traditional concepts of deterrence will not work against a terrorist enemy whose avowed tactics are wanton destruction and the targeting of innocents; whose so–called soldiers seek martyrdom in death and whose most potent protection is statelessness. The overlap between states that sponsor terror and those that pursue WMD compels us to action.[23]

In other words, American policy–makers claimed that the traditional defence–dominant balance, prevailing throughout the Cold War because of the mutually–assured–destruction principle accepted by both the US and the USSR, had been supplanted by a new, offence–dominant balance, on account of the weapons of mass destruction possessed by rogue states and terrorists. If we abide by Van Evera's opinion that shifts in the offence–defence balance have a large effect on the risk of war (Van Evera, 1998), it is *a priori* credible to ascribe Operation Iraqi Freedom to the heightened security dilemma felt by the US. As America was confronted with an adversary representing a new kind of threat and saw itself as a victim of defensive vulnerability, the country was doomed to pursue an aggressive, but actually defensive, form of expansionism in order to successfully cope with a potentially offensive aggressor. Which leads us to address two important and correlated questions. What about the reality of America's defensive vulnerability? And supposing that the US was indeed vulnerable, was this due to the offence–dominant weapon technologies possessed by Iraq?

The 9/11 attacks clearly revealed America's vulnerability in the asymmetric conflict it had been in with the terrorist conglomeration Al'Qaeda since the first bomb attack against the World Trade Center in 1993. The small number of terrorist activists linked to Osama Bin Laden have killed some 3,000 people and caused billions of dollars of material damage. Since 12th September, 2001, the US, in order to protect its territory, has been forced to contemplate the necessity of watching over some '600,000 bridges, 170,000 water systems, more than 2,800 power plants (104 of them nuclear), 190,000 miles of interstate pipelines for natural gas, 463 sky–scrapers … nearly 20,000 miles of borders, airports, stadiums, train tracks'.[24] Richard Betts is right to assert that the offence–defence ratio in the US–Al'Qaeda relationship is favourable for offence by 100 to 1, given that 'each competent terrorist will have much greater individual impact than each good counterterrorist, that each dollar invested in a terrorist plot will have a higher payoff than each dollar expended on counterterrorism, and that only small numbers of competent terrorists need survive and operate to keep the threat to American society uncomfortably high'.[25] This analysis corroborates the hypothesis of Operation Iraqi Freedom as a form of defensive expansionism. It was indeed in the interest of the US to profit from the advantages conferred by the revolution in military affairs and wage an offensive war on the adversary's territory instead of trying to protect its own territory, most probably in vain.

America's vulnerability was even greater if one takes into consideration, on top of the commercial airliners turned into deadly weapons by Muhammad Atta and his accomplices, the weapons of mass destruction Iraq allegedly possessed, or was bent on acquiring. These weapons, including the nuclear bomb, were indeed likely to give rise to a specific kind of security dilemma, called a 'survival dilemma' by Stephen Van Evera (Van Evera, 1999: 248).

During the Cold War, Van Evera recalls, the existence of nuclear weapons favoured the defensive over the offensive option not because of the intrinsic nature of the nuclear revolution but, because after the destruction of Hiroshima and Nagasaki, the nuclear powers adopted the deterrence doctrine, synonymous with a no–first–use policy. The pacifying effect of nuclear weapons, called the 'sturdy child of terror' by Winston Churchill, was due to the nuclear powers' sensitivity to the suicidal costs implied by the possible use of the 'absolute weapon',[26] tantamount to mutually assured destruction (MAD). In all logic, the defence–dominant balance would turn into an offence–dominant balance if nuclear weapons were possessed by political actors who did not adhere to the no–first–use doctrine and/or were not sensitive to the costs of possible nuclear retaliation.

> New dangers arise as MAD's pacifying effects disappear. These dangers stem from the possibility of wanton violence by non–deterrable rogue states and from fears of such violence among normal states. Non–deterrable states … can destroy even those they cannot conquer. All states lie at the mercy of their violent impulses, even those with secure nuclear deterrents and strong conventional defences. War could erupt either from violence by these non–deterrable states or from forceful moves by normal states to forestall their violence (Van Evera, 1998: 248).

When we read Van Evera, we cannot help feeling that, some two to four years before 9/11 and Operation Iraqi Freedom, he had anticipated exactly what was going to happen. The US could be considered to be what he called a 'normal state' and Iraq had indeed been defined as a 'rogue state' by the US administration. For instance, in his Cincinnati statement delivered on 7th October, 2002, George W. Bush declared that, according to UN inspectors, Iraq had produced 'two to four times' the 30,000 litres of anthrax and other lethal biological agents Saddam Hussein had officially acknowledged, after the defection of several heads of Iraq's military industries in 1995. The US President stressed that 'we know that the regime has produced thousands of tons of chemical agents, including mustard gas, sarin nerve gas, VX nerve gas'. According to him, 'Iraq possesses ballistic missiles with a likely range of hundreds of miles – far enough to strike Saudi Arabia, Israel, Turkey, and other nations – in a region where more than 135,000 American civilians and service members live and work'. He also emphasised that 'we know that Iraq and the Al'Qaeda terrorist network share a common enemy – the United States of America. We know that Iraq and Al'Qaeda have had high–level contacts that go back a decade. Some Al'Qaeda leaders who fled Afghanistan went to Iraq. … Iraq could decide on any given day to provide a biological or chemical weapon to a terrorist group or individual terrorists. Alliance with terrorists could allow the Iraqi regime to attack America without leaving any fingerprints'. In his State of the Union Address on 28th January, 2003, he repeated that 'Saddam Hussein aids and protects terrorists, including members of Al'Qaeda', advanced new figures, partially different from those put forward some months before, relating to Iraq's biological and chemical armament and recalled that 'the International Atomic Energy Agency confirmed in the 1990s that Saddam Hussein had an advanced nuclear weapons development program, had a design for a nuclear weapon and was working on five different methods of enriching uranium for a bomb', that 'the British government has learned that Saddam Hussein recently sought significant quantities of uranium from Africa'; that 'our intelligence sources tell us that he has attempted to purchase high–strength aluminium tubes suitable for nuclear weapons production'. On 5th February, 2003, Colin Powell addressed the Security Council and repeatedly accused Iraq of possessing banned materials. In his plea to prove that the US was really confronted with an unknown threat 'at the crossroads of radicalism and technology',[27] he backed up his accusations with satellite photos and tape recordings.

Unfortunately for the US administration, such arguments were proved wrong by empirical evidence. In the domain of Iraq's military capacities, Saddam Hussein had biological and chemical weapons; he also had a nuclear weapon programme. However, he possessed neither nuclear arms nor intercontinental missiles that could strike US territory. He did not even possess intermediate–range missiles that could target America's regional allies. According to neutral sources, he merely possessed 25 SCUD ballistic missiles with a maximum range of 150 kilometres, in accordance with the UN Security resolution 687 (1991).[28] In other words, ascribing Operation Iraqi Freedom to an increased defensive vulnerability felt by the US because of an offensive advantage benefiting Iraq requires that at least one of the two following hypotheses should be confirmed. Either Iraq really aimed at producing, or acquiring, ballistic missiles that could strike America's regional allies' territories and was likely to launch these missiles armed with the chemical or bacteriological warheads it already possessed, or with nuclear warheads it would potentially produce or acquire; or Saddam Hussein was ready to supply terrorist networks such as Al'Qaeda with samples of the biological or chemical weapons he already possessed, and even samples of nuclear weapons if ever he managed to acquire a nuclear arsenal.

Let me start with the second hypothesis, already existing or potential future links between Saddam Hussein and Osama Bin Laden. George W. Bush's administration has never been able to produce the slightest evidence of these alleged links and such links were highly improbable.

Osama Bin Laden is a radical fundamentalist, and he detests secular leaders like Saddam. Similarly, Saddam has consistently repressed fundamentalist movements within Iraq. Given this history of enmity, the Iraqi dictator is unlikely to give Al'Qaeda nuclear weapons, which it might use in ways he could not control. Intense US pressure, of course, might eventually force these unlikely allies together, just as the United States and Communist Russia became allies during World War II. Saddam would still be unlikely to share his most valuable weaponry with Al'Qaeda, because he could not be confident it would not be used in ways that place his own survival in jeopardy. During the Cold War, the United States did not share all its WMD expertise with its own allies, and the Soviet Union balked at giving nuclear weapons to China despite their ideological sympathies and repeated Chinese requests. No evidence suggests Saddam would act differently (Mearsheimer & Walt, 2003: 58).

However, Saddam could have a non–rational motivation instead. That was exactly what the White House contended: it inferred Iraq's aggressive intentions from its past behaviour, which it ascribed to its dictatorial regime (see Chapter four). Now, it is far from sure that Saddam's past behaviour proves his irrationality, without even mentioning the fact that the willingness to acquire nuclear weapons *per se* does not necessarily equate with the willingness to use them.[29] Saddam Hussein actually was not a worse 'serial aggressor' (Mearsheimer & Walt, 2003: 52) than Israel or Egypt. His war against Iran, whose objective was to redefine Iraq's border, was a rational decision when considering the window of opportunity represented by the relative weakness of the Ayatollah's regime after the Islamic Revolution. As for his attack against Kuwait, he had admittedly miscalculated both America's refusal to accept his *fait a ccompli* and Moscow's willingness to support his aggression. But such mistakes rather stemmed from traditional misperceptions than irrationality. They were not completely absurd, given America's post–Vietnam unwillingness to launch military adventures and the existence of a mutual aid treaty with the USSR. Above all, Saddam's behaviour during Operation Desert Storm tended, if anything, to prove his rationality. He did not arm the SCUD missiles he launched at Israel with chemical or bacteriological warheads, as he was well aware, after George H. Bush's warnings, of Israel's devastating retaliatory measures. Finally, when his eventual defeat was merely a question of time, he did not hesitate to look for a diplomatic solution in order to avoid a land invasion of his territory by Coalition troops.

To sum up, the US was certainly vulnerable but this vulnerability hardly stemmed from an offensive–dominant balance benefiting Iraq. All the more so if we compare the respective military capacities – infantry, tanks, aircraft, submarines, ballistic missiles of any range, fissile material, etc. – possessed by the three so–called rogue states in 2002. Iraq was, by far, less dangerous than North Korea and even Iran (see the data in Howard, 2004). Strangely enough, however, America agreed to negotiate with the other two members of the so–called axis of evil, either directly as in the case of North Korea – a move initiated by Clinton – or indirectly, as with Iran, the European Union acting as an intermediary.

* * *

How then can we explain such a difference in approaches? The answer can be found in the offence–defence theory. According to Van Evera, the risks of war due to an offence–dominant balance are likely to be higher in two cases. First, war can be initiated by a revisionist state which wants to profit from a window of opportunity by attacking preventively. Secondly, war can be launched by a satisfied state in an attempt to avoid the negative consequences of a window of vulnerability, due to its adversary's offensive advantage. If the analysis I have proposed in the previous pages is right, then the second hypothesis, advanced by the White House in order to justify its use of armed force, is hardly convincing. It logically remains to be seen whether the first hypothesis is plausible. What if the US profited from an offensive advantage and adopted the option of opportunistic expansionism?

From the theoretical perspective developed by Van Evera who upholds the idea that 'temperate powers are tempted to attack if the offence is strong' and specifies that, in the case of an offence–dominant balance, the wars that 'do not stem from the security dilemma' (Van Evera, 1999: 123, 117) are also favoured, the first hypothesis is corroborated in my case study. In the years 2002–3, the US was the largest military power in the world's history, although it was vulnerable to asymmetric attacks by terrorist activists. It clashed with a country, Iraq, weakened by twelve years of economic embargo and various inspections, though temporarily suspended, and whose territory was partially controlled – north of the 36th Parallel – by the American and British air forces. In other words, the US benefited from a massive military power advantage, disproportionate if we compare it with the case of Iran and North Korea. An attack against Iraq was possible precisely because of Baghdad's incapacity to deter the US or retaliate. Can it then be asserted that Operation Iraqi Freedom was a military intervention by an aggressive power that perceived conquest as both easy and not costly and rejected the resort to peaceful conflict resolution, given the expected utility of the military operation?

If we remember the statements made by the American authorities, who were eager to spread 'the true faith … corresponding to (their) interpretation of life and history' (Aron, 2003: 74) in defining themselves as 'a friend to the people of Iraq' and aiming at transforming a dictatorship into a prosperous and free democracy, we can legitimately wonder whether George W. Bush's America, far from being a temperate status quo power guided by its sole security objectives, might not have been tempted by opportunistic expansionism, representative of an imperialist form of adventurism. I will scrutinise this hypothesis in the following chapter. If it proves to be empirically corroborated, then Operation Iraqi Freedom might well be 'a war the Bush administration chose to fight but did not have to fight' (Mearsheimer & Walt, 2003: 59).

NOTES

1 P. Jessup, 'The Monroe Doctrine in 1940', *American Journal of International Law*, 34, N° 4 (October 1940), pp. 704–11.

2 Heraclitus, *Fragment 53*. Quoted in W. Palaver, 'Europe's Political Economy: A Discussion of its Economic and Political Theologies', http://www.uibk.ac.at/theol/leseraum/texte/83.html.

3 Quoted by Richard Betts, 'Must War Find A Way?', *International Security*, 24, N° 2 (Fall 1999), pp. 166–198.

4 Saint Augustine, *The City of God*: Book XIX, 12. Source: http://www.newadvent.org/fathers /120.htm.

5 Needless to say that Aron uses the words 'enemies' and 'rivals' interchangeably, as he refers to the commonsense meaning, without giving to them the specific definitions I have borrowed from Wendt.

6 Remarks of George W. Bush at the Cincinnati Museum Center, October 7, 2002.

7 See 'War with Iraq Is Not in America's National Interest', Op–ed page of the *New York Times*, 26th September, 2002, signed by 33 prominent US realist scholars of international

relations, notably R. Betts, D. Copeland, R. Jervis, C. Kaufmann, J. Levy, J. Mearsheimer, B. Posen, R. Schweller, J. Snyder, S. Van Evera, S. Walt, and K. Waltz. Also see John Mearsheimer & Stephen Walt, 'An Unnecessary War', *Foreign Policy*, N° 134 (January–February 2003), pp. 51–9, as well as Kenneth Waltz's interview with H. Kreisler, 10th February, 2003, part of the University of California at Berkeley's Institute of International Studies' Conversations with History, http://globetrotter.berkeley.edu/people3/Waltz/waltz–con0.html.

8 A parallel can be made with the position adopted by Hans Morgenthau against the Vietnam War, 'We Are Deluding Ourselves in Vietnam', *New York Times Magazine*, 18th April, 1965. See J. Mearsheimer, 'Hans Morgenthau and the Iraq War: Realism Versus Neo–Conservatism', Conference held in Munich on 28th October, 2004 http://www.opendemocracy.net/democracy–americanpower/morgenthau_2522.jsp.

9 See the definitions of security and insecurity proposed by A. Wolfers, 'National Security as an Ambiguous Symbol' in Wolfers, 1962: 150.

10 Liberals do not accept this pessimistic outlook on the implacable nature of the security dilemma. They state that co–operation and security regimes contribute to abating the security dilemma, especially if they are initiated by the hegemonic state. See Chapter three, which deals more specifically with the Soviet–American Cold–War security dilemma.

11 J. Mearsheimer is an offensive realist and his conception of the security dilemma does not correspond to the conception defended by defensive realists such as Waltz, Jervis or Van Evera. According to defensive realists, the vicious circle of insecurity and power accumulation incites states to look for optimal security, compatible with the security of adversary states, instead of striving for maximum security, tantamount to insecurity for adversaries because of its counterproductive impact. According to Mearsheimer, the security dilemma on the contrary prevents states from accepting the status quo until they become hegemonic powers (regional hegemons in Mearsheimer's specific, i.e. geopolitical, sense), thus inciting them to strive for ever more military power.

12 Lewis Richardson, *Statistics of Deadly Quarrels* (Chicago: Quadrangle, 1960).

13 Stuart Bremer, 'Dangerous Dyads: Conditions Affecting the Likelihood of Interstate War', *Journal of Conflict Resolution*, 36, N° 2 (June 1992), pp. 309–41.

14 Paul Diehl, 'Geography and War: A Review and Assessment of the Empirical Literature', *International Interactions*, 17, N° 1 (February 1991), pp. 11–27.

15 John Vasquez, 'Why Do Neighbours Fight? Proximity, Interaction or Territoriality?', *Journal of Peace Research*, 32, N°3 (May 1995), pp. 277–93; J. Vasquez, 'Distinguishing Rivals That Go To War From Those That Do Not', *International Studies Quarterly*, 40, N°4 (December 1996), pp. 531–58. Vasquez does not hesitate to assert that thanks to the geographical distance separating the US from the USSR, there was almost no risk of the Cold War turning into an actual armed conflict.

16 See K. Holsti, *Peace and War*, op. cit.

17 Kenneth Boulding, *Conflict and Defense* (New York: Harper and Row, 1962: 262).

18 Needless to say, the nature of armaments has an impact on the loss of strength–gradient, as modern weapons and transport capabilities reduce the obstacle of distance.

19 See also, among numerous other references, Sean Lynn Jones, 'Offense–Defense Theory and Its Critics', *Security Studies*, 4, N°4 (Summer 1995), pp. 660–91, as well as Charles Glaser

& Chaim Kaufmann, 'What Is the Offense–Defense Balance And How Can We Measure It?', *International Security*, 22, N° 4 (Spring 1998), pp. 44–82.

20 In the following paragraphs, I will sum up Van Evera's theory. For the needs of my demonstration in this chapter, I will focus on the sole military factors of the offence–defence military balance, whereas Van Evera's balance is also affected by other determinants, such as geography, domestic political and social factors, and the nature of diplomacy. For further details, see S. Van Evera, 'Offense, Defense, and the Causes of War', *International Security*, 22, N° 4 (Spring 1998), pp. 5–43, and *The Causes of War: Power and the Roots of Conflict, op. cit.*

21 Van Evera stresses that in 1914, the subjective perception of the offence–defence balance and the cult of the offensive as expressed in the German von Schlieffen Plan, prevailed over the objective reality of this balance, which was defence–dominant because of the combined effects of machine guns, railway networks and entrenchments. See his article 'The Cult of the Offensive and the Origins of the First World War', *International Security*, 9, N° 1 (Summer 1984), pp. 58–107.

22 George W. Bush, State of the Union Address, January 28, 2003.

23 The National Security Strategy of the United States, *op. cit.*

24 Richard Betts, 'The Soft Underbelly of American Primacy: Tactical Advantages of Terror', *Political Science Quarterly*, 117, N° 1 (Spring 2002), pp. 19–36.

25 *Ibid.*

26 Bernard Brodie, *The Absolute Weapon* (New York: Harcourt Brace, 1946).

27 The National Security Strategy of the United States, *op. cit.*

28 See, besides Hans Blix, *Disarming Iraq: The Search for Weapons of Mass Destruction* (London: Bloomsbury, 2004), the report of the Center for Strategic and International Studies published on July 21, 2002, edited by Anthony Cordesman: 'Iraqi War Fighting Capabilities: A Dynamic Net Assessment', available at http://www.csis.org/burke/mb/iraq_dynamic.pdf.

29 On the various reasons inciting states to acquire nuclear weapons, see Scott Sagan, 'Why Do States Build Nuclear Weapons?', *International Security*, 21, N° 3 (Winter 1996–97), pp. 54–86.

chapter eight | domestic politics and sinister imperialism

The vast expenditure on armaments, the costly wars, the grave risks and embar-
rassments of foreign policy, the checks upon political and social reform within
Great Britain, though fraught with great injury to the nation, have served well the
present interests of certain industries and professions.
(John Hobson[1])

While Operation Iraqi Freedom may be viewed as a form of opportunistic, rather
than defensive, expansionism, its origins should not be looked for only in the context of American–Iraqi interactions. Indeed, it was in the US that the military technologies and doctrines that nurtured America's offensive dominance were first
elaborated. If we extend our inquiry into this elaboration beyond the aspects that
pertain specifically to the offence–defence balance, it becomes essential to address
the question whether 'the internal organization' (Waltz, 1959: 81) of the US might
be an independent variable likely to explain Operation Iraqi Freedom.

The hypothesis that war can be explained by domestic factors relative to the
working of the initiating states' political regimes is indirectly accepted by some
realists. For instance, the Prussian general Carl von Clausewitz (1809–1830: Book
1, §2, §24), who defined war as 'an act of violence to compel our opponent to fulfil our will', likened politics, of which war was 'the mere continuation ... by other
means', to the foreign policy of a state, exclusively guided by its national interest.

> That policy unites in itself, and reconciles all the interests of internal adminis-
> trations ... is presupposed, for it is nothing in itself, except a mere representa-
> tive and exponent of all these interests towards other states (Clausewitz,
> 1809–1830, Book 8, VI)

In other words, and in accordance with the realist state–as–unitary–actor approach
prioritising foreign policy as high politics, Clausewitz claimed that explanations
of foreign policy in general, and wars in particular, had to be looked for in the
interest of a state 'towards other states', i.e. in its international environment.[2]

Clausewitz nonetheless implicitly admitted that a foreign policy could also be
driven by domestic motives, or considerations of low politics.

> That policy may take a false direction, and may promote unfairly the ambitious ends, the private interests, the vanity of rulers, does not concern us here; for ... we can only look at policy here as the representative of the interests generally of the whole community (*Ibid*).

Obviously, the nuance – 'does not concern us *here*; for ... we can only look at policy *here* ...' (emphasis added) – is tantamount to Clausewitz acknowledging that there may be other motives than 'the interests generally of the whole community' but not taking them into account in his analysis.[3]

In this chapter, I will take Clausewitz at his word, so to speak, and analyse whether Operation Iraqi Freedom can indeed be considered to be a war intimately linked to the 'ambitious ends, the private interest (and) the vanity' of 'rulers' in the Bush administration.[4]

For that purpose, I will appeal to the liberal paradigm in international relations. Liberals ascribe war first and foremost to the political programmes of specific state leaders. In the heyday of liberalism, two authors notably dedicated their major writings to analysing the internal causes of two wars of the time – John Hobson, who focused on the Anglo–Boer War in Southern Africa in his 1902 essay 'Imperialism: A Study' (Hobson, 1965 (1902)); and Joseph Schumpeter, who analysed World War One in his essay 'The Sociology of Imperialisms', first published in 1919 (Schumpeter, 1951 (1919)). Since then, liberal theories have been updated and enriched. Indeed Andrew Moravcsik has proposed a very convincing general 'liberal theory of international politics' (Moravscik, 1997), while Jack Snyder has substantially reviewed the specifically liberal version of imperialism (Snyder, 1991).[5]

By applying the various findings of these authors to the present case study, I will show that Operation Iraqi Freedom is indeed an imperialist war, on account of its very nature, as it is a war fought by a state against another state in order to exert its – admittedly indirect – political control over the conquered territory; and because of its origins, as it can be related to the material and ideational interests of a small minority of societal actors represented within the Bush administration.

* * *

John Locke was the founding father of liberal internationalism, not only because he refused Hobbes's conception of the state of nature as 'a state of enmity, malice, violence and mutual destruction' (see Chapter four), but also because he ultimately ascribed the 'state of peace, good–will, mutual assistance and preservation', prevailing among political units, to individuals' private interests. According to Locke, the 'bonds that hold ... the princes of the world', i.e. the treaties they sign and agreements they conclude in order to regulate their mutual relations, were grounded on 'the great and chief end of men's uniting into commonwealths, and putting themselves under government, [which] is the preservation of their property', i.e. their possessions, wealth, liberty and lives (Locke, 1690: 16, §195; 7, §85).

In his view, all things being equal, the interests of property were better served in times of peace than in times of war and so governments, whose objective was to satisfy the interests and rights of the individuals who collectively formed civil society, were thus led to adopt a policy of peaceful conflict resolution rather than resort to armed force, which remained exceptional.

Consequently, the tenets of the contemporary liberal approach to international politics consider the fundamental actor of international relations to be the rational, risk–averse individual who, striving to promote his property – existing prior to the formation of a political unit – entrusts the government with the task of guaranteeing that his own interests will be furthered. Whereas realists claim that the state is the main actor, as it was created through the social contract precisely with a view to protecting that security which individuals were unable to guarantee by themselves in the pre–social state, liberals assert that 'the fundamental actors in international politics are … rational and risk–averse … individuals and private groups' (Moravcsik, 1997: 516), whose rights, needs, values and ideas, existed before, and independently from, the state they came to belong to as citizens. State authorities are thus the mere representatives of particular societal interests, which they are commissioned to defend and promote, and which individuals are unable to fulfil more efficiently, that is, at a lower cost.

Since it is conceived of merely a mechanism for the defence of the various interests and values of a civil society, the state is, of course, far from being a unitary actor embodied in a head of state, or head of government, and acting in the name of national interest. In a civil society, there is no spontaneous harmony and homogeneity in the definition and promotion of the interests and values of its various members. As resources are scarce in a society marked by competition, individuals, who may resort to differentiated means in order to promote their diverging or contending values and interests, do not hesitate to further them, either alone or through collective action. Consequently, in matters of international politics, as well as domestic, political decision–making is 'constrained by the underlying identities, interests, and power of individuals and groups (inside and outside the state apparatus) who constantly pressure the central decision makers to pursue policies consistent with their preferences' (518). The foreign policy of a state is not a continuous, coherent undertaking motivated by the defence and promotion of the national interest and shaped by the international distribution of power. It is but a succession of particular decisions that reflect the interests and values of the specific societal groups that can impose their views on the decision–making process.

In any political unit, access to political authority by the various members of the civil society is channelled through the state's political institutions. In logic then, the political regime of a state would play a fundamental role in shaping diplomatic action and decisions. The political regime is in fact the crucial variable determining a state's foreign behaviour. Contrary to Waltz's[6] claim that political units are 'like units' because they are constrained by the anarchical structure of international politics to adopt self–help behaviour, liberals contend that democracies, autocracies and totalitarian states will adopt different behaviour on the international scene, because they represent different interpretations and combinations of the security and welfare interests and values of their respective predominant members.

Generally speaking, a non–democratic state will behave more aggressively than a democratic state, as the minority that exerts monopolistic sway over political authority can oblige the dominated majority to bear the costs of a war. Symmetrically, risk aversion – a typical feature among ordinary people – accounts for the fact that a democracy will be incited *a priori* to adopt a peaceful behaviour on the international scene, as citizens have no interest in letting their government launch wars whose costs they may have to assume. This is most clearly explained by Immanuel Kant in his essay 'Perpetual Peace'.

> The republican constitution … gives a favourable prospect for … perpetual peace. The reason is this: if the consent of the citizens is required in order to decide that war should be declared (and in this constitution it cannot but be the case), nothing is more natural than that they would be very cautious in commencing such a poor game, decreeing for themselves all the calamities of war. Among the latter would be: having to fight, having to pay the costs of war from their own resources, having painfully to repair the devastation war leaves behind, and, to fill up the measure of evils, load themselves with a heavy national debt that would embitter peace itself and that can never be liquidated on account of constant wars in the future. But, on the other hand, in a constitution which is not republican, and under which the subjects are not citizens, a declaration of war is the easiest thing in the world to decide upon, because war does not require of the ruler, who is the proprietor and not a member of the state, the least sacrifice of the pleasures of his table, the chase, his country houses, his court functions, and the like. He may, therefore, resolve on war as on a pleasure party for the most trivial reasons, and with perfect indifference leave the justification which decency requires to the diplomatic corps who are ever ready to provide it (Kant, 1795, §II).

But accepting the general rule is not tantamount to saying that a dictatorial regime *per se* is revisionist,[7] or that a democratic regime is intrinsically a pacific one. In the case of a democracy, it is possible for an active and bellicose minority either to bypass the majority's interest in intrinsically peaceful behaviour or to convince it that waging a war is in the interest of the nation as a whole.[8] Imperialism is a particular case in point of such a bypassing strategy.

Besides the more common and ideological meaning attached to it, imperialism is a core concept in the explanation of wars fought by democracies as proposed by liberal thinkers, though the concept has also been used mainly by Marxists[9] and, incidentally, by realists.[10]

The first liberal author was John Hobson, who defined imperialism as a 'policy of expansion' through which a state '(annexes) or otherwise (asserts) political sway over vast portions of Africa and Asia … and elsewhere' (Hobson, 1965: 15). Hobson's starting point was Britain's colonial expansion in the late nineteenth century. Focusing on the Second Anglo–Boer War of 1899–1902, Hobson linked British imperialism and the economic crisis affecting Great Britain at the time. According to his analysis, the crisis was due to the tendency of British capitalists to underpay their employees in order to increase their profits. The underpaid vast majority of the British population could not purchase the goods produced by British industries, which caused under–consumption. Under–consumption led to over–production and economic stagnation turned into a self–reinforcing phenomenon, as growing savings capacities were not re–invested on account of the already existing over–production. In order to get out of the rut, British capitalists might have raised wages, in order to boost consumption, absorb over–production, and create new investment opportunities but, for political and economic reasons, some refused to accept both a decrease in the unitary profit rate and the very principle of sharing out the country's welfare. They chose instead to conquer new overseas markets in order to export their over–production and invest their savings. In doing so, a minority of British financial and industrial firms transformed the prevailing liberal capitalism into expansionist imperialism, as they did not hesitate to pressure the British government to protect these new markets against rival states, bent on promoting their own capitalist interests, and conquer new territories, which meant new investment opportunities.

Hobson upheld the idea that imperialism was a sinister drift of a liberal economic system, due to the egotism of some sectional interests, marked by a pre–capitalist and aristocratic, rather than truly bourgeois, capitalist mentality. 'Although the new imperialism has been bad business for the nation, it has been good business for certain classes and certain trades within the nation' (Hobson, 1965: 46).

Schumpeter was the second liberal who used the concept of imperialism. He defined it 'as the objectless disposition on the part of a state to unlimited forcible expansion' (Schumpeter, 1951: 7). He made a similar link between this tendency 'toward forceful expansion, without definite ... limits' (83) of the purposes and the needs of domestic policy. In his view, imperialism had nothing to do with modern capitalism. Quite on the contrary, it was the heirloom of the pre–capitalist past, a form of atavism of the social structure and of individual emotional habits. From the ancient empires to the absolute monarchies, imperialism had been inherent in the 'vital needs of situations that moulded peoples and classes into warriors – if they wanted to avoid extinction', and it had been facilitated by subsidiary factors such as the 'domestic interests of ruling classes' and 'the influence of all those who stand to gain individually from a war policy' (83–4). In modern times, however, the efficient working demands of capitalist economies furthered the emergence of a general feeling opposed to warlike undertakings and favouring pacific means of conflict resolution, which resulted in the progressive disappearance of war as a social phenomenon. The persistence of imperialism in the early twentieth century, argued Schumpeter, in a direct reference to World War One and the role played by Prussian landowners in the political decision–making process of Imperial Germany on the eve of 1914, was due to the fact that 'a class oriented toward war maintained itself in a ruling position' thanks to its ability to ally itself with 'the pro–military interests among the bourgeoisie' (129). In a way, as the Egyptian war–making aristocrats and mercenaries had done in the past, the Junker caste, which owed its existence to the necessity of consolidating the emerging Prussian monarchical state threatened by the occupation of North–Eastern Germany after the Thirty Years War, was to invent a new war – i.e. World War One – two centuries later in order to justify the no–longer–rational social privileges it strove to perpetuate.

If we leave aside the specific historical context and normative dimensions of the work of Hobson and Schumpeter, both convinced that liberal capitalism was essentially inherently peaceful, the following general conclusions can be drawn from their analyses. First, imperialism can be defined as the predisposition of a state to resort to armed force in order to conquer territory over which it can exert its political authority. Secondly, in the specific case of democratic states, imperialism can be linked to the existence of some sinister domestic interests. Though a democratic state is *a priori* not exposed to imperialist temptations, it may resort to an imperialist war if particular societal actors successfully shape the state's foreign policy with a view to promoting their sectional interests.

This leads us to the question that necessarily stems from Hobson and Schumpeter's assertions. How can a minority, intent on launching a war, impose its will upon the majority, in a democracy, defined *a priori* by the domination of the majority's will and interest? How does it succeed in forcing the majority to endorse its choices? Hobson and Schumpeter proposed some tentative answers. According to the first author, imperialists 'exercise [...control ...] over the body of public opinion through the press which ... is becoming more and more their obedient instrument' (Hobson, 1965: 60). In Schumpeter's view, the atavistic military is able to ally itself with those members of the ruling bourgeois class interested in expansionism. Both authors stressed the hypocritical rhetoric presenting an imperialist war as either 'a defensive war' (Schumpeter, 1951: 93) or as a war fought for in the name of 'national destiny' (Hobson, 1965: 209). These explanations have recently been taken up and improved by Jack Snyder.

Snyder's starting point is that, in a recent past, various great powers have been unable to resist the temptation of imperial(ist) (over–)expansion detrimental to their objective long–term interests – Great Britain during the Victorian period, Imperial Germany in the early twentieth century, Imperial Japan in the 1930s and 1940s, Post–Stalinist USSR in Africa and Central and South–East Asia, or the USA during the Vietnam War. This imperial temptation is due to the myth that a state's security can only be achieved through expansion. Notably developed through the 'domino' doctrine, the 'best defence is a good offence' principle and the 'paper tiger' analogy, the 'myth of empire' is in itself 'a product of the political and propagandistic activities of imperialist groups' (Snyder, 1991: 17). It is nothing more than a rationalisation process for the material and ideological interests of groups who 'derive parochial benefits from expansion, from military preparations associated with expansion, or from the domestic political climate brought about by intense political competition' (31).

More exactly, myths of empire enable imperialist groups to promote their respective private interests through the state's foreign policy. Thanks to their superior political resources, 'owing to their ability to organise for collective action, their monopolies on information, and their ties to the state' (31), these imperialist groups successfully hijack state policies in various ways. First, they gain control over national policy by joining in log–rolled coalitions, trading favours so that each group can get what it wants most, whereas the costs are shared by the whole society through taxes imposed by the state. The pressure they exert upon policy–makers is all the more efficient as it is difficult for the opposition to mobilise efficiently, because the costs implied by political decisions are not immediately perceptible by the individual citizen. Secondly, they take advantage of their quasi–monopoly on information and expertise, thanks to their strategic positioning close to government sources. Selling myths of empire is indeed easier for coalitions who can exploit the credibility of state resources and do not hesitate to 'support favourable politicians, buy journalists, and fund mass organizations and think tanks' (36). Thirdly, they penetrate vital sectors of the administration, thus constraining the state leadership – no longer 'a unitary rational actor, but rather the manager of a heterogeneous coalition' (17) – to satisfy the interests of the various groups represented within the government and oppose any adjustment of political options, should the costs of imperialist action increase.

According to Snyder, imperialist groups are more likely to 'pervert national policy in the pursuit of private interests' (14) in cartelised political systems, such as imperial Germany and Japan, than in democracies, which are characterised by a pluralist dispersion of political power, institutional checks and balances and the existence of elected authorities accountable to citizens. Nonetheless, democracies can also be the victim of state hijacking, as democratic institutions do not always function so as to enable and support genuine opposition to sinister interests. The decision–making process in diplomatic and strategic affairs tends to be secretive, which is supposedly necessary to cope with an anarchical environment, and the average voter, unaware of his, or the nation's, true interests, is given biased information as a result.

Snyder published his book a dozen years before Operation Iraqi Freedom but his conclusions can be applied directly to account for America's decision to go to war against Iraq in 2003. Operation Iraqi Freedom was indeed an imperialist war in the sense of the above definition. Through the use of military force, the American objective was to conquer Iraq in order to bring it under US political control. The US successfully drove Saddam Hussein from power and set up a provisional government by transferring political power to an Iraqi government whose very survival depended – and still depends – on the presence of some 150,000 troops occupying Iraq.[11] Operation Iraqi Freedom was also an imperialist war because it was in all likelihood launched by certain specific private interests close to the Bush administration.

I mentioned in Chapter seven that the White House was unable to produce the slightest evidence to support its claims about the existence of weapons of mass destruction in Iraq when it started considering the prospect of a military intervention. As a matter of fact, no such weapons have ever been found, either by the UN and IAEA inspectors or by American soldiers deployed in Iraq.[12] Consequently, it cannot be said that the US administration was impelled to go to war with Iraq by the alleged presence of weapons of mass destruction, or by Saddam Hussein's refusal to allow UN inspection. George W. Bush's decision to attack Iraq did not originate either in the post 9/11 trauma, or in his coming to office in 2001. I contend that the origins of Operation Iraqi Freedom are to be found in the early 1990s, as an extension of Operation Desert Storm. Indeed, during the first Gulf War, some members of George H. Bush's administration, notably Secretary of State Dick Cheney and Undersecretary of Defense Paul Wolfowitz, vainly tried to convince the President of the necessity of overthrowing Saddam Hussein's regime.[13] In 1998, after Saddam Hussein stopped cooperating with the UN disarmament inspectors, thus inciting the UN to withdraw them, not only Wolfowitz and Cheney but also Donald Rumsfeld and Richard Perle, – to name some of the most prominent members of the neo–conservative think–tank Project for a New American Century[14] – jointly signed a letter urging President Clinton to implement 'a strategy ... including military steps ... for removing Saddam's regime from power'.[15]

This fact is of crucial importance. All these political personalities became members of George W. Bush's administration in 2002–3. The White House's new organisation chart clearly revealed the joint presence of three groups of politicians representing the major intellectual approaches to foreign policy:[16] the pragmatist realists with Colin Powell, Secretary of State and former Chief of Staff during Operation Desert Storm, and, to a lesser degree, Condoleezza Rice, Head of the National Security Council; the nationalist hardliners such as Donald Rumsfeld, Secretary of Defense, and Vice–President Dick Cheney; and the neo–conservatives, with Paul Wolfowitz, number two at the Defense Department, and Richard Perle, head of the Pentagon's Defense Policy Board. In the competition to influence White House decisions, Dick Cheney played a key role because President Bush heavily relied on his political experience for the conduct of US policy. Cheney promoted the appointments of Rumsfeld and Wolfowitz to the Defense Department, where neo–conservative Douglas Feith also held an important position. Cheney chose another neo–conservative, Lewis Libby, as his delegate to the White House meetings, and sent two other neo–conservatives, Richard Armitage and Stephen Hadley, to the State Department.[17] In addition there were the nationalist hawk, John Bolton, Under–Secretary for Arms Control, and the neo–conservative Elliot Abrams, Special Assistant to the President. All in all, however, the hardliners and neo–cons were not more numerous than the pragmatists. Moreover, the two groups did not share the same vision of the US foreign–policy strategy. Whereas the nationalist hawks of the Rumsfeld generation, immersed in Cold War ideology, favoured a defensive policy protecting 'fortress America' from exterior threats, younger neo–conservatives were convinced of the necessity for, and capacity of, the US to reshape the exterior world in accordance with America's values and interests, with a view to perpetuating its primacy by eliminating any opposition. In spite of their diverging views, however, the hawks and neo–cons had one common conviction – their belief in American exceptionalism – and one common objective – their desire to get rid of America's tradition of multilateral *Realpolitik*, which had prevailed during the Cold War and the first Gulf crisis[18] and which was still the preferred strategy of Powell and Rice. It was the terrorist attacks of 9/11 that gave them the opportunity to convince George W. Bush that the war option was the '*prima* rather than the *ultima ratio*' (Schumpeter, 1951: 38).

George W. Bush had in fact been elected on an isolationist programme. During a TV debate with Al Gore, he had stressed the necessity for the US to keep a low profile on the international scene. 'If we are an arrogant nation, they will resent us. If we are a humble nation, but strong, they will welcome us'. On 21st August, 2002, he was still simply shrugging off rumours about a possible war against Iraq, which he called 'a kind of a churning'. But the newly adopted National Security Strategy of the United States of America (2002) was a harbinger of things to come, i.e. the progressive acknowledgement by the US president of the necessity of a pre–emptive, in fact preventive (see Chapter five), war against rogue states in general and Iraq in particular.

This evolution was not the sign of any incoherence or irrationality on the part of George W. Bush. It simply reflected the internal struggle between the various factions within his administration and the final victory of the neo–conservatives, hailing America's primacy and proclaiming the necessity for the US to assume its imperial role by spreading democracy, by force if necessary.

> What's the point of being the greatest, most powerful nation in the world and not having an imperial role? ... The most powerful nation always had an imperial role. ... I think it would be natural for the United States ... to play a far more dominant role in world affairs. Not what we're doing now but to command and to give orders as to what is to be done.[19]

The war against Iraq was the concrete implementation of the neo–conservatives' political programme.

> To many, the idea of America using its power to promote changes of regime in nations ruled by dictators rings of utopianism. In fact, it is eminently realistic. There is something perverse in declaring the impossibility of promoting democratic change abroad in the light of the record of the past three decades. After we have already seen dictatorships toppled in such unlikely places as the Philippines, Indonesia, Chile, Nicaragua, Paraguay, Taiwan and South Korea, how utopian is it to imagine a change of regime in a place like Iraq?[20]

However, neo–conservative ideas would not have prevailed without the support of the nationalist hawks.[21] How then is it possible to account for the emergence of such a necessarily short–lived coalition – if we consider Cheney and Rumsfeld's scepticism towards the 'democratic domino doctrine' championed by neo–conservatives?

Snyder's log–rolling concept provides the answer. In their common fight against the multilateral realists, nationalist hardliners reached some form of bargain with the neo–conservatives. They accepted the neo–conservative nation–building programme in Iraq in exchange for the satisfaction of their own demands. As these demands were obviously secret and classified, we can only speculate on their content but a simple analysis of the non–military aspects of Operation Iraqi Freedom shows that they most probably pertained to the promotion of the interests of big American oil and engineering companies and of the sub–contracting activities of the US Army – to private security firms, for example.

Let us have a closer look at the case of nationalist hardliner Dick Cheney. As early as 25th March, 2003, that is, only one week after the beginning of Operation Iraqi Freedom, Halliburton, the world's major oilfield supply company, obtained the main contracts for the rebuilding of Iraqi facilities and the distribution of Iraqi oil, without any competitive bidding. Interestingly enough, Cheney had been Halliburton's CEO from 1995 to 2000, before retiring during the presidential election. Donald Rumsfeld was, more particularly, the representative of the US Army's interests. Since the end of the Cold War, and in a more concrete way since the first armed interventions in Bosnia and Kosovo, private security firms had been increasingly entrusted with tasks that were traditionally carried out by conventional armies, such as, for instance, the protection of high–ranking officers or civil personalities – Paul Bremer, to be more precise – weapon–maintenance and a number of missions ranging from military support operations to the recruitment and training of military personnel.[22] We could paraphrase Schumpeter and say that mercenaries and private security groups, originally created to compensate for the drop in military budgets subsequent to the fall of the Berlin Wall and the disappearance of the Soviet threat, call for wars in order to advance their own profit, if not ensure their own survival. And last, the US President himself, as well as the Bush family, had close links with some private interests – not only in the oil sector. On 2nd May, 2003, one day after he had made his famous 'Mission Accomplished' statement on board USS Lincoln and declared Operation Iraqi Freedom was over, he made a speech in a United Defense Industries armament factory – one of the Pentagon's most important suppliers. The main shareholder of UDI was the Carlyle Group, the largest private equity firm located in Washington, DC, and former employer of both George Bush senior and junior.

Such evidence tends to corroborate the hypothesis of Operation Iraqi Freedom as an imperialist war. George W. Bush's America proved to be a cartelised political system, in Michael Walzer's sense.[23] In Walzer's view, a just democracy, has 'good fences' separating the political, economic, judicial and media spheres; but it ceases to be a democracy (and becomes cartelised) when those with great resources, economic for instance, can convert their dominant position in the market into opportunities and privileges in another sphere – the political sphere for example – by purchasing honour or buying political office, through the colonisation of the administration or the financing of electoral campaigns.[24]

The absence of separation between the political sphere and the media sphere is further evidence of the imperialist nature of Operation Iraqi Freedom. It makes it possible to understand how sinister private interests defended by the neo–conservative–hardliner coalition and the societal factions linked to them have successfully passed as America's national interest in the eyes of American citizens.

On 29th April, 2004, Dick Cheney expressed his gratitude to Fox News for the quality of its coverage of the electoral campaign of the forthcoming presidential election of November 2004. And he did that for a very good reason. Throughout the Iraqi crisis, American media in general, and Fox News Channel in particular, had relayed the US administration's vision to the American public, negating the role of a pluralistic press in a democracy, which is supposed to guarantee 'access to a broad range of viewpoints' (Snyder, 1991: 39).

This is confirmed by the analysis of opinion polls. Asked in a Chicago Council on Foreign Relations Poll in June 2002 about their position on invading Iraq, 65 per cent of the respondents said the United States 'should only invade Iraq with UN approval and the support of its allies'; 20 per cent declared 'the US should invade Iraq even if we have to go it alone'; and 13 per cent thought that 'the US should not invade Iraq'. A year after, in a May 2003 poll conducted by the Program on International Policy Attitudes/Knowledge Networks, a majority of 68 per cent said that 'the US made the right decision … in going to war with Iraq' (Kull *et al.*, 2003–4). The mood theory or 'Almond–Lippmann consensus'[25], compatible with the realist theory of international politics, provides a tentative explanation for this reversal in trends. According to this theory, general public opinion is, at worst, indifferent to foreign affairs, or, at best, essentially marked by unstable and capricious mood reactions, disapproving in the first place and then approving a given policy – for instance the use of armed force against Iraq – or vice versa. The mood theory has however been disproved by empirical research showing that the average citizen is likely to show real interest in foreign affairs, at least at specific moments, and that public opinion on foreign affairs issues is mostly coherent over time – a coherence through time correlated to the general public's exposure to the information from either governmental sources or media coverage.[26]

A detailed analysis of what happened during the Iraqi crisis confirms these findings. Indeed, the more people believed that weapons of mass destruction had been discovered in Iraq, that there were proved links between Saddam Hussein and Osama bin Laden, and that other states, including the Arab countries, supported America's intervention, the more they approved Operation Iraqi Freedom. Obviously, these beliefs were wrong. But they cannot be explained by an alleged lack of interest in foreign affairs issues by American citizens. On the contrary, they clearly evidence the impact of the media on citizens' opinions. Indeed, among those who were favourable to the use of force against Iraq, those who primarily watched Fox News were 2.0 times more likely to believe that the US had found evidence of the links between Saddam Hussein and Al'Qaeda, 1.6 times more likely to be convinced that WMDs had been found, 1.7 times more likely to believe that world opinion supported the American will to go to war, and 2.1 times more likely to have at least one of these three misperceptions. Even worse, the risk of misperception in this specific part of the population was significantly correlated to their level of attention to news (Kull *et al.*, 2003).

In other words, American media[27] contributed to shaping public opinion in accordance with the administration's vision of the crisis. Admittedly, it was not really a risky venture. In the aftermath of the 9/11 terrorist attacks, the American general public was 'psychologically primed to accept the myths of empire' (Snyder, 2003)[28] and receptive to the idea of a necessary pre–emptive/preventive war against Iraq in order to avoid a new Munich. It is nonetheless true that the media played the role of real 'mass communication weapons'[29], in the service of the Bush administration whose policy they supported without batting an eyelid. Suffice it to mention the number of platforms respectively offered to the supporters of Operation Iraqi Freedom and to its opponents, the origins of their information – mostly from CIA sources – the fact that France became the 'usual suspect' for the difficulties encountered at the UN, on account of its systematic obstructionism, not to mention the omnipresence of the American flag on TV screens throughout the crisis.

The Fox effect, which can be defined as 'a form of collusion between a government and an aligned medium in order to convey live propaganda to public opinion by means of fear',[30] was hardly balanced by the behaviour of America's political community. According to Snyder, 'representative branches of government have the right to extract information from state bureaucracies' (Snyder, 1991: 39), thus checking the administration's typical tendency to monopolise information in periods of crises. George Kennan had already advanced this idea in the 1950s, claiming that a 'democratic society' such as the US 'cannot plan a preventive war' because 'it [democracy] leaves no room for conspiracy in the great matters of state' (quoted in Schweller, 1992: 244–5). This general rule was disproved by the Democrats' failure to oppose the Bush administration's war plans. According to Chaim Kaufman, 'not one of the more than 30 senators and 100 representatives who attended hearings in July–October 2002 [challenged] administration claims concerning Hussein's intentions or the supposed Iraqi nuclear threat'.[31]

George W. Bush also took advantage of the post–9/11, 'rally–round–the–flag' effect[32] to set the agenda of the US Congress. Boosted by a substantial rise in his overall approval rate after the terrorist attacks,[33] he decided to stage a vote in Congress on a resolution authorising the use of armed force against Iraq, on the eve of the mid–term elections in November 2002. In so doing, he clearly made Iraq a major stake in the coming elections. The plan worked even better than expected. Democrats not only accepted Bush's agenda, though the Democratic majority in Senate could have asked for the vote to be postponed in the absence of any objective proof of Iraqi WMDs, but they also authorised the President to 'use the armed forces of the US *as he determines* to be necessary and appropriate in order to defend the national security of the US against the continuing threat posed by Iraq ...'[34] (emphasis added). For fear of being accused of betraying America's vital interest, they justified their attitude by invoking the direct threat Iraq was supposed to represent for America's security, though polls in October 2002 suggested that 69 per cent of Americans thought the national economy should be given priority in the President's agenda.[35]

* * *

According to Louis Fisher, this attitude was reminiscent of the Tonkin Gulf Resolution passed almost unanimously by the US Congress in 1964. In both cases, representatives 'authorized military force' and hypocritically 'hoped that it would not be necessary'. In both cases, they 'chose to trust in the President, not in themselves. Instead of acting as the people's representatives and preserving the republican form of government, they gave the President unchecked power' (Fisher, 2003: 405).

The comparison with the Vietnam War is very interesting within the framework of the present essay, i.e. the analysis of the potential impact of Operation Iraqi Freedom on the international order. As 'the costly failure of US state–building in Vietnam bequeathed a legacy of profound aversion to the use of force to remake other societies in our own image',[36] Jack Snyder claims that the Vietnam War is a good illustration of the fact that democratic institutions can eventually recover their virtues, thus putting an end to imperial(ist) (over–) expansion. Seen from this perspective, Operation Iraqi Freedom would be a mere parenthesis in history, unlikely profoundly to change America's attitude to the world or leave a durable mark on the international order of the twenty–first century.

However, I contend that Operation Iraqi Freedom can also be compared to another imperialist war fought by another democracy, namely Britain's Boer War. By 'producing beneficial reforms and reassessments' (Kennedy, 1989: 524), the Boer War admittedly proved to be reversible. It nevertheless heralded the irresistible decline of Britain as a hegemonic power. In the next chapter I will try to apply this hypothesis to Operation Iraqi Freedom and adopt the approach of the hegemonic power cycle theory.

NOTES

1   Hobson, 1965 (1902): 46.

2   On this point, see Raymond Aron, *Penser la guerre, Clausewitz* (Paris: Gallimard, 1976), volume 2, pp. 225 *sqq*. Aron stresses Clausewitz's state–centrism in defining foreign policy as 'the intelligence of the personified state'.

3   Kenneth Waltz concedes a similar nuance. In his article 'The Origins of War in Neorealist Theory', after criticising liberals and Marxists for linking 'the outbreak of war or the prevalence of peace to the internal qualities of states', he emphasises that 'although neorealist theory does not explain why particular wars are fought, it does explain war's dismal occurrence

through the millennia. Neorealists point not to the ambitions or the intrigues that punctuate the outbreak of individual conflicts but instead to the existing structure within which events, whether by design or accident, can precipitate open clashes of arms'. In other words, he implicitly admits that a particular decision to go to war can be explained at the unit–level of analysis, i.e. the 'internal structure of states' (Waltz, 1959: 80).

4   A first version of this chapter was published in French in the journal *Etudes internationales* *35*, N° 4 (December 2004), pp. 667–87: 'Prendre Clausewitz au mot: Une explication libérale de Liberté en Irak'.

5   I claim that Jack Snyder's essay can be considered to be substantially liberal. Obviously, his analysis is compatible with defensive realism because it implicitly postulates the existence of an 'authentic' national interest and normatively rejects a state's illusory and counterproductive overexpansion. However, he refuses state–centrism by looking inside the 'black box'. He also pinpoints the explanation of a state's overexpansion temptations by stressing the role of imperialist factions' particular interests and political moves, on the same lines as Kenneth Waltz's 'second image'. Moreover, in his essay there are explicit references to Hobson and Schumpeter (pp. 14–15).

6   According to Kenneth Waltz, states are 'like units' (Waltz, 1979: 95–7), stimulated by the anarchic structure of the international system to 'behave in ways that tend toward the creation of balances of power' (118).

7   See Chapter two. The Holy Alliance members' converging political interests in the defence of the *status quo* contributed to their overall peaceful behaviour, despite their non–democratic, or non–republican, regime.

8   Andrew Moravcsik proposes a second explanation of the possible warlike behaviour of a democracy, relative to the 'configuration of interdependent state preferences'. A state, argues Moravcsik, has to adapt its behaviour to the behaviour of other states defending their own combination of societal interests. For instance a democracy, confronted with a dictatorial regime, may be forced to adopt a warlike behaviour. This argument, in line with the democratic peace theory, notably defended by Michael Doyle and Bruce Russett, was taken up by the Bush administration, in its presentation of Operation Iraqi Freedom as a defensive war aiming at anticipating an asymmetric attack from a dictatorship with an offensive advantage. See Chapter seven for a refutation of this theory.

9   The main Marxist reference remains Lenin, in his essay 'Imperialism, the Highest Stage of Capitalism', http://www.marxists.org/archive/lenin/works/1916/imp–hsc/. According to Lenin, 'imperialism is capitalism at that stage of development at which the dominance of monopolies and finance capital is established; in which the export of capital has acquired pronounced importance; in which the division of the world among the international trusts has begun; in which the division of all territories of the globe among the biggest capitalist powers has been completed.' Among the many updates of classical international Marxism, Johan Galtung's theory of structural imperialism should be mentioned. In his article 'A Structural Theory of Imperialism', *Journal of Peace Research*, 8, N° 2 (1971), pp. 81–117, he broadly defines imperialism as 'a dominance relation ... between nations', and distinguishes five types of imperialism: economic, political, military, communication, and cultural.

10   According to Hans Morgenthau in *Politics among Nations*, an imperialist policy is a 'policy devised to overthrow the *status quo*', and as such it has to be distinguished from the two other

strategies adopted by states in their struggle for power: the policy of the *status quo* and the policy of prestige (Morgenthau, 2005: 64). Raymond Aron's conception of imperialism is closer both to the commonsense meaning and to the liberal conception. In his essay *Peace and War*, imperialism is defined as 'the diplomatic–strategic behaviour of a political unit which constructs an empire, that is, subjects foreign populations to its rule' (Aron, 2003: 259).

11 Iraq's return to sovereignty on 28th June, 2004, and the elections held afterwards, did not put an end to what Hobson calls the 'political sway' exerted by the US.

12 Many months after Operation Iraqi Freedom, British authorities – followed by their American counterparts – finally acknowledged that there were no weapons of mass of destruction in Iraq. As early as 9th May, 2003, in an interview given to Sam Tannenhaus of *Vanity Fair*, Paul Wolfowitz had admitted that the pretext of an alleged threat from Iraq because of its weapons of mass destruction had been chosen because it was the only one likely to create a consensus within the Bush administration in favour of a military operation. 'The truth is that for reasons that have a lot to do with the US government bureaucracy we settled on the one issue that everyone could agree on, which was weapons of mass destruction as the core reason.'

13 As early as 1991, Paul Wolfowitz and his assistant, Scooter Libby, had elaborated the Defense Planning Guidance to 'set the nation's direction for the next century'. Wolfowitz's and Libby's ideas – which were abandoned by President Clinton – called for the necessary replacement of the classic containment strategy by 'pre–emption' and 'unilateralism'. This programme was to influence directly the National Security Strategy adopted in September 2002.

14 On its website, http://www.newamericancentury.org/, the Project for the New American Century describes itself as 'a non–profit educational organization dedicated to a few fundamental propositions: that American leadership is good both for America and for the world; and that such leadership requires military strength, diplomatic energy and commitment to moral principle.'

15 Letter to Bill Clinton, 26 January, 1998, http://www.newamericancentury.org/ iraqclintonletter.htm.

16 See Gary Rosen (ed.), *The Right War? The Conservative Debate on Iraq* (Cambridge: Cambridge University Press, 2005), for an anthology of the different points of view expressed in the US during the Iraqi crisis.

17 Stephen Fidler & Gerard Baker, 'America's Democratic Imperialists: How the Neo–Conservatives Rose from Humility to Empire in Two Years', *Financial Times*, March 6, 2003. See also Ivo Daalder & James Lindsay, *America Unbound: The Bush Revolution in Foreign Policy* (Washington: Brookings Institution Press, 2003), and James Mann, *Rise of the Vulcans: The History of Bush's War Cabinet* (London: Penguin, 2004).

18 Bush senior and his Secretary of State, James Baker, can be considered to have acted as pragmatist realists during the first Gulf crisis. Colin Powell, the Head of the Joint Chiefs of Staff, had explicitly opposed any action destined to overthrow Saddam's regime. During the 2000 electoral campaign, Condoleezza Rice recommended a classical containment strategy against Iraq and other rogue regimes. See her article 'Campaign 2000: Promoting the National Interest', *Foreign Affairs* 79, N° 1 (January–February 2000), p. 61: 'One thing is clear: the United States must approach regimes like North Korea resolutely and decisively. The Clinton administration has failed here, sometimes threatening to use force and then backing down, as it often has with Iraq. These regimes are living on borrowed time, so there

need be no sense of panic about them. Rather, the first line of defense should be a clear and classical statement of deterrence – if they do acquire weapons of mass destruction, their weapons will be unusable because any attempt to use them will bring national obliteration. Second, we should accelerate efforts to defend against these weapons. This is the most important reason to deploy national and theater missile defenses as soon as possible, to focus attention on U.S. homeland defenses against chemical and biological agents, and to expand intelligence capabilities against terrorism of all kinds'.

19 Irving Kristol, quoted by Corey Robin, 'Remembrance of Empires Past: 9/11 and the End of the Cold War', in Irving Schrecker (ed.), *Cold War Triumphalism: The Misuse of History after the Fall of Communism* (New York: The New Press, 2004), p. 275. Irving Kristol is the godfather of the neo–conservatives, whose two major representatives are his son, William Kristol, and Robert Kagan. For one of the first and most complete expressions of the neo–conservative programme, see their article 'Toward a Neo–Reaganite Foreign Policy', *Foreign Affairs* 75, N° 4 (July–August 1996), pp. 18–32. See also the websites of their foundations and think tanks, notably The Committee on the Present Danger and The Project for the New American Century, where their most important documents are published on line, for instance '*Rebuilding America's Defenses*' and '*Present Dangers: Crisis and Opportunity in American Foreign and Defence Policy*'. For periodicals, see *The Weekly Standard* and *The National Interest*. The most interesting neo–conservative essays include Max Boot, *The Savage Wars of Peace. Small Wars and the Rise of American Power* (New York: Basic Books, 2002); Robert Kagan, *Paradise and Power: America versus Europe in the Twenty–First Century* (London: Atlantic, 2003); Robert Kaplan, *Warrior Politics: Why Leadership Demands a Pagan Ethos* (New York: Random House, 2002). For essays advancing the idea of a necessary attack against Iraq, see Sidney Pollack, *The Gathering Storm: The Case for Invading Iraq* (New York: Random House, 2002) and David Frum & Richard Perle, *An End to Evil: How to Win the War on Terror* (New York: Random House, 2003). Interesting synthetic analyses of the neo–conservative movement can be found in Alex Callinicos, *The New Mandarins of American Power: The Bush Administration's Plans for the World* (Cambridge: Polity Press, 2003); Gary Dorrien, *Imperial Designs: Neo–Conservatism and the New Pax Americana* (New York: Routledge, 2004); Alain Frachon & Daniel Vernet, *L'Amérique messianique: Les guerres des néo–conservateurs* (Paris: Seuil, 2004); Stefan Halper & Jonathan Clarke, *America Alone: The Neo–Conservatives and the Global Order* (Cambridge: Cambridge University Press, 2004); Ghassan Salamé, *Quand l'Amérique refait le monde* (Paris: Fayard, 2005).

20 Robert Kagan & William Kristol, 'The Present Danger', *The National Interest*, No. 59 (Spring 2000), pp. 57–69.

21 See Robert Gilpin, 'War Is Too Important to Be Left to Ideological Amateurs', *International Relations*, 19, N° 1 (March 2005), pp. 5–18.

22 See Peter Singer, *Corporate Warriors: The Rise of the Privatized Military Industry* (Ithaca: Cornell University Press, 2004). 'Corporate' soldiers account for the second largest military contingent in Iraq, more numerous, for instance, than the British contingent.

23 See Michael Walzer, *Spheres of Justice: A Defence of Pluralism and Equality* (Oxford: Robertson, 1983).

24 According to the French newspaper *Le Monde*, 2nd–3rd November, 2003 quoting the Center

for Public Integrity, the 71 firms which obtained the biggest contracts in Iraq and in Afghanistan were among the most important financial supports of George W. Bush's electoral campaign.

25 See Gabriel Almond, *The American People and Foreign Policy* (New York: Praeger, 1950); and Walter Lippman, *Essays in Public Philosophy* (New York: New American Library, 1956).

26 See the most representative work of this research, Benjamin Page & Robert Shapiro, *The Rational Public: Fifty Years of Trends in Americans' Policy Preferences* (Chicago: University of Chicago Press, 1992).

27 Things were not fundamentally different in the written press, on which I will not focus, given its low reception rate by the average American citizen.

28 In this article, Snyder updates his book published twelve years before and applies his theory to the Iraqi crisis. He rightly stresses the importance of the supposed link between Saddam Hussein and Osama bin Laden as presented by the Bush administration. Exploiting the potential threat from Iraq, a country weakened by twelve years of economic sanctions, could hardly have convinced American public opinion. Conversely, the idea that the American territory could be hit by weapons supplied by Saddam to terrorist networks ready to use them against the US, was much more credible after 9/11. See Chaim Kaufmann, 'Threat Inflation and the Failure of the Marketplace of Ideas: The Selling of the Iraq War', *International Security* 29, No. 1 (Summer 2004), pp. 5–48. In his essay Kaufmann stresses the impact of the alleged link between Saddam Hussein and terrorist groups on the Democrats' final decision not to criticise the arguments put forward by the Bush administration. Kaufmann' statement also confirms the opinion advanced in the fifties by Bernard Brodie (quoted in Schweller, 1992: 242), who claimed that war was very unpopular in the US, and that 'dramatic fear' was a necessary condition for the spreading of the idea of a preventive war among the general public.

29 See Jean–Marie Charon and Arnaud Mercier (eds), *Armes de communication massive: Informations de guerre en Irak: 1991–2003* (Paris: Editions du CNRS, 2004).

30 Divina Frau–Meigs, 'L'effet Fox contre l'effet CNN: Le journalisme américain entre surveillance et propagande', in J.–M. Charon & A. Mercier (eds), *Armes de communication massive, ibid.* pp. 188–96.

31 C. Kaufman, 'Threat Inflation and the Failure of the Marketplace of Ideas', *op. cit.* See also Nancy Kassop, 'The War Powers and Its Limits', *Presidential Studies Quarterly* 33, No. 3 (September 2003), pp. 509–29; James Lindsay, 'Deference and Defiance: The Shifting Rhythms of Executive–Legislative Relations in Foreign Policy', *Presidential Studies Quarterly* 33, No. 3 (September 2003), pp. 530–46.

32 See Kathleen Murray & Christopher Spinosa, 'The Post–9/11 Shift in Public Opinion: How Long Will It Last?', in Eugene Wittkopf & James McCormick (eds), *The Domestic Sources of American Foreign Policy: Insights and Evidence*, 4th edition (Lanham: Rowman & Littlefield, 2004). The 'rally–round–the–flag–effect' concept is due to John Mueller, *War, Presidents and Public Opinion* (New York: Wiley, 1973).

33 This approval rate, measured by the Gallup Institute – 'Do you approve or disapprove of the way George W. Bush is handling his job as President?' – went from 51 per cent on 10th September, 2001, to 91 per cent on 22nd September, 2001. It was the highest approval rate of an American President since the first Gallup poll conducted during Franklin Roosevelt's mandate.

34 House Joint Resolution 114 [107], voted by the US Congress on 16th October, 2002. This resolution followed the Senate Joint Resolution 23 [107], adopted on 18th September, 2001, also called 'Authorization for the Use of Military Force'. 'The President is authorized to use all necessary and appropriate force against those nations, organizations, or persons he determines planned, authorized, committed, or aided the terrorist attacks that occurred on September 11, 2001, or harboured such organizations or persons, in order to prevent any future acts of international terrorism against the United States by such nations, organizations or persons' (emphasis added).

35 Opinion poll published in the *New York Times*, 7th October, 2002, quoted in Fisher, 2003.

36 Jeffrey Record, 'The Limits and Temptations of America's Conventional Primacy', *Survival* 47, No. 1 (Spring 2005), pp. 33–49.

chapter nine | power cycles and hegemonic decline

Rome fell, Babylon fell; Scarsdale's turn will come.
(Paul Kennedy[1])

The United States today controls a greater share of world power than any other country since the emergence of the nation–state system. Nevertheless, recent US Presidents George H. Bush and Bill Clinton still cultivated allies and strove to maintain large coalitions. They considered such strategies the best way for the United States to secure desired behaviour from others, minimize costs to the nation, and most smoothly manage a complex and contentious world. By contrast, the fundamental objective of the current Bush doctrine, which seeks to universalize US values and defend preventively against new, non–traditional threats, is the establishment of US hegemony, primacy, or empire. This stance was precipitated both by the election of George W. Bush (who brought to the Presidency a more unilateral outlook) and the terrorist attacks of September 11, 2001. ... We can only speculate on what a President Al Gore would have done in the same situation; but while Gore probably would have invaded Afghanistan, he most likely would not have adopted anything like the Bush doctrine. To some extent, then, the new assertiveness of US hegemony is accidental, the product of a reaction of personalities and events. Yet deeper factors reveal that if this shift in policy was an accident, it was also an accident waiting to happen. The forceful and unilateral exercise of US power is not simply the by–product of September 11, the Bush administration, or some shadowy neoconservative cabal – it is the logical outcome of the current unrivalled US position in the international system (Jervis, 2003a: 83–4).[2]

In this analysis of Operation Iraqi Freedom, Robert Jervis reminds us of the basic principle of any scientific research in social sciences that must go beyond the surface reasons of an event in order to grasp its fundamental causes. Jervis claims that the decision to go to war against Saddam Hussein is reducible neither to the bilateral interactions between Washington and Baghdad nor to the personality of American policy–makers or the specificities of America's foreign–policy decision–making process but pertains to systemic factors relative to the current evolution of the contemporary international power configuration. He thus revives the method used by Thucydides, who ascribed the structural cause of the Peloponnesian War to the shift in the power relations between Athens and Sparta.

There is however one major difference between Jervis and Thucydides. The Greek historian took into account the dynamics of the power distribution through the way the Spartans perceived it, and stressed the subjective fear inspired in them by the objective reality of Athenian growth. Such a causal relationship is absent in Jervis's analysis. He considers America's decision to resort to armed force to be 'the logical outcome' of America's primacy and explains it by the objective fact of today's unipolar system, independently of any awareness, perception, or interpretation of this position by the actors concerned.

> Power is checked most effectively by counterbalancing power, and a state that is not subject to severe external pressures tends to feel few restraints at all. Spreading democracy and liberalism throughout the world has always been a US goal, but having so much power makes this aim a more realistic aim. It is not as if the Middle East has become suddenly more fertile ground for American ideals; it's just that the US now has the means to impose its will (Jervis, 2003a: 84).

Jervis postulates that a unipolar power is bound to yield to imperial temptation, which is invalidated by the historical records of two preponderant powers – the United Kingdom in 1815, and the US in the contemporary period (see Chapters two and three). In the immediate post–WWII years and at the end of the Cold War, the US twice benefited from a huge advantage of power resources, without resorting to military means in order to shape the world according to its interests. In the present study of the systemic level of analysis in my search for the fundamental causes of Operation Iraqi Freedom, I acknowledge the relevance of Jervis's opinion but will not start from his hypothesis of a 'compulsive empire' (Jervis, 2003a: 82) inherent in the very structure of a unipolar system. Quite on the contrary, I contend that the transformation of the US into an imperial(ist) America is not due to the emergence of a unipolar moment but rather that it is the deep conviction shared by America's policy–makers that the forthcoming evolution of the international power configuration will no longer be favourable for America's interests that has led them to adopt an imperial(ist) strategy.

The hypothesis echoes the liberal theory of the international institutional order and the realist theory of the power cycles I have already applied in the first part of this essay. According to these theories, a preponderant power is interested in organising a stable international order, thanks to its outstanding power resources, and willing to do so, by associating the satisfied secondary powers with the benefits of this order. When read *a contrario*, this hypothesis is tantamount to saying that the self–restraint of a preponderant power comes to an end when it thinks that the existing power disparity declines. In that case, it is no longer in the interest of the dominant power to maintain the order, as rival powers' relative gains are perceived to be greater than its own.

From a systemic perspective, Operation Iraqi Freedom thus appears to be the result of the US progressive shift from a 'benevolent hegemon' to a 'predatory hegemon'.[3] The US has abandoned the soft–power option, hoping that resorting to hard power will help maintain US primacy by postponing its relative decline, both in economic matters – the control of the Middle East oil resources that are vital to global economic prosperity – and on political issues, concerned as the US is by the rise of China as the future peer competitor east of the Greater Middle East.

* * *

The main theory[4] that accounts for the causes of war at the systemic level of the international power distribution, or more exactly at the level of the policy–makers' perception of the evolution of this power distribution, is the power cycle theory[5], notably the power transition theory proposed by Kenneth Organski and his disciples[6] and the hegemonic war theory theorised by Robert Gilpin (Gilpin, 1981 and 1989) among others.[7]

According to Organski and Gilpin, the international system, which is anarchical because of the absence of any central authority above states, is nonetheless hierarchical *de facto*. One of the great powers exerts its domination over the others thanks to the preponderance of its material resources. The pre–eminent power strives to perpetuate such a hierarchical system, first and foremost through the rules of the international game it proposes and diffuses. While these norms are accepted by some secondary powers, i.e. the powers that benefit from the existing order and are satisfied with the status quo, they have to be imposed, through force if necessary, on dissatisfied, or revisionist secondary powers intent on changing the prevailing order. As long as the unipolar structure persists, as long as the preponderant power can bear the costs implied by the management of the international system, and as long as the satisfied secondary powers are given their fair share of the benefits of the existing order, the dominant power will succeed in preserving a stable international order and preventing the outbreak of a general war opposing the major powers, even if this sometimes leads to limited wars against trouble–making minor powers.

However, the preponderant power's material advantage is not permanent. On account of the law of uneven growth rates, the predominant state's economic growth will slow down at a given moment as the secondary states' growth rate progressively increases, each power respectively entering the growth cycle at different moments. Moreover, the costs implied by the management of the international order penalise the preponderant power, whereas secondary powers can free ride: benefiting from the global public goods provided by the international order – such as political and economic stability – without having to share the burden of their preservation. Following this double evolution, a secondary power will sooner or later catch up with the predominant power, and match and even outmatch its resources. There will then be a transition phase in the power cycle, marked by parity between two or more powers, with a higher war risk if the rising power is what Organski calls 'a contender', i.e. a dissatisfied challenger.[8]

War may be the direct outcome of the evolution of the power relations between the declining hegemonic power and the rising contender. The rising power might wish to accelerate the historical process and initiate a war against the declining power in order to become top dog. Conversely the hegemonic power, facing up to the growing threat of the rising power but persuaded that it is still more powerful, might be tempted to launch a preventive war in order to check its challenger before it is too late – that was Sparta's option, which led to the Peloponnesian War. But war can also be the indirect outcome of an escalation process transforming a local armed conflict into a major war. Either an armed intervention in the immediate neighbourhood of the rising challenger, launched by the hegemonic power, within the scope of its order–keeping operations, increases the intensity of the security dilemma felt by the challenger, thus prompting it to resort to war for the sake of its threatened security. Alternatively, an armed intervention initiated by the rising challenger, within the scope of its expansionist policy, compels the still–hegemonic power to intervene in order to maintain the existing order, leading to an armed confrontation between the two protagonists. This happened twice in the twentieth century – when Great Britain declared war on Imperial, and subsequently on Nazi, Germany, which had attacked its neighbours, directly in 1939 and indirectly in 1914 as Austria's ally.

In any case, the general war occurring during a transition phase is what Gilpin calls a 'hegemonic war', from which a new international order will emerge, characterised by a new hierarchy and new norms proposed by the new preponderant power. The new pre–eminent power is not necessarily the rising challenger, which is often defeated by the coalition of satisfied powers during the armed confrontation, but could be a third–party state – either a member of the winning coalition, such as the US after the two World Wars, or an outsider taking advantage of the decisive weakening of both the hegemon and the contender, such as Macedonia after the Peloponnesian War.

In the light of this summary, the power cycle theory thus distinguishes two types of war: hegemonic wars that pit the declining hegemonic power and its satisfied allies against the rising revisionist contender, for the preservation of the existing order as opposed to its transformation; and limited wars that merely aim at preserving the status quo, and oppose the hegemonic power and its allies to a trouble–making regional power.

From the perspective of the present study, the power cycle theory amounts *a priori* to considering Operation Iraqi Freedom as a limited intervention with a view to preserving the international order. It has taken the form of an armed confrontation opposing the hegemonic power to a state that attacked Iran in 1980 and Kuwait in 1990, thus behaving twice in a revisionist way, and challenged the international order by its perceived reluctance to respect the UN Security Council's resolutions relative to its disarmament since 1991. In a way, to take up Carl Schmitt's words, Iraqi Freedom was merely 'the execution of an irksome or disturbing agent, a troublemaker who is rendered harmless by all the modern technical means – for example police bombing' (Schmitt, 2001: 125). We just have to replace the words 'troublemaker' by 'rogue state', and 'police bombing' by 'surgical strikes' and 'smart weapons', and Schmitt's description can be used to describe America's intervention against Iraq, although it was written more than fifty years before.[9]

However, such an interpretation tends to overlook the fact that Operation Iraqi Freedom has been a revisionist undertaking from the start, as it has indeed revived all at once the enmity principle, the preventive–war doctrine and unilateralism (see Chapters four, five and six). While it can undoubtedly be asserted that Operation Desert Storm was an international police operation waged against a state guilty of 'having perpetrated an aggression, a criminal attack' (Schmitt, 2001: 125) against another sovereign state, Kuwait, Operation Iraqi Freedom can hardly be considered to have been similarly aiming at preserving the international order. America's war against Iraq is a revisionist war, both in the sense given by Hans Morgenthau to his concept of imperialist policy – a war aiming at changing the status quo — and also from the standpoint of America's grand–strategy tradition – the adoption of an empire's predatory strategy to the detriment of a hegemon's past self–restraint strategy. It has meant the shift from a diplomacy resorting to indirect forms of consensual direction to a policy of domination through coercion.[10] Now, a war which is waged by a preponderant power but which violates the international norms previously proposed by the selfsame preponderant power, thus breaking off with its own past behaviour, does not fit the limited–war concept of the power cycle theory. The behaviour of a hegemonic power deciding to act unilaterally against a trouble–maker, despite its interest in adopting self–restraint or, at least, in forming a coalition with the majority of the other satisfied powers, may seem to be irrational, precisely because such behaviour is likely to subvert the hegemony acknowledged by the other members of the international society.

Does that mean that the power cycle theory is irrelevant and inoperative as a systemic approach to the potential causes of Operation Iraqi Freedom? I do not think so; this theory proposes another interesting research hypothesis, thanks to its economic variant, the so–called 'hegemonic stability' theory.

In its original version, proposed by Charles Kindleberger in his analysis of the international economic systems of the nineteenth century and the post–WWII period, the hegemonic stability theory presupposes the necessary existence of 'a stabiliser, one stabiliser' for a stable international economic system (Kindleberger, 1973: 305). According to Kindleberger, the stabiliser exerts a benevolent leadership. For example, the United Kingdom during the nineteenth century guaranteed the emergence of a liberal international economy. After 1945, the US contributed to the consolidation of this liberal international economy by transforming it into a regulated liberal international economy through the creation of the Bretton Woods institutions. Conversely, when there is no such stabiliser, as in the 1920s and 1930s which were marked by the absence of any benevolent leader who was both able and willing to pay the costs of maintaining the global public good – a stable international economy

– the world economy is in a state of depression, as was the case during the post–1929 years, the transition period between the British and the American leadership.

It is this last hypothesis which has been taken up and revisited by Gilpin in his own analyses of the international political economy (Gilpin, 1987).[11] Gilpin stresses the fact that the benevolent leadership exerted by the world's economic leader is waning when its resource preponderance is in relative decline.

A hegemon is necessary to the existence of a liberal international economy. ... It is valid to probe the motivations that the hegemon may have to create and sustain a liberal international economy. ... I believe that the United States has been motivated by enlightened self–interest and security objectives. The United States has assumed leadership responsibilities because it has been in its economic, political, and even ideological interest to do so, or at least it has believed this to be the case. To secure these long–term interests, the United States has been willing to pay the short–term and additional costs of supporting the international economic and political system. However, because of the free–rider problem, the hegemon does tend to pay far more than its share of the costs of maintaining the public good over the long run. In addition, economic benefits to other states may be disproportionately favourable because of the larger size of the hegemon's market. The hegemonic country as a whole can lose economically through the opening of its market [... and thus ...] is increasingly tempted to take advantage of its position as its power declines, as occurred with the United States in the 1980s. ... When the United States launched the Bretton Woods system of fixed exchange rates, implemented the Marshall Plan, and took the lead in the GATT negotiations on trade liberalization, it acted in enlightened self–interest. The United States as well as other countries gained through the lowering of trade and other economic barriers. ... The United States had ideological, political, and strategic motives to seek a liberal world economy; it desired to promote its values abroad, to create a secure international order, and to strengthen political ties with its allies. For two decades following the Second World War, the United States, largely for political and security reasons, subordinated many of its parochial economic interests to the economic well–being of its alliance partners ..., eschewed the temptation to exercise its political and economic power for nationalistic ends. Indeed, the United States created an international economy of which others could take full advantage. In the late 1960s, however, the United States began to pursue economic policies that were more self–centred ... Beginning with the escalation of the war in Vietnam and continuing in the Reagan administration, with its massive budget deficit, the United States exploited its hegemonic position in ways that released inflationary forces and contributed to global economic instability. Although other countries can certainly be faulted for equally self–serving behaviour, the American hegemon undermined its own legitimacy and the acceptance of its rule when it failed to fulfil what others considered to be its leadership responsibilities. By the 1980s, the United States was pursuing protectionist, macroeconomic, and other policies that would be identified as appropriate to what Conybeare has called a 'predatory hegemon' ..., less willing to subordinate its own interests to those of its allies; instead, it tended more and more to exploit its hegemonic status for its own narrowly defined purposes (Gilpin, 1987: 88–90, 345).

In concrete terms, Gilpin states that from the 1970s onwards the US has resorted to mercantilist competition, economic regionalism, and sectoral protectionism (394 *sqq*).[12]

It would probably be exaggerated to establish a direct parallel between mercantilist values in international economy and Hobbesian values in international politics, although the mercantilist view of international trade as a zero–sum game that is the mere continuation of warfare by other means against a competitor, instead of a partner, is close to the enmity principle.[13] In the same vein, no immediate comparison can be made between the cult of preventive war and the adoption of protectionist measures, although a protectionist strategy aims at compensating for a lack of economic competitiveness, just as a preventive war aims at preventing an unfavourable strategic imbalance. In both cases, actors strive to anticipate the excessive build–up of the capacities or resources of the adversary. The potential comparison between the creation of regional blocs in the economic sphere and the unilateralist option in international politics seems to be more relevant. Indeed, they both imply abandoning multilateral practices, regional blocs furthering the establishment of special relations with a limited number of privileged partners to the detriment to the most favoured nation's clause, while unilateralism favours coalitions to the detriment of the collective–security principle.

However irrelevant these parallels may be, it seems heuristically interesting to apply hegemonic stability theory to the present study in order to find tentative explanations for the apparently irrational behaviour of the US during the Iraqi crisis. If the American administration decided to go to war against Iraq, though it meant violating the international norms of appropriate behaviour it had contributed to establishing and consolidating in the interest of a peaceful and smooth *Pax Americana*, it was because American authorities believed that they were no longer in a position to maintain the international order through their soft power, on account of America's declining power preponderance over the secondary powers of the international system. In other words, from the perspective of the systemic level of analysis, Operation Iraqi Freedom can be viewed as the expression of America's relative decline or, more exactly, the consequence of the way American elites perceived this relative decline. The Bush administration resorted to armed force because it wanted to exploit America's current supremacy in an attempt to re–create its past preponderance or, at least, postpone the moment when its rising challengers would catch up and eventually overtake it.

The following pages will show that this hypothesis is corroborated, both by the objective evolution of the international power distribution and by the subjective political statements on such evolution made by American authorities.

In a comparative analysis of the situation of the objective power capacities of the US and the other powers, the unipolar structure of the current international system appears as an established fact for any observer, whatever power index is chosen – Gross Domestic Product, military expenditure, a combination of the two elements, with other power components, material or non material.[14] In 2001[15], American GDP amounted to 10,082 billion dollars, against 5,560 billion dollars for China, 3,450 for Japan, 2,174 for Germany, 1,510 for France, 1,470 for Great Britain, and 1,200 for Russia. In other words, China represented a little more than half of the American economic power, Japan slightly more than a third, Germany a little more than a fifth, etc. If we now turn to military expenditure,[16] the US spent 399 billion dollars, China 56, France 46.5, Japan 39.5, Germany 38.8 and the United Kingdom 31.7. In other words, the American military budget was higher than the total military spending of the five most important secondary military powers, which seems to confirm the assertion made by William Wohlforth, after many others.[17]

> The system is unambiguously unipolar. The US enjoys a much larger margin of superiority over the next most powerful state or, indeed, all other great powers combined than any leading state in the last two centuries. Moreover, the US is the first leading state in modern international history with decisive preponderance in all the underlying components of power: economic, military, technological, and geopolitical (Wohlforth, 1999).

However, absolute figures are less relevant than their dynamic evolution over time. America's power position has to be compared both to its own past and to the evolution of the respective positions of the other powers. I will show that the prediction made by Paul Kennedy, who asserted in 1988 that

> it simply has not been given to any one society to remain permanently ahead of all the others, because that would imply a freezing of the differentiated patterns of growth rates, technological advance, and military developments which has existed since time immemorial (Kennedy, 1989: 689),

seems to fit the current power dynamics perfectly.

If we consider the development of America's economic power, its current pre–eminence is hardly comparable to the predominant position of the US both in the immediate post–WWII period and after the collapse of the USSR. Indeed, in 1950 the American GDP represented 30.6 per cent of the Gross World Product but fell to 23.9 per cent in 1960, 22.1 per cent in 1970, 20.8 per cent in 1980, and 19.9 per cent in 1990.[18] The same trend continued after the end of the Cold War, in spite of a temporary recovery after the collapse of the planned economies of the Soviet bloc. In 1991, America's GDP represented 25.4 per cent of the Gross World Product and the percentage fell to 21.2 ten years after.[19] If we now compare the evolution of America's economic position relative to the other great powers' economies (The

USSR (Russia since 1991), Great Britain, Germany, France, Japan, and China), rather than to the world economy, we reach the same conclusion. In 1950, America's GDP was equivalent to 45 per cent of the total gross national product of the world's seven greatest economies; this share slowly diminished and fell to 39.8 per cent in 1960, 37.2 per cent in 1970, 36.7 per cent in 1980, and 34.3 per cent in 1990. After the end of the Cold War, America's share rose to 41 per cent in 1994 and 1998, before going down to 39.6 per cent in 2002.[20] We can indeed speak of a relative decline of America's economic power over the long term, even if we do not take into account America's exceptional preponderance in 1945 and the temporarily favourable circumstances in the early 1990s.

This temporary recovery was of course a consequence of the collapse of the Soviet Union, America's main challenger during the Cold War. The Soviet Union's GDP, which amounted to 20.2 per cent of America's GDP in 1945, successively rose to 35.7 per cent in 1955, 41.3 in 1965, and 45 per cent in 1975. It then fell to 41 per cent in 1980, 38.9 per cent in 1985, and 36.4 per cent in 1990, before collapsing to 10.7 per cent in 1994 and 7 per cent in 1998, and climbing once again to 13 per cent in 2002.[21]

The most notable evolution since the end of the Cold War, however, is less related to the collapse of the Soviet–Russian economy than to the respective evolution of the two major economies of Japan and China, which have become America's main economic challengers since the beginning of the Soviet–Russian economic decline at the end of the Brezhnev era. Competition from Japan has slackened, as Japan's GDP, which represented 43 per cent of America's GDP in 1991, fell to 37 per cent in 1998 and 34.1 per cent in 2002. Conversely, China's economic power has steadily improved when compared to America's economy. The country's GDP, which represented a mere 44.2 per cent in 1994 and 51.2 per cent in 1998, amounted to 55 per cent of America's GDP in 2002. To put it briefly, the US has been going through a period of relative economic decline, and China has superseded the USSR and Japan as America's main economic challenger.[22]

In matters of military expenditure, the USSR was America's peer competitor[23] throughout the Cold War. Considering its initial inferiority in 1945, with a military budget representing a mere 10 per cent of America's total military expenditure, the USSR's decision to match America's military resources as quickly as possible gave rise to a never–ending arms race between the two protagonists who tried to outmatch each other.[24] Times have radically changed since 1991, as China, America's most serious economic challenger today, did not significantly increase its military budget, at least until 2002.[25]

What conclusion can be drawn from these various observations? The present–day situation of the US is utterly different from what it was in the Cold War period. During the Cold War, the Soviet Union's military capacities were no real cause for concern in the US, on account of the economic weakness of the Communist regime. John Mueller has convincingly showed that, in addition to its nuclear deterrence, the production capacities of Detroit guaranteed America's long–term supremacy over an adversary bound to disappear sooner or later.[26] It was no coincidence that America's one and only imperial parenthesis – the Vietnam war – should have taken place during the best years of Soviet economic performance – the decade 1965–75. If we except this period, the USSR was no real threat to America's pre–eminence, either directly or indirectly through its aid programmes to proxy states. Paradoxically though it may seem, China's economic growth, combined with its fairly weak level of military expenditure, is a greater challenge for the US in the long term.

According to the power cycle theory, the temporary dissociation between the economic growth of a country and the increase in its military capacities is an integral part of a typical power transition process. There is first a time–lag between the economic growth which occurs at the point in time 't', 't+1', 't+2', etc., and the increase in military spending which takes place at the point in time 't+n'. It is thus logical that in the early twenty–first century China should not have substantially increased its military budget yet. Secondly, and more significantly, it is precisely because China has not increased its military expenditure that the country has been in a position to boost its economic growth, thus paving the way for a future built–up of its military arsenal in a mid– to long–term perspective, as exemplified by China's gross fixed capital formation rate since 1990 – over 35 per cent per year – against America's – less than 20 per cent. It is thus not surprising that the various economic scenarios all foresee China's catching up with America's economic power in the near future. For instance, Organski's disciples[27] assert that, by 2015–25, China will be America's main contender, in the strict sense given to this concept.[28]

The most important thing is that America's authorities believe in this scenario. Admittedly, in the National Security Strategy adopted in September 2002, we can read that 'today, the United States enjoys a position of unparalleled military strength and great economic and political influence'(National Security Strategy, 2002). But the scenario of a potential confrontation with a new peer competitor can be traced back to the mid 1990s. For example, the 1997 Quadrennial Defense Review acknowledged the fact that 'in the period beyond 2015, there is the possibility that a regional great power or global peer competitor may emerge', namely China, because of its 'potential to become a major military power in Asia'. Although the 2001 Quadrennial Defense Review, published three weeks after 9/11, was more contradictory, emphasising that 'the United States will not face a peer competitor in the near future' while admitting that in Asia 'the possibility exists that a military competitor with a formidable resource base will emerge', George W. Bush, in his Graduation Speech at West Point, on 1st June, 2002, unambiguously mentioned America's intention 'to keep military strengths beyond challenge, thereby making the destabilizing arms races of other eras pointless'.

Obviously, such statements would indeed be pointless if there were no perceived risk of a potential arms race likely to threaten American supremacy. And the political unit which may challenge America's military primacy is obviously neither Iraq nor Al'Qaeda or whatever other terrorist network, but China.[29] Operation Iraqi Freedom can therefore be analysed from the perspective of

America's perception of the rise of China as its future peer competitor. From an economic standpoint, America's control of Iraq will supposedly permit the US to guarantee free access to oil resources indispensable to the growth of the US economy and to the wealth and stability of the world economy. From a strategic point of view, America's control of Iraq is supposed to achieve China's containment in order to prevent it from taking advantage of its future status as a regional power to challenge America's preponderance.

In the previous chapter, I have considered the private, and indeed sinister, interests of American oil and engineering firms to be credible causes of Operation Iraqi Freedom, furthered as it were by the presence of direct or indirect representatives of these firms in the Bush administration. However, these private interests cannot be separated from America's national interest in the domain of oil resources, as 'the birth and development of the oil industry is not an affair of state; it essentially is a story of private businessmen' in the US (Noël, 2003).[30] To put it bluntly, what is good for the oil industrialists is good for America. All the more so as, since Reagan's presidency, the deregulation of the oil market, which has meant the end of the system of import and price–control favourable for producers and the adoption of a system of price and import liberalisation favourable for consumers and refiners, has resulted in an increased dependency on foreign oil resources, a situation which is likely to worsen in the future.[31] Just as America's oil industrialists, the whole American economy and the American population are interested in having a secure access to oil resources[32] if indeed 'the American way of life is not negotiable'.[33]

It is not only America's prosperity but the stability of the world economy that is at stake. This stability is linked to free access to the oil reserves of the Middle East, which account for 40 per cent of the world's energy consumption. As the acceptance of America's hegemony by the secondary satisfied powers also depends on the capacity of the US to guarantee the stability of the oil market, which is the prime mover of their economic wealth, it may be said that the US had, and still has, another good reason to control the Middle East – Iraq's oil reserves are four times larger than America's reserves and two–thirds of the world's global oil reserves are located in the Middle East.

To sum up, seen from a systemic level of analysis, Operation Iraqi Freedom can be considered to be an armed intervention aiming at transforming Iraq into a definitely safe oil supplier, both directly through America's presence and indirectly via a now America–friendly Iraqi member of OPEC. In a way, Operation Iraqi Freedom is just another step in a century–long story, being all at once a continuation of Operation Desert Storm whose objective was to prevent Saddam Hussein from controlling Kuwait's oil resources and possibly ogling Saudi Arabia's oil reserves; an application in real conditions of the Carter Doctrine, adopted after the overthrowing of the Shah's regime by Iranian Islamists, which proclaimed America's will to defend America's vital interests in the Middle East region, including the use of military force if necessary; a remake on a larger and public scale of the Anglo–American covert action to remove Mohammad Mossadegh, guilty of having nationalised the Iranian oil industry, from the leadership of the Iranian government in 1953; and a legacy of the Truman Doctrine, whose immediate background was the Turkish and Iranian crises in 1946 due to the Soviets' designs on the Bosporus and Northern Iran. In other words, it is a limited war whose economic stakes, apparently local, do have a global scope.

Beyond its global economic dimension, Operation Iraqi Freedom also has a global strategic scope. The address made by President George W. Bush to the people of Iraq on 4th April, 2003

> The government of Iraq, and the future of your country, will soon belong to you. ... We will end a brutal regime ... so that Iraqis can live in security. We will respect your great religious traditions, whose principles of equality and compassion are essential to Iraq's future. We will help you build a peaceful and representative government that protects the rights of all citizens. And then our military forces will leave. Iraq will go forward as a unified, independent, and sovereign nation that has regained a respected place in the world. You are a good and gifted people, the heirs of a great civilization that contributes to all humanity

echoes the rhetoric used by the British General F. S. Maude at the head of his troops when they marched into Baghdad on 19th March, 1917.

> Our armies do not come into your cities and lands as conquerors or enemies, but as liberators. ... It is [not] the wish of [our] government to impose upon you alien institutions. ... [It is our wish] that you should prosper even as in the past, when your lands were fertile, when your ancestors gave to the world literature, science, and art, and when Baghdad city was one of the wonders of the world. ... It is [our] hope that the aspirations of your philosophers and writers shall be realized and that once again the people of Baghdad shall flourish, enjoying their wealth and substance under institutions which are in consonance with their sacred laws and their racial ideals.[34]

As early as 1917, the stakes were intimately both economic and strategic, as Britain could not accept the German railway project that, linking Berlin to Baghdad via Byzantium, threatened its control over the crucial oil resources and its access to the Suez Canal, the gateway to Africa and India. And what was true in 1917 is still true today, even independently of the link established by the power cycle theory between economic wealth at the point in time 't' and military power at the point in time 't+n'.

By occupying Iraq, the US has completed the system of military bases it already possessed in the Near and Middle East, ranging from Turkey, a member of NATO, to the Gulf monarchies, and Israel. Seen from the standpoint of the mere regional security complex, this network of bases can directly be used to cope with the other regional rogue state, Iran. Simultaneously, the occupation of Iraq has made it possible for the US to reduce its military presence in Saudi Arabia, accused by

Islamic fundamentalists of betraying the Ummah in accepting heathens on Islamic soil.

However, if it is true that the security complex of a hegemonic power is, by essence, global, then the positioning of American bases in the Middle East cannot be explained without taking into account the network of military bases which already exist in the Horn of Africa, the Indian Ocean (Djibouti, Diego Garcia), and Central Asia (Pakistan, Afghanistan, Tajikistan, Uzbekistan, Kyrgyzstan).[35] Of course, the new scale implies a new adversary; and this adversary is China, a country the US wishes to 'encircle to try to keep it from expanding' (Mearsheimer 2001: 400)[36] on its Western flank, given that it is already contained on its Eastern marches, from South Korea to Australia via Japan, Taiwan, and Singapore.

This is a hypothesis which could be indirectly deduced from John Mearsheimer's prospective analysis. Starting from the assumption that China's economy will steadily grow at a rate twice greater than America's growth rate, Mearsheimer believes that the US will be forced to maintain its military presence in Asia in order to 'make sure that China does not become a peer competitor. Japan and Russia are unlikely to have the wherewithal to contain China, even if India, South Korea and Vietnam were to join the balancing coalition' (Mearsheimer 2001: 400). In the book he wrote in 2001, Mearsheimer made no allusion to Iraq. He only referred to North–East Asia, and considered India to be a mere peripheral actor on the Western border of the Middle Kingdom. However, he criticised the way Clinton managed the question of China and the efforts made by the US president to integrate China into the capitalist world economy and in the international institutions such as the WTO, with a tentative view to transforming it into a democratic and prosperous, i.e. satisfied, power.[37] Convinced as he was that 'a wealthy China would not be a status quo power but an aggressive state determined to achieve regional hegemony', Mearsheimer strongly advised US policy–makers 'to reverse course and do what (they) can to slow the rise of China'. Alluding to the decision made by George W. Bush's administration to increase America's arms sales to Taiwan, he did not hesitate to conclude that 'there are signs that the new Bush administration has taken the first steps in this direction' (402).

I argue that Operation Iraqi Freedom is another of these 'signs'. This would of course be a strange irony of fate, as Mearsheimer – who opposed the Iraqi war – argued that a classical containment and deterrence strategy would be efficient to successfully cope with Saddam Hussein, whatever weapons he might have had at his disposal (see Chapter seven). But seen from Mearsheimer's view – America's preponderance depends on its capacity to prevent the rise of an Asian hegemon – the occupation of Iraq was eminently logical. As they perceived a future decline of America's primacy, American policy–makers, in their efforts to maintain the existing status quo, had an interest in waging a proto–systemic war that could reinforce the containment of a future peer competitor they could no longer hope to strangle in the cradle.

* * *

However, such a venture may well lead the US sooner or later to face up to the risk of imperial overexpansion. This is indeed the fate of all declining hegemonic powers, according to the power cycle theory. Bound to forestall any challenge to their primacy, hegemonic powers are led to allocate an increasing share of their resources to unproductive military expenditure, thus eventually subverting the economic dynamics at the origin of their preponderance; all the more so as 'one of the few constancies in history is that the scale of commitment on military spending has always risen' (Kennedy, 1989: 570).

For the time being, the US is not yet a victim of this historical 'constancy' – which presupposes that military spending is non–productive – this explanation would be simplistic. Even if American military spending dramatically increased during the years preceding Operation Iraqi Freedom, from 267 billion dollars in 1997 to 399 in 2001,[38] it represented less than 4 per cent of America's GDP in 2001, against a rate of more than 9 per cent during the Korea and Vietnam Wars. However, the US may jump out of the frying pan into the fire: it may avoid the first risk but still remains exposed to what Arthur Stein, in another context, calls the 'hegemon's dilemma'.[39] Either the US resorts to armed force, as for instance against Iran or North Korea, at the risk of antagonising China – whose security dilemma would necessarily be intensified by such military actions – and irritating its European allies because of Europe's preference for a management of the system by soft power methods;[40] or Operation Iraqi Freedom remains an exception, in which case America's attitude may easily be interpreted as a sign of weakness by those actors who want to overthrow the status quo and are tempted to go on harassing the US.

To ask these questions is to anticipate the consequences of Operation Iraqi Freedom and wonder about its possible impact on the international order, a topic I will deal with in the concluding chapter.

NOTES

1   Paul Kennedy, in *The Rise and Decline of Great Powers*, paraphrases a quip of the Irish playwright G. B. Shaw, by replacing Hindhead, a stockbroker township south of London prospering in the early twentieth century while other parts of the British economy were stagnating, by Scarsdale, a northern suburb of New York City (Kennedy, 1989: 689).

2   Jervis uses the term 'hegemony' as an equivalent to empire, both being defined by a primacy in material, and notably military, resources.

3   The opposition between 'benevolent' and 'predatory' hegemon was first made by John Conybeare, quoted in Gilpin, 1987: 90. Like Jervis, Gilpin refers to the general meaning of 'hegemony' in the sense of material primacy. In my view, the expression 'benevolent hegemon' is a tautology, while the expression 'predatory hegemon' is a combination of contradictory terms.

4   There is of course another systemic theory of war – the balance of power theory – according to which risks of war are greater when there is an imbalance of power, because of the temptation of any preponderant power to use its resources. As I have shown in the first part of

this essay that this theory lacks logical coherence and is, moreover, invalidated by the historical record of the seventeenth and eighteenth centuries, I cannot but reject this theory. Accepting it would mean agreeing with Jervis's analysis, which I have criticised in the opening pages of this chapter.

5   In this chapter I will not apply John Ikenberry's liberal international institutional order theory. Though this theory posits the self–restraint of the preponderant power as the indispensable condition for a stable international order, it does not propose any analysis of the consequences of the absence, or the decline, of such self–restraint, and does not address the case of a preponderant power resorting to aggressive behaviour.

6   See Organski, 1958: Organski & Kugler, 1980; J. Kugler & D. Lemke (eds), *Parity and War: Evaluations and Extensions of The War Ledger* (Ann Arbor: University of Michigan Press, 1996); Tammen *et al.*, 2000.

7   There are many other variants of cyclical theories of world politics, such as the world leadership cycle theory proposed by George Modelski and William Thompson: G. Modelski, 'Long Cycles of World Leadership', in W. Thompson (ed.), *Contending Approaches to World System Analysis* (London: Sage, 1983), pp. 115–139; G. Modelski & W. Thompson, 'Long Cycles and Global War', in M. Midlarsky (ed.), *Handbook of War Studies, op. cit.,* pp. 23–54; W. Thompson (ed.), *Great Power Rivalries* (Columbia: South Carolina University Press, 1998); the relative power cycle theory proposed by Charles Doran: C. Doran, 'Power Cycle Theory and the Contemporary State System', in W. Thompson (ed.), *Contending Approaches to World System Analysis, op. cit.,* pp. 165–82; C. Doran *et al.,* 'Power Cycle Theory and Global Politics', Special issue of the *International Political Science Review*, 24, N° 1 (January 2003); and the long cycle theory proposed by Joshua Goldstein in J. Goldstein, *Long Cycles: Prosperity and War in the Modern Era* (New Haven: Yale University Press, 1988).

8   If the rising power is a satisfied power, a peaceful transition is then possible.

9   The first German edition of Carl Schmitt's '*Nomos* of the Earth in the International Law of *Jus Publicum Europaeum*' was published in 1950, but the main ideas of the book had been conceived in the 1920s, before being revisited in the immediate post–WWII period.

10   The essays dealing with America's possible change from a hegemonic to an imperial stance are countless. The most interesting ones include Andrew Bacevich, *American Empire: The Realities and Consequences of US Diplomacy* (Cambridge: Harvard University Press, 2002); Zbigniew Brzezinski, *The Choice: Global Domination or Global Leadership* (New York: Basic Books, 2004); Michael Cox (ed.), 'Forum on the American Empire', *Review of International Studies*, 30, N° 4 (October 2004); Niall Ferguson, *Colossus: The Rise and Fall of the American Empire* (London: Allen Lane, 2004); Chalmers Johnson, *The Sorrows of Empire. Militarism, Secrecy, and the End of the Republic* (New York: Verso, 2004); Charles Kupchan, *The End of the American Era: US Foreign Policy and the Geopolitics of the 21st Century* (New York: Vintage, 2003); Michael Mann, *Incoherent Empire* (London: Verso, 2003); John Newhouse, *Imperial America. The Bush Assault on the World Order* (New York: Knopf, 2003).

11   See also R. Gilpin, *The Challenge of Global Capitalism* (Princeton: Princeton University Press, 2000), and R. Gilpin, *Global Political Economy: Understanding the International Economic Order* (Princeton: Princeton University Press, 2001).

12 On the parallel between the US and Great Britain one century before, P. O'Brien & A. Clesse (2002), recall that during its relative decline in the late nineteenth century, Great Britain also adopted egoistic behaviour and hardly showed any interest in preserving the smooth working of the free–trade system.

13 For a summary of the mercantilist doctrine, see R. Gilpin, 1987: 31 and R. Aron, *Peace and War*, 2003: 245.

14 In adopting two power indexes, the GDP and the part of the GDP affected to military spending, I follow the method adopted in most current research programmes. The tradition was initiated in Organski & Kugler, 1980.

15 I have taken the figures of the year 2001 according to the hypothesis that the American decision to go to war against Iraq was taken in 2002, when only the 2001 data were available to American authorities. The data have been taken from the CIA World Factbooks, which measure the GDP on a purchasing power parity basis.

16 The figures for American military expenditure are for the year 2001, while the other figures concern the year 2002. There are no figures on Russian military expenditure in the CIA World Factbook for the year 2002.

17 For instance, Charles Krauthammer has claimed as early as 1990 that 'the immediate post–Cold War world ... is unipolar', and that 'the center of world power is the unchallenged superpower, the United States' (Krauthammer, 1991).

18 Calculations are made on the basis of the data published in Angus Maddison, *Monitoring the World Economy 1820–1992* (Paris: OECD, 1995). There are no figures concerning 1945 in Maddison's research, but this does not matter in the perspective of our research work, as they are biased in favour of the US because the economies of the other states were totally destroyed during World War Two.

19 Figures taken from the yearbook *L'état du monde*, Paris, La Découverte. The figures differ from Maddison's data, but the established trend is the same – the weight of America's economy in the world economy has slowly but steadily diminished.

20 Calculations made on the basis of the figures of the CIA World Factbooks for the years concerned.

21 Calculations made on the basis of the figures published in A. Maddison, *Monitoring the World Economy 1820–1992, op. cit.*, for the 1945–1990 period, on the basis of the figures of the CIA World Factbooks for the period since 1994. The post–Cold War figures concern Russia alone.

22 If we consider the economic weight of the European Union, which is superior to the US, it may be surprising not to consider the EU as an economic challenger of the US. In fact, within the framework of the present study which approaches economic prosperity as a power asset in the sole perspective of its potential political and strategic use, there is no reason why I should mention the EU, which is no unitary actor but a political dwarf and a military worm though it is an economic giant. *A fortiori*, if the EU is split into its various national components, no nation is likely to represent an economic challenge to the US. Of course, things would be different in the case of a politically unified Europe, with a real Common Foreign and Security Policy.

23 I do of course use this expression retroactively.

24 On the contrast between (Soviet–)Russia's economic weakness and the importance of its

military expenditure, see Georges Sokoloff, *La puissance pauvre* (Paris: Fayard, 1993), who has convincingly unearthed the contradictions of the (Soviet–)Russian idol with feet of clay.

25 This statement is pretty poor, but no other conclusion can be drawn from the existing figures, given the opaqueness of Chinese military figures. It is quite plausible that American authorities interpret this lack of clarity as a sign of China's willingness to become a military power.

26 John Mueller, *Retreat from Doomsday: The Obsolescence of Major War* (New York: Basic Books, 1989), pp. 112 *sqq.*

27 See Tammen *et al.* 2000: 153 *sqq.* Tammen *et al.* also take into account India as another economic giant in a more or less far future. Besides the possible political troubles in China, the emergence of India as a great power is likely to have an impact on the proposed scenario, as indeed it might be used by American diplomats as an asset in America's game against China, exactly as was the case with China in America's game against the USSR in the 1970s and 1980s.

28 Even before the years 2015–25, the most recent figures confirm this scenario. According to the CIA World Factbook, the Chinese GDP amounted to 10,170 billion dollars in 2006, against America's 13,130 billion. In other words, in 2006 the Chinese GDP represented 77 per cent of America's GDP, instead of approximately 55 per cent four years before.

29 Since the French edition of this essay, the 2006 Quadrennial Defense Review explicitly considers China to be America's main adversary in the future. 'Of the major and emerging powers, China has the greatest potential to compete militarily with the United States and field disruptive military technologies that could over time offset traditional US advantages in the absence of US counter strategies'.

30 The various figures quoted in this chapter are taken from the same issue of the journal *Questions internationales.*

31 See the *Report of the National Energy Policy Development Group* published on 17th May, 2001, entitled 'Reliable, Affordable and Environmentally Sound Energy for America's Future', also called 'The Cheney Report'.

32 This general interest has contributed to explaining the Democrats' reluctance to criticise George W. Bush's choices – cf. Chapter eight.

33 A statement made by George H. Bush during the Earth Summit held in Rio de Janeiro on June 1992.

34 Quoted in Niall Ferguson, 'Hegemony or Empire?', *Foreign Affairs*, 82, N°5 (September–October 2003), pp. 154–61.

35 Oil supplies are also at stake in Central Asia. Up to the mid–1990s, with the possible transport of oil from the Caspian Sea region to the Indian Ocean, the US supported the Taliban they saw as a potentially stabilising force in a country torn by civil war following the retreat of the Red Army.

36 I shall only refer to the analyses by J. Mearsheimer, without quoting the massive literature relative to the Chinese threat that has recently been published in the US, from the general public essay by Richard Bernstein & Ross Munro, *The Coming Conflict with China* (New York: Knopf, 1997), to the countless articles dedicated to this topic in scientific reviews, such as *International Security* for instance.

37 Whereas Mearsheimer criticises any policy aiming at integrating China in the world economy, Tammen *et al.*, 2000, approve such a policy. The difference is due to the fact that

Mearsheimer is not a defensive power cycle realist but an offensive balance of power realist, convinced that any power, whatever its domestic regime, is bound to take the offensive if it is not contained by a hegemonic power. According to Mearsheimer, whose theory contains a significant geopolitical dimension, the only possible hegemon is, by necessity, a regional hegemon, because 'the stopping power of water' prevents any power from conquering substantial territories situated on other continents. The US is such a regional hegemon, as it has no rival in the Western Hemisphere. It is the only regional hegemon of human history. As the possible emergence of another regional hegemon would threaten America's overall pre–eminence, the only strategy for the US is to prevent the emergence of any other regional hegemon on another continent, notably China in Asia, thanks to a policy of active presence in Asia and dynamic alliances with Asian countries.

38 Since then, American military spending has kept increasing. In 2006, America's military budget amounts to more than 546 billion dollars according to the estimates of the SIPRI Yearbook, *Armaments, Disarmaments and International Security* (Oxford: Oxford University Press, 2007).

39 Arthur Stein, 'The Hegemon's Dilemma: Great Britain, the United States and the International Economic Order', *International Organization* 38, No. 2 (Spring 1984), pp. 355–86.

40 The main books published recently on the American–European troubled partnership include David Andrews (ed.), *The Atlantic Alliance under Stress: US–European Relations after Iraq* (Cambridge: Cambridge University Press, 2005); Matthew Evangelista & Vittorio Parsi (eds), *Partners or Rivals? European–American Relations after Iraq* (Milan: Vita e Pensiero, 2005); Philip Gordon & Jeremy Shapiro, *Allies at War: America, Europe and the Crisis over Iraq* (New York: McGraw–Hill, 2004); Gustav Lindström *et al.*, *Shift or Rift? Assessing EU–US Relations after Iraq* (Paris: European Union Institute for Security Studies, 2003); Peter Merkl, *The Rift Between America and Old Europe: The Distracted Eagle* (London: Routledge, 2005).

conclusion | the open anarchy

History … is always richer in content, more varied, more multiform, more lively and ingenious than is imagined …
(Lenin[1])

Can it be said that Operation Iraqi Freedom is a mere accident or a harbinger of things to come – the 'bright future of war'?[2] Does this opportunistic and imperialist war, with its proto–systemic potentialities, signal a sea change that calls into question the maturing process of international anarchy? Or will it have negligible impact on the long–term pacification trend of international politics?

There is of course no definitive answer to this question. In social science, predicting the future is a vain undertaking[3] because of the unpredictable nature of human behaviour and the self–negating and self–fulfilling potentialities of stated prophecies. Indeed, actors might be tempted to adopt the necessary behaviour for a prediction to come true, being interested in the predicted benefits resulting from it, while other actors will do the contrary. Recent best–sellers on the future of American power – whether they predict the decline of America as a great power (Kennedy, 1989), the advent of a new American century[4] or the breakdown of the American empire[5] – have all been contested or criticised as soon as they were published. In the same vein, forecasts on the coming international systems have been refuted, whether they heralded forthcoming anarchy,[6] the end of history[7] or the clash of civilizations.[8] Authors have all made the same error – they have forgotten Lenin's warning about history's ingenuity.

This is particularly true in the field of international relations, in which the impact of what Marx calls the subjective factor in history should not be underestimated because of the open and undetermined nature of international anarchy. Anarchy is an empty structure, which implies the absence of any central authority. It entails a much wider field of possible actions than domestic politics, in which political action is predominantly embedded in, and shaped by, shared norms as a rule. It thus seems unjustified to criticise international scholars for failing to foresee major events such as the end of the Cold War or, *a fortiori*, the 9/11 terrorist attacks.

I will, however, try to resist the temptation of merely asserting that the main objective of scientific research is to explain and that predicting is not the ultimate aim of a theory.[9] Indeed, since Hans Morgenthau, 'the major theoretical approaches that have shaped the discipline of international relations … have all had in common, as one of their principal objectives, the anticipation of the future'.[10] In an attempt to avoid the dangers of making prophecies[11] I propose three scenarios based not on extrapolations of past tendencies but on the analysis of the causes of Operation Iraqi Freedom presented in the previous chapters.

* * *

According to the synthetic conclusion that can be drawn from the analyses proposed in these previous chapters, Operation Iraqi Freedom can be considered to be a voluntarist subjective initiative furthering the pursuit of material and ideological interests relative to American domestic and foreign policy, against a background of objective determining factors – the short–term evolution of the offence–defence balance and the long–term evolution of America's unipolar hegemony. Starting from Machiavelli's assertion that 'fortune to the extent of one half is the arbiter of our actions, but … she permits us to direct the other half' (Machiavelli, 1513: XXV), I will tentatively deduce the impact of Operation Iraqi Freedom on the international society and its consolidation process from America's virtue. There are thus two alternatives – either the US abandons the *Machtpolitik* it opted for in its war against Iraq or it goes on adhering to Hobbesian values.

It is perfectly possible that the US will take a step backwards so Operation Iraqi Freedom remains a mere parenthesis in history, on a par with the Vietnam War. Two factors may corroborate such a liberal scenario, in both the scientific and the normative sense of the word 'liberal'. If the number of US casualties keeps increasing in Iraq, turning this war into a military quagmire, American public opinion, including the elites, the media and the electoral body, may well change opinions and refuse to support any further adventurous expansionism by voting for a new political direction. American policy–makers, whatever their partisan orientation, may be tempted to adopt a new course and call for the return of *Realpolitik* and multilateralism, spurred on by the emergence of new log–rolling coalitions or influenced by America's allies, who might convince the US that gains obtained in the hard–power sphere will be paid for by as many losses in the soft–power domain.

However, we cannot exclude the possibility that the US will persist in its imperial(ist) expansionism. In that case, two other scenarios are possible.

The 'declinist' scenario is the same as the 'imperial–overstretch' scenario as defined by power cycle theory. According to this hypothesis, the US will eventually exhaust its forces, because of its commitment to a multiplicity of armed interventions, and this will undermine US economic dynamism, thus offering its major challenger, China, or its main ally, Europe, the opportunity of overtaking it. The power cycle theory forecasts a hegemonic war, in case of parity with a still–dissatisfied China. Such a war should, logically, benefit Europe, provided that, in the meantime,

Europe has become politically united. A pacific transition is also possible, however, with a democratic China, or a politically unified Europe, overtaking the US.

The 'imperial' scenario is the exact opposite of the imperial–overstretch hypothesis, i.e. the success of America's expansionism and its progressive transformation into an empire. This hypothesis, which is cherished by America's neo–conservatives, is rather neglected by mainstream scholars, probably because of the a–historical, eurocentrist, state–centrist and anarchophile approaches that characterise their research work.[12] International relations scholars focus almost exclusively on the interstate system born in the Eurasian continent in the mid seventeenth century. They thus ignore, forget, or neglect two major facts that a more global historical perspective should restore to favour. First, throughout human history, Empire has been the predominant form of political organisation in pre– and extra–Westphalian societies. Secondly, imperial universalism has been seen by many Western political thinkers – from Greek Stoics to Dante – as the best form of political organisation.

* * *

Anyone remembering the Napoleonic or Hitlerian tragedies knows very well that the imperial legend will go on preying on people's minds, even among the best and brightest. The policy adopted in the near future by the US towards Iran, or North Korea will help us have a clearer idea of the attraction it might have for contemporary America.

NOTES

1　Lenin, *Left Wing Communism: an Infantile Disorder* (1920). Source: http://www.marxists.org/archive/lenin/works/pdf/Lenin_Left_wing_Communism.pdf. The full quote is 'History as a whole, and the history of revolution in particular, is always richer in content, more varied, more multiform, more lively and ingenious than is imagined by even the best parties, the most class conscious vanguards of the most advanced classes.'

2　Allusion to Philippe Delmas, *Le bel avenir de la guerre* (Paris: Gallimard, 1995).

3　On the problem of forecasting in international relations see N. Choucri & T. Robinson (eds), *Forecasting in International Relations: Theory, Methods, Problems, Prospects* (San Francisco: Freeman, 1978); J. Freeman and B. Job, 'Scientific Forecasts in International Relations: Problems of Definition and Epistemology', *International Studies Quarterly*, 23, N°1 (March 1979), pp. 113–43; C. Doran, 'Why Forecasts Fail: The Limits of Potential and of Forecasting in International Relations and Economics', *International Studies Review*, 1, N°2 (Summer 1999), pp. 11–41; S. Bernstein, R. N. Lebow, J. G. Stein & S. Weber, 'God Gave Physics the Easy Problems: Adapting Social Science to an Unpredictable World', *European Journal of International Relations*, 6, N°1 (March 2000), pp. 43–76; G. Quester, *Before and After the Cold War: Using Past Forecasts to Predict the Future* (London: F. Cass, 2002); C. Fettweis, 'Evaluating International Relations, Crystal Balls: How

Predictions of the Future Have Withstood Fourteen Years of Unipolarity', *International Studies Review*, 6, N°1 (March 2004), pp. 79–104.

4   Alfredo Valladao, *The Twenty–First Century Will Be American*, (London: Verso, 1996).

5   Emmanuel Todd, *After the Empire: the Breakdown of the American Order* (New York: Columbia University Press, 2003).

6   Robert Kaplan, 'The Coming Anarchy', *The Atlantic Monthly*, 273, N°2 (February 1994), pp. 44–76.

7   Francis Fukuyama, *The End of History and the Last Man* (New York: The Free Press, 1992).

8   Samuel Huntington, *The Clash of Civilisations and the Remaking of World Order* (New York: Simon & Schuster, 1997).

9   See David Singer, *Models, Methods and Progress in World Politics: A Peace Research Odyssey* (Boulder: Westview, 1990).

10   John Gaddis, 'International Relations Theory and the End of the Cold War', *International Security*, 17, N°3 (Winter 1992–1993), pp. 5–58.

11   On the opposition between scholar and prophet, see Max Weber, *The Vocation Lectures: Politics as Vocation, Science as Vocation* (1919) (Indianapolis: Hackett, 2004).

12   On these unquestioned postulates of International Relations as a discipline, see Buzan & Little, 2000: 16 *sqq*.

select bibliography and online sources

Note: Full publication details of works cited in the text by author–date references are in the bibliography. Historical and classical sources have been cited from online sources, which are listed following the bibliography.

Aron, Raymond, 2003, *Peace and War: A Theory of International Relations* (1962), London: Transaction Publishers.

Aron, Raymond, 1967, 'Qu'est–ce qu'une théorie des relations internationales?', *Revue française de science politique*, 17 (5): 837–61.

Badie, Bertrand, 2004, *L'impuissance de la puissance: Essai sur les incertitudes et les espoirs des nouvelles relations internationales*, Paris: Fayard.

Baldwin, David (ed.), 1993, *Neo–realism and Neo–liberalism: the Contemporary Debate*, New York: Columbia University Press.

Battistella, Dario, 2004, 'Liberté en Irak ou le retour de l'anarchie hobbienne', *Raisons politiques*, 13: 59–78.

Battistella, Dario, 2004, 'L'ordre international: Portée théorique et conséquences pratiques d'une notion réaliste', *Relations internationales et stratégiques*, 54: 89–98.

Battistella, Dario, 2004, 'Prendre Clausewitz au mot: Une explication libérale de Liberté en Irak', *Etudes internationales*, 35 (4): 667–87.

Battistella, Dario, 2006, *Théories des relations internationales*, Paris: Presses de Sciences Po, 2nd edition.

Battistella, Dario, 2006, *Retour de l'état de guerre*, Paris: A. Colin.

Bull, Hedley, 1995, 'Society and Anarchy in International Relations' (1966), in James Der Derian (ed.), *International Theory: Critical Investigations*, Basingstoke: Palgrave Macmillan: 75–93.

Bull, Hedley, 2002, *The Anarchical Society: A Study of Order in World Politics* (1977), Basingstoke: Palgrave Macmillan, 3rd edition.

Bull, Hedley and Watson, Adam (eds), 1984, *The Expansion of International Society*, Oxford: Oxford University Press.

Buzan, Barry, 2007, *People, States and Fear* (1991, 2nd edition), Colchester: ECPR Press.

Buzan, Barry and Little, Richard, 2000, *International Systems in World History*,

Oxford: Oxford University Press.

Charon, Jean–Marie and Mercier, Arnaud (eds), 2004, *Armes de communication massive: Informations de guerre en Irak: 1991–2003*, Paris: Editions du CNRS.

Christensen, Thomas, and Snyder, Jack, 1990, 'Chain Gangs and Passed Bucks: Predicting Alliance Patterns in Multipolarity', *International Organization*, 44 (2): 137–68.

Claude, Inis, 1962, *Power and International Relations*, New York: Random House.

Cox, Robert, 1983, 'Gramsci, Hegemony and International Relations', *Millennium* 12 (2): 162–75.

Crucé, Emeric, 2004, *Le Nouveau Cynée ou Discours des occasions et moyens d'établir une paix générale et la liberté de commerce pour tout le monde* (1623), Rennes: Presses Universitaires de Rennes.

Delcourt, Barbara, Denis Duez and Eric Remacle (eds), 2004, *La guerre d'Irak: Prélude à un nouvel ordre international?*, Bruxelles: P.I.E. Peter Lang.

Ferguson, Niall, 2003, 'Hegemony or Empire?', *Foreign Affairs*, 82 (5): 154–61.

Fischer, Markus, 1992, 'Feudal Europe, 800–1300: Communal Discourse and Conflictual Practices', *International Organization*, 46 (2): 427–66.

Fisher, Louis, 2003, 'Deciding on War against Iraq: Institutional Failures', *Political Science Quarterly*, 118 (3): 389–410.

Gaddis, John, 1987, *The Long Peace*, Oxford: Oxford University Press.

Gilpin, Robert, 1981, *War and Change in War Politics*, Princeton: Princeton University Press.

Gilpin, Robert, 1987, *The Political Economy of International Relations*, Princeton: Princeton University Press.

Gilpin, Robert, 1989, 'The Theory of Hegemonic War', in Robert Rotberg and Theodore Rabb (eds), *The Origin and Prevention of Major Wars*, Cambridge: Cambridge University Press: 15–37.

Grieco, Joseph, 1988, 'Anarchy and the Limits of Cooperation', *International Organization*, 42 (3): 485–507.

Gross, Leo, 1948, 'The Peace of Westphalia: 1648–1948', *American Journal of International Law*, 42 (1): 20–41.

Gulick, Edward, 1967, *Europe's Classical Balance of Power*, New York: Norton.

Haine, Jean–Yves, 2003, 'The Imperial Moment', *Cambridge Review of International Affairs*, 16 (3): 485–511.

Haine, Jean–Yves, 2004, *Les Etats–Unis ont–ils besoin d'alliés?*, Paris: Plon.

Hassner, Pierre and Vaïsse, Justin, 2003, *Washington et le monde: Dilemmes d'une superpuissance*, Paris: Editions Autrement.

Herz, John, 1950, 'Idealist Internationalism and the Security Dilemma', *World Politics*, 2 (2): 157–80.

Hobson, John, 1965, *Imperialism. A Study* (1902), Ann Arbor: University of Michigan Press.

Howard, Peter, 2004, 'Why Not Invade North Korea? Threats, Language Games, and US Foreign Policy', *International Studies Quarterly*, 48 (4): 805–28.

Ikenberry, John, 2001, *After Victory: Institutions, Strategic Restraint and the Rebuilding of Order after Major Wars*, Princeton: Princeton University Press.

Jervis, Robert, 1976, *Perception and Misperception in International Relations*, Princeton: Princeton University Press.

Jervis, Robert, 1978, 'Cooperation under the Security Dilemma', *World Politics*, 30 (2): 167–214.

Jervis, Robert, 1983, 'Security Regimes', in S. Krasner (Ed.), *International Regimes*, Ithaca: Cornell University Press: 173–94.

Jervis, Robert, 1985, 'From Balance to Concert. A Study of International Security Cooperation', *World Politics*, 38 (1): 58–79.

Jervis, Robert, 2003a, 'The Compulsive Empire', *Foreign Policy*, 137: 83–7.

Jervis, Robert, 2003b, 'Understanding the Bush Doctrine', *Political Science Quarterly*, 118 (3): 265–388.

Kaufmann, Chaim, 2004, 'Threat Inflation and the Failure of the Marketplace of Ideas: The Selling of the Iraq War', *International Security*, 29 (1): 5–48.

Kennedy, Paul, 1989, *The Rise and Fall of the Great Powers: Economic Change and Military Conflict from 1500 to 2000* (1988), London: Fontana.

Kindleberger, Charles, 1973, *The World in Depression 1929–1939*, Berkeley: University of California Press.

Kissinger, Henry, 1957, *A World Restored: Metternich, Castlereagh and the Problems of Peace 1812–1822*, Boston: Houghton Mifflin.

Kissinger, Henry, 1994, *Diplomacy*, New York: Simon & Schuster.

Krauthammer, Charles, 1990–1991, 'The Unipolar Moment', *Foreign Affairs*, 70 (5): 23–33.

Kull, Steven, Ramsay, Clay and Lewis, Evan, 2003–2004, 'Misperceptions, the Media, and the Iraq War', *Political Science Quarterly*, 118 (4): 569–98.

Levy, Jack, 1987, 'Declining Power and the Preventive Motivation for War', *World Politics*, 40 (1): 82–107.

Lindemann, Thomas, 2004, 'Les guerres américaines dans l'après–guerre froide: Entre intérêt national et affirmation idenditaire', *Raisons politiques*, 13: 37–57.

Livet, George, 1972, *Guerre et paix de Machiavel a Hobbes*, Paris: A. Colin.

Lundestad, Geir, 1986, 'Empire by Invitation? The United States and Western Europe 1945–1952', *Journal of Peace Research*, 22 (3): 263–77.

Lundestad, Geir, 1998, *Empire by Integration: The United States and European Integration 1945–1997*, Oxford: Oxford University Press.

Meadwell, Hudson, 2001, 'The Long Nineteenth Century in Europe: Reinterpreting the Concert System', *Review of International Studies*, 27 (Special Issue): 165–89.

Mearsheimer, John, 2001, *The Tragedy of Great Power Politics*, New York: Norton.

Mearsheimer, John and Walt, Stephen, 2003, 'An Unnecessary War', *Foreign Policy*, 134: 51–9.

Mesnard, Pierre, 1977, *L'essor de la philosophie politique au XVIème siècle*,

Paris: Vrin.

Moravcsik, Andrew, 1997, 'Taking Preferences Seriously: A Liberal Theory of International Politics', *International Organization*, 51 (4): 513–53.

Morgenthau, Hans, 2005, *Politics among Nations: The Struggle for Power and Peace* (1948), New York: MacGraw–Hill, 7th edition.

Noël, Pierre, 2003, 'Les Etats–Unis et le pétrole': De Rockefeller à la guerre du Golfe', *Questions internationales*, 2: 30–7.

Nye, Joseph, 1987, 'Nuclear Learning and US–Soviet Security Regimes', *International Organization*, 41 (3): 371–402.

Nye, Joseph, 1990, *Bound to Lead: the Changing Nature of American Power*, New York: Basic Books.

O'Brien, Patrick, and Clesse, Armand (eds), 2002, *Two Hegemonies: Britain 1846–1914 and the United States 1941–2001*, Aldershot: Ashgate.

Organski, Kenneth, 1958, *World Politics*, New York: Knopf.

Organski, Kenneth and Kugler, Jacek, 1980, *The War Ledger*, Chicago: University of Chicago Press.

Paul, T.V., Wirtz, James and Fortmann, Michael (eds), 2004, *Balance of Power: Theory and Practice in the 21st Century*, Stanford: Stanford University Press.

Roberts, Adam, 2003, 'Law and the Use of Force after Iraq', *Survival*, 45 (2): 31–56.

Ruggie, John, 1994, 'Third Try at World Order? America and Multilateralism after the Cold War', *Political Science Quarterly*, 109 (4): 553–70.

Ruggie, John, 1998, *Constructing the World Polity: Essays on International Institutionalization*, London: Routledge.

Schmitt, Carl, 1996, *The Concept of the Political* (1932), Chicago: University of Chicago Press.

Schmitt, Carl, 2001, *Le nomos de la terre dans le droit des gens du jus publicum europaeum* (1950), Paris: PUF.

Schroeder, Paul, 1994, *The Transformation of European Politics 1763–1848*, Cambridge: Cambridge University Press.

Schroeder, Paul, 2002, 'Iraq. The Case against Pre–emptive War', *The American Conservative*, October 21: 12–27.

Schumpeter, Joseph, 1951, 'The Sociology of Imperialisms' (1919), in J. Schumpeter, *Imperialism and Social Classes*, Oxford: Basil Blackwell: 1–130.

Schweller, Randall, 1992, 'Domestic Structure and Preventive War: Are Democracies More Pacific?', *World Politics*, 44 (2): 235–69.

Schweller, Randall, 1994, 'Bandwagoning for Profit: Bringing the Revisionist State Back In', *International Security*, 19 (1): 72–107.

Smith, Michael, 1992, 'Liberalism and International Reform', in Terry Nardin and David Mapel (eds), *Traditions of International Ethics*, Cambridge: Cambridge University Press: 201–24.

Smouts, Marie–Claude, Battistella, Dario and Vennesson, Pascal, 2006,

Dictionnaire des relations internationales, Paris: Dalloz, 2nd edition.

Snyder, Jack, 1991, *Myths of Empire: Domestic Politics and International Ambition*, Ithaca: Cornell University Press.

Snyder, Jack, 2003, 'Imperial Temptations', *The National Interest*, 71: 29–40.

Sofka, James, 2001, 'The Eighteenth Century International System: Parity or Primacy?', *Review of International Studies*, 27 (Special Issue): 147–63.

Soutou, Georges–Henry, 2001, *La guerre de cinquante ans: Les relations Est–Ouest 1943–1990*, Paris: Fayard.

Tammen, Ronald *et al.*, 2000, *Power Transitions: Strategies for the 21st Century*, New York: Chatham House Publishers.

Van Evera, Stephen, 1998, 'Offense, Defense, and the Causes of War', *International Security*, 22 (4): 5–43.

Van Evera, Stephen, 1999, *The Causes of War: Power and the Roots of Conflict*, Ithaca: Cornell University Press.

Vasquez John, and Henehan, Marie, 1999, *The Scientific Study of Peace and War: A Text Reader*, Lanham: Lexington Books.

Wallace, Michael, 1979, 'Arms Races and Escalation: Some New Evidence', *Journal of Conflict Resolution*, 23 (1): 3–16.

Walt, Stephen, 1987, *The Origins of Alliances*, Ithaca: Cornell University Press.

Waltz, Kenneth, 1959, *Man, the State, and War*, New York: Columbia University Press.

Waltz, Kenneth, 1979, *Theory of International Politics*, New York: McGraw–Hill.

Waltz, Kenneth, 1989, 'The Origins of War in Neorealist Theory', in Robert Rotberg and Theodore Rabb (eds), *The Origin and Prevention of Major Wars*, Cambridge: Cambridge University Press: 37–52.

Walzer, Michael, 1991 (1977), *Just and Unjust Wars: A Moral Argument with Historical Illustrations*, New York: Basic Books, 2nd edition.

Walzer, Michael, 2004, *Arguing about War*, New Haven: Yale University Press.

Watson, Adam, 1992, *The Evolution of International Society*, London: Routledge.

Wendt, Alexander, 1992, 'Anarchy Is What States Make of It', *International Organization* 49 (2): 391–425.

Wendt, Alexander, 1999, *Social Theory of International Politics*, Cambridge: Cambridge University Press.

Wight, Martin, 1992, *International Theory: The Three Traditions*, Leicester: Leicester University Press.

Wohlforth, William, 1999, 'The Stability of a Unipolar World', *International Security*, 24 (1): 5–41.

Wolfers, Arnold, 1962, *Discord and Collaboration: Essays on International Politics*, Baltimore: Johns Hopkins University Press.

Zacher, Mark, and Matthews, Richard, 1995, 'Liberal International Theory: Common Threads, Divergent Trends', in Charles Kegley (ed.), *Controversies in International Relations Theory: Realism and the Neoliberal Challenge*, New York: Saint Martin's: 107–50.

ONLINE REFERENCES FOR PRIMARY SOURCES

Bacon, Francis, 1597, *On Empire*,
    http://www.authorama.com/essays–of–francis–bacon–20.html
Bodin, Jean, 1576, *Six Books of the Commonwealth*,
    http://www.constitution.org/bodin/bodin_.htm
Bush, George W. various years, various speeches,
    http://www.whitehouse.gov
Clausewitz, Carl von, 1809–1830, *On War*,
    http://www.gutenberg.org/files/1946/1946–h/1946–h.htm
Grotius, Hugo, 1625, *On the Law of War and Peace*,
    http://oll.libertyfund.org/?option=com_staticxt&staticfile=show.php%3Fp
    erson=3775&Item=28
Hobbes, Thomas, 1651, *Leviathan*,
    http://www.gutenberg.org/dirs/etext02/lvthn10.txt
Hume, David, 1752, 'Of the Balance of Power',
    http://www.econlib.org/library/LFBooks/Hume/hmMPL30.html
Kant, Immanuel, 1795, 'Perpetual Peace: A Philosophical Sketch',
    http://www.constitution.org/kant/perpeace.htm
Locke, John, 1690, *Two Treatises of Government*,
    http://oll.libertyfund.org/index.php?option=com_staticxt&staticfile=show.
    php%3Ftitle=222&layout=html
Machiavelli, Niccolo, 1513, *The Prince*,
    http://www.constitution.org/mac/prince00.htm
Machiavelli, Niccolo, 1518, *Discourses on Livy*,
    http://www.constitution.org/mac/disclivy.txt
Mill, John Stuart, 1859, 'A Few Words on Non–intervention',
    http://www.libertarian.co.uk/lapubs/forep/forep008.pdf
National Security Strategy of the United States, 2002,
    http://www.whitehouse.gov/nsc/nss.html
Rousseau, Jean–Jacques, 1754, 'Discourse on the Origin of Inequality among Men',
    http://www.constitution.org/jjr/ineq.htm
Rousseau, Jean–Jacques, 1760, 'A Lasting Peace',
    http://oll.libertyfund.org/?option=com_staticxt&staticfile=show.php%3Ftitle
    =1010&chapter=144254&layout=html&Itemid=27
Tocqueville, Alexis de, 1831–1835, *Democracy in America*,
    http://xroads.virginia.edu/~Hyper/DETOC/toc_indx.html
Thucydides, 411 BC, *The Peloponnesian Wars*,
    http://www.gutenberg.org/dirs/etext04/plpwr10.txt
Vattel, Emer de, 1758, *The Law of Nations*,
    http://www.constitution.org/vattel/vattel.htm
United Nations, 1945, *Charter of the United Nations*,
    http://www.un.org/aboutun/charter/
United Nations Security Council resolutions,
    http://www.un.org/documents/scres.htm

index